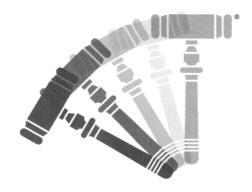

Casenote® Legal Briefs

CIVIL PROCEDURE

Keyed to Courses Using

Subrin, Minow, Brodin, Main, and Lahav's
Civil Procedure:
Doctrine, Practice, and Context

Fourth Edition

Wolters Kluwer
Law & Business

Copyright © 2012 CCH Incorporated.

Published by Wolters Kluwer Law & Business in New York.

Wolters Kluwer Law & Business serves customers worldwide with CCH, Aspen Publishers, and Kluwer Law International products. (www.wolterskluwerlb.com)

To contact Customer Service, e-mail customer.service@wolterskluwer.com, call 1-800-234-1660, fax 1-800-901-9075, or mail correspondence to:

Wolters Kluwer Law & Business
Attn: Order Department
P.O. Box 990
Frederick, MD 21705

Printed in the United States of America.

1 2 3 4 5 6 7 8 9 0

ISBN 978-1-4548-0516-8

About Wolters Kluwer Law & Business

Wolters Kluwer Law & Business is a leading global provider of intelligent information and digital solutions for legal and business professionals in key specialty areas, and respected educational resources for professors and law students. Wolters Kluwer Law & Business connects legal and business professionals as well as those in the education market with timely, specialized authoritative content and information-enabled solutions to support success through productivity, accuracy and mobility.

Serving customers worldwide, Wolters Kluwer Law & Business products include those under the Aspen Publishers, CCH, Kluwer Law International, Loislaw, Best Case, ftwilliam.com and MediRegs family of products.

CCH products have been a trusted resource since 1913, and are highly regarded resources for legal, securities, antitrust and trade regulation, government contracting, banking, pension, payroll, employment and labor, and healthcare reimbursement and compliance professionals.

Aspen Publishers products provide essential information to attorneys, business professionals and law students. Written by preeminent authorities, the product line offers analytical and practical information in a range of specialty practice areas from securities law and intellectual property to mergers and acquisitions and pension/benefits. Aspen's trusted legal education resources provide professors and students with high-quality, up-to-date and effective resources for successful instruction and study in all areas of the law.

Kluwer Law International products provide the global business community with reliable international legal information in English. Legal practitioners, corporate counsel and business executives around the world rely on Kluwer Law journals, looseleafs, books, and electronic products for comprehensive information in many areas of international legal practice.

Loislaw is a comprehensive online legal research product providing legal content to law firm practitioners of various specializations. Loislaw provides attorneys with the ability to quickly and efficiently find the necessary legal information they need, when and where they need it, by facilitating access to primary law as well as state-specific law, records, forms and treatises.

Best Case Solutions is the leading bankruptcy software product to the bankruptcy industry. It provides software and workflow tools to flawlessly streamline petition preparation and the electronic filing process, while timely incorporating ever-changing court requirements.

ftwilliam.com offers employee benefits professionals the highest quality plan documents (retirement, welfare and non-qualified) and government forms (5500/PBGC, 1099 and IRS) software at highly competitive prices.

MediRegs products provide integrated health care compliance content and software solutions for professionals in healthcare, higher education and life sciences, including professionals in accounting, law and consulting.

Wolters Kluwer Law & Business, a division of Wolters Kluwer, is head-quartered in New York. Wolters Kluwer is a market-leading global information services company focused on professionals.

Format for the Casenote® Legal Brief

Nature of Case: This section identifies the form of action (e.g., breach of contract, negligence, battery), the type of proceeding (e.g., demurrer, appeal from trial court's jury instructions), or the relief sought (e.g., damages, injunction, criminal sanctions).

Fact Summary: This is included to refresh your memory and can be used as a quick reminder of the facts.

Rule of Law: Summarizes the general principle of law that the case illustrates. It may be used for instant recall of the court's holding and for classroom discussion or home review.

Facts: This section contains all relevant facts of the case, including the contentions of the parties and the lower court holdings. It is written in a logical order to give the student a clear understanding of the case. The plaintiff and defendant are identified by their proper names throughout and are always labeled with a (P) or (D).

Party ID: Quick identification of the relationship between the parties.

Concurrence/Dissent: All concurrences and dissents are briefed whenever they are included by the casebook editor.

Analysis: This last paragraph gives you a broad understanding of where the case "fits in" with other cases in the section of the book and with the entire course. It is a hornbook-style discussion indicating whether the case is a majority or minority opinion and comparing the principal case with other cases in the casebook. It may also provide analysis from restatements, uniform codes, and law review articles. The analysis will prove to be invaluable to classroom discussion.

Issue: The issue is a concise question that brings out the essence of the opinion as it relates to the section of the casebook in which the case appears. Both substantive and procedural issues are included if relevant to the decision.

Holding and Decision: This section offers a clear and in-depth discussion of the rule of the case and the court's rationale. It is written in easy-to-understand language and answers the issue presented by applying the law to the facts of the case. When relevant, it includes a thorough discussion of the exceptions to the case as listed by the court, any major cites to the other cases on point, and the names of the judges who wrote the decisions.

Quicknotes: Conveniently defines legal terms found in the case and summarizes the nature of any statutes, codes, or rules referred to in the text.

Palsgraf v. Long Island R.R. Co.

Injured bystander (P) v. Railroad company (D)

N.Y. Ct. App., 248 N.Y. 339, 162 N.E. 99 (1928).

NATURE OF CASE: Appeal from judgment affirming verdict for plaintiff seeking damages for personal injury.

FACT SUMMARY: Helen Palsgraf (P) was injured on R.R.'s (D) train platform when R.R.'s (D) guard helped a passenger aboard a moving train, causing his package to fall on the tracks. The package contained fireworks which exploded, creating a shock that tipped a scale onto Palsgraf (P).

🏛 RULE OF LAW
The risk reasonably to be perceived defines the duty to be obeyed.

FACTS: Helen Palsgraf (P) purchased a ticket to Rockaway Beach from R.R. (D) and was waiting on the train platform. As she waited, two men ran to catch a train that was pulling out from the platform. The first man jumped aboard, but the second man, who appeared as if he might fall, was helped aboard by the guard on the train who had kept the door open so they could jump aboard. A guard on the platform also helped by pushing him onto the train. The man was carrying a package wrapped in newspaper. In the process, the man dropped his package, which fell on the tracks. The package contained fireworks and exploded. The shock of the explosion was apparently of great enough strength to tip over some scales at the other end of the platform, which fell on Palsgraf (P) and injured her. A jury awarded her damages, and R.R. (D) appealed.

ISSUE: Does the risk reasonably to be perceived define the duty to be obeyed?

HOLDING AND DECISION: (Cardozo, C.J.) Yes. The risk reasonably to be perceived defines the duty to be obeyed. If there is no foreseeable hazard to the injured party as the result of a seemingly innocent act, the act does not become a tort because it happened to be a wrong as to another. If the wrong was not willful, the plaintiff must show that the act as to her had such great and apparent possibilities of danger as to entitle her to protection. Negligence in the abstract is not enough upon which to base liability. Negligence is a relative concept, evolving out of the common law doctrine of trespass on the case. To establish liability, the defendant must owe a legal duty of reasonable care to the injured party. A cause of action in tort will lie where harm, though unintended, could have been averted or avoided by observance of such a duty. The scope of the duty is limited by the range of danger that a reasonable person could foresee. In this case, there was nothing to suggest from the appearance of the parcel or otherwise that the parcel contained fireworks. The guard could not reasonably have had any warning of a threat to Palsgraf (P), and R.R. (D) therefore cannot be held liable. Judgment is reversed in favor of R.R. (D).

DISSENT: (Andrews, J.) The concept that there is no negligence unless R.R. (D) owes a legal duty to take care as to Palsgraf (P) herself is too narrow. Everyone owes to the world at large the duty of refraining from those acts that may unreasonably threaten the safety of others. If the guard's action was negligent as to those nearby, it was also negligent as to those outside what might be termed the "danger zone." For Palsgraf (P) to recover, R.R.'s (D) negligence must have been the proximate cause of her injury, a question of fact for the jury.

▶ ANALYSIS
The majority defined the limit of the defendant's liability in terms of the danger that a reasonable person in defendant's situation would have perceived. The dissent argued that the limitation should not be placed on liability, but rather on damages. Judge Andrews suggested that only injuries that would not have happened but for R.R.'s (D) negligence should be compensable. Both the majority and dissent recognized the policy-driven need to limit liability for negligent acts, seeking, in the words of Judge Andrews, to define a framework "that will be practical and in keeping with the general understanding of mankind." The Restatement (Second) of Torts has accepted Judge Cardozo's view.

Quicknotes

FORESEEABILITY A reasonable expectation that change is the probable result of certain acts or omissions.

NEGLIGENCE Conduct falling below the standard of care that a reasonable person would demonstrate under similar conditions.

PROXIMATE CAUSE The natural sequence of events without which an injury would not have been sustained.

Wolters Kluwer Law & Business is proud to offer *Casenote® Legal Briefs*—continuing thirty years of publishing America's best-selling legal briefs.

Casenote® Legal Briefs are designed to help you save time when briefing assigned cases. Organized under convenient headings, they show you how to abstract the basic facts and holdings from the text of the actual opinions handed down by the courts. Used as part of a rigorous study regimen, they can help you spend more time analyzing and critiquing points of law than on copying bits and pieces of judicial opinions into your notebook or outline.

Casenote® Legal Briefs should never be used as a substitute for assigned casebook readings. They work best when read as a follow-up to reviewing the underlying opinions themselves. Students who try to avoid reading and digesting the judicial opinions in their casebooks or online sources will end up shortchanging themselves in the long run. The ability to absorb, critique, and restate the dynamic and complex elements of case law decisions is crucial to your success in law school and beyond. It cannot be developed vicariously.

Casenote® Legal Briefs represents but one of the many offerings in Legal Education's Study Aid Timeline, which includes:

- *Casenote® Legal Briefs*
- *Emanuel® Law Outlines*
- *Emanuel® Law in a Flash* Flash Cards
- *Emanuel® CrunchTime® Series*
- *Siegel's Essay and Multiple-Choice Questions and Answers Series*

Each of these series is designed to provide you with easy-to-understand explanations of complex points of law. Each volume offers guidance on the principles of legal analysis and, consulted regularly, will hone your ability to spot relevant issues. We have titles that will help you prepare for class, prepare for your exams, and enhance your general comprehension of the law along the way.

To find out more about Wolters Kluwer Law & Business' study aid publications, visit us online at *www.wolterskluwerlb.com* or email us at *legaledu@wolterskluwer.com*. We'll be happy to assist you.

How to Brief a Case

A. Decide on a Format and Stick to It

Structure is essential to a good brief. It enables you to arrange systematically the related parts that are scattered throughout most cases, thus making manageable and understandable what might otherwise seem to be an endless and unfathomable sea of information. There are, of course, an unlimited number of formats that can be utilized. However, it is best to find one that suits your needs and stick to it. Consistency breeds both efficiency and the security that when called upon you will know where to look in your brief for the information you are asked to give.

Any format, as long as it presents the essential elements of a case in an organized fashion, can be used. Experience, however, has led *Casenote® Legal Briefs* to develop and utilize the following format because of its logical flow and universal applicability.

NATURE OF CASE: This is a brief statement of the legal character and procedural status of the case (e.g., "Appeal of a burglary conviction").

There are many different alternatives open to a litigant dissatisfied with a court ruling. The key to determining which one has been used is to discover *who is asking this court for what.*

This first entry in the brief should be kept as *short as possible.* Use the court's terminology if you understand it. But since jurisdictions vary as to the titles of pleadings, the best entry is the one that addresses who wants what in this proceeding, not the one that sounds most like the court's language.

RULE OF LAW: A statement of the general principle of law that the case illustrates (e.g., "An acceptance that varies any term of the offer is considered a rejection and counteroffer").

Determining the rule of law of a case is a procedure similar to determining the issue of the case. Avoid being fooled by red herrings; there may be a few rules of law mentioned in the case excerpt, but usually only one is *the* rule with which the casebook editor is concerned. The techniques used to locate the issue, described below, may also be utilized to find the rule of law. Generally, your best guide is simply the chapter heading. It is a clue to the point the casebook editor seeks to make and should be kept in mind when reading every case in the respective section.

FACTS: A synopsis of only the essential facts of the case, i.e., those bearing upon or leading up to the issue.

The facts entry should be a short statement of the events and transactions that led one party to initiate legal proceedings against another in the first place. While some cases conveniently state the salient facts at the beginning of the decision, in other instances they will have to be culled from hiding places throughout the text, even from concurring and dissenting opinions. Some of the "facts" will often be in dispute and should be so noted. Conflicting evidence may be briefly pointed up. "Hard" facts must be included. Both must be *relevant* in order to be listed in the facts entry. It is impossible to tell what is relevant until the entire case is read, as the ultimate determination of the rights and liabilities of the parties may turn on something buried deep in the opinion.

Generally, the facts entry should not be longer than three to five *short* sentences.

It is often helpful to identify the role played by a party in a given context. For example, in a construction contract case the identification of a party as the "contractor" or "builder" alleviates the need to tell that that party was the one who was supposed to have built the house.

It is always helpful, and a good general practice, to identify the "plaintiff" and the "defendant." This may seem elementary and uncomplicated, but, especially in view of the creative editing practiced by some casebook editors, it is sometimes a difficult or even impossible task. Bear in mind that the *party presently* seeking something from this court may not be the plaintiff, and that sometimes only the cross-claim of a defendant is treated in the excerpt. Confusing or misaligning the parties can ruin your analysis and understanding of the case.

ISSUE: A statement of the general legal question answered by or illustrated in the case. For clarity, the issue is best put in the form of a question capable of a "yes" or "no" answer. In reality, the issue is simply the Rule of Law put in the form of a question (e.g., "May an offer be accepted by performance?").

The major problem presented in discerning what is *the* issue in the case is that an opinion usually purports to raise and answer several questions. However, except for rare cases, only one such question is really the issue in the case. Collateral issues not necessary to the resolution of the matter in controversy are handled by the court by language known as *"obiter dictum"* or merely *"dictum."* While dicta may be included later in the brief, they have no place under the issue heading.

To find the issue, ask *who wants what* and then go on to ask *why did that party succeed or fail in getting it.* Once this is determined, the "why" should be turned into a question.

The complexity of the issues in the cases will vary, but in all cases a single-sentence question should sum up the issue. *In a few cases,* there will be two, or even more rarely, three issues of equal importance to the resolution of the case. Each should be expressed in a single-sentence question.

Since many issues are resolved by a court in coming to a final disposition of a case, the casebook editor will reproduce the portion of the opinion containing the issue or issues most relevant to the area of law under scrutiny. A noted law professor gave this advice: "Close the book; look at the title on the cover." Chances are, if it is Property, you need not concern yourself with whether, for example, the federal government's treatment of the plaintiff's land really raises a federal question sufficient to support jurisdiction on this ground in federal court.

The same rule applies to chapter headings designating sub-areas within the subjects. They tip you off as to what the text is designed to teach. The cases are arranged in a casebook to show a progression or development of the law, so that the preceding cases may also help.

It is also most important to remember to *read the notes and questions* at the end of a case to determine what the editors wanted you to have gleaned from it.

HOLDING AND DECISION: This section should succinctly explain the rationale of the court in arriving at its decision. In capsulizing the "reasoning" of the court, it should always include an application of the general rule or rules of law to the specific facts of the case. Hidden justifications come to light in this entry: the reasons for the state of the law, the public policies, the biases and prejudices, those considerations that influence the justices' thinking and, ultimately, the outcome of the case. At the end, there should be a short indication of the disposition or procedural resolution of the case (e.g., "Decision of the trial court for Mr. Smith (P) reversed").

The foregoing format is designed to help you "digest" the reams of case material with which you will be faced in your law school career. Once mastered by practice, it will place at your fingertips the information the authors of your casebooks have sought to impart to you in case-by-case illustration and analysis.

B. Be as Economical as Possible in Briefing Cases

Once armed with a format that encourages succinctness, it is as important to be economical with regard to the time spent on the actual reading of the case as it is to be economical in the writing of the brief itself. This does not mean "skimming" a case. Rather, it means reading the case with an "eye" trained to recognize into which "section" of your brief a particular passage or line fits and having a system for quickly and precisely marking the case so that the passages fitting any one particular part of the brief can be easily identified and brought together in a concise and accurate manner when the brief is actually written.

It is of no use to simply repeat everything in the opinion of the court; record only enough information to trigger your recollection of what the court said. Nevertheless, an accurate statement of the "law of the case," i.e., the legal principle applied to the facts, is absolutely essential to class preparation and to learning the law under the case method.

To that end, it is important to develop a "shorthand" that you can use to make marginal notations. These notations will tell you at a glance in which section of the brief you will be placing that particular passage or portion of the opinion.

Some students prefer to underline all the salient portions of the opinion (with a pencil or colored underliner marker), making marginal notations as they go along. Others prefer the color-coded method of underlining, utilizing different colors of markers to underline the salient portions of the case, each separate color being used to represent a different section of the brief. For example, blue underlining could be used for passages relating to the rule of law, yellow for those relating to the issue, and green for those relating to the holding and decision, etc. While it has its advocates, the color-coded method can be confusing and time-consuming (all that time spent on changing colored markers). Furthermore, it can interfere with the continuity and concentration many students deem essential to the reading of a case for maximum comprehension. In the end, however, it is a matter of personal preference and style. Just remember, whatever method you use, underlining must be used sparingly or its value is lost.

If you take the marginal notation route, an efficient and easy method is to go along underlining the key portions of the case and placing in the margin alongside them the following "markers" to indicate where a particular passage or line "belongs" in the brief you will write:

N   (NATURE OF CASE)
RL (RULE OF LAW)
I   (ISSUE)
HL (HOLDING AND DECISION, relates to the RULE OF LAW behind the decision)
HR (HOLDING AND DECISION, gives the RATIONALE or reasoning behind the decision)
HA (HOLDING AND DECISION, APPLIES the general principle(s) of law to the facts of the case to arrive at the decision)

Remember that a particular passage may well contain information necessary to more than one part of your brief, in which case you simply note that in the margin. If you are using the color-coded underlining method instead of marginal notation, simply make asterisks or checks in the margin next to the passage in question in the colors that indicate the additional sections of the brief where it might be utilized.

The economy of utilizing "shorthand" in marking cases for briefing can be maintained in the actual brief writing process itself by utilizing "law student shorthand" within the brief. There are many commonly used words and phrases for which abbreviations can be substituted in your briefs (and in your class notes also). You can develop abbreviations that are personal to you and which will save you a lot of time. A reference list of briefing abbreviations can be found on page xii of this book.

C. Use Both the Briefing Process and the Brief as a Learning Tool

Now that you have a format and the tools for briefing cases efficiently, the most important thing is to make the time spent in briefing profitable to you and to make the most advantageous use of the briefs you create. Of course, the briefs are invaluable for classroom reference when you are called upon to explain or analyze a particular case. However, they are also useful in reviewing for exams. A quick glance at the fact summary should bring the case to mind, and a rereading of the rule of law should enable you to go over the underlying legal concept in your mind, how it was applied in that particular case, and how it might apply in other factual settings.

As to the value to be derived from engaging in the briefing process itself, there is an immediate benefit that arises from being forced to sift through the essential facts and reasoning from the court's opinion and to succinctly express them in your own words in your brief. The process ensures that you understand the case and the point that it illustrates, and that means you will be ready to absorb further analysis and information brought forth in class. It also ensures you will have something to say when called upon in class. The briefing process helps develop a mental agility for getting to the *gist* of a case and for identifying, expounding on, and applying the legal concepts and issues found there. The briefing process is the mental process on which you must rely in taking law school examinations; it is also the mental process upon which a lawyer relies in serving his clients and in making his living.

Abbreviations for Briefs

acceptance	acp	offer	O
affirmed	aff	offeree	OE
answer	ans	offeror	OR
assumption of risk	a/r	ordinance	ord
attorney	atty	pain and suffering	p/s
beyond a reasonable doubt	b/r/d	parol evidence	p/e
bona fide purchaser	BFP	plaintiff	P
breach of contract	br/k	prima facie	p/f
cause of action	c/a	probable cause	p/c
common law	c/l	proximate cause	px/c
Constitution	Con	real property	r/p
constitutional	con	reasonable doubt	r/d
contract	K	reasonable man	r/m
contributory negligence	c/n	rebuttable presumption	rb/p
cross	x	remanded	rem
cross-complaint	x/c	res ipsa loquitur	RIL
cross-examination	x/ex	respondeat superior	r/s
cruel and unusual punishment	c/u/p	Restatement	RS
defendant	D	reversed	rev
dismissed	dis	Rule Against Perpetuities	RAP
double jeopardy	d/j	search and seizure	s/s
due process	d/p	search warrant	s/w
equal protection	e/p	self-defense	s/d
equity	eq	specific performance	s/p
evidence	ev	statute	S
exclude	exc	statute of frauds	S/F
exclusionary rule	exc/r	statute of limitations	S/L
felony	f/n	summary judgment	s/j
freedom of speech	f/s	tenancy at will	t/w
good faith	g/f	tenancy in common	t/c
habeas corpus	h/c	tenant	t
hearsay	hr	third party	TP
husband	H	third party beneficiary	TPB
injunction	inj	transferred intent	TI
in loco parentis	ILP	unconscionable	uncon
inter vivos	I/v	unconstitutional	unconst
joint tenancy	j/t	undue influence	u/e
judgment	judgt	Uniform Commercial Code	UCC
jurisdiction	jur	unilateral	uni
last clear chance	LCC	vendee	VE
long-arm statute	LAS	vendor	VR
majority view	maj	versus	v
meeting of minds	MOM	void for vagueness	VFV
minority view	min	weight of authority	w/a
Miranda rule	Mir/r	weight of the evidence	w/e
Miranda warnings	Mir/w	wife	W
negligence	neg	with	w/
notice	ntc	within	w/i
nuisance	nus	without	w/o
obligation	ob	without prejudice	w/o/p
obscene	obs	wrongful death	wr/d

Table of Cases

Introduction

Quick Reference Rules of Law

United States v. Hall

United States (P) v. Criminal defendant (D)

472 F.2d 261 (5th Cir. 1972).

NATURE OF CASE: Appeal from guilty verdict of contempt charge following nonjury trial.

FACT SUMMARY: As part of a desegregation plan, a federal district court issued a restraining order that was violated by Hall (D) who was not a party to the original segregation suit.

🏛 RULE OF LAW
A federal district court has power to punish for contempt a person who violates its order even though the person punished is not a party to the litigation out of which the case arose.

FACTS: As part of a desegregation plan, a federal district court issued an interim ex parte order restraining unauthorized persons from entering certain school grounds. The court served notice on Hall (D) who, nevertheless, went upon the grounds, stating his purpose was to violate the desegregation order. Hall (D) was not a party to the segregation suit.

ISSUE: Does a federal district court have power to punish for contempt a person who violates the court's order even though the person punished is not a party to the litigation out of which the order arose?

HOLDING AND DECISION: (Wisdom, J.) Yes. The activities of Hall (D) threatened the rights of the parties as adjudicated in the underlying desegregation suit, which had established that the original plaintiffs had a constitutional right to attend a desegregated school. The activities of persons contributing to racial disorder, which was the goal of Hall (D) in entering the school premises, imperiled the court's fundamental power to make a binding adjudication between the parties properly before it. Because school desegregation orders often strongly excite community passions, such orders, like in rem orders, are particularly vulnerable to disruption by an indefinable class of persons who, like Hall (D), are neither parties nor acting at the instigation of parties. Affirmed.

▶ ANALYSIS

Although a literal reading of Rule 65(d) of the Federal Rules of Civil Procedure forbids federal courts to issue in rem type injunctions against persons not parties nor acting in concert with parties to a suit, the instant court noted that federal courts continue to issue such injunctions because they possess the power to do so at common law and because Rule 65(d) was intended to embody rather than to limit their common-law powers.

■═■

Quicknotes

EX PARTE A proceeding commenced by one party without providing any opposing parties with notice or that is uncontested by an adverse party.

INJUNCTION A court order requiring a person to do or prohibiting that person from doing a specific act.

IN REM An action against property.

■═■

Goldberg v. Kelly

Recipients of financial aid (P) v. New York State (D)

397 U.S. 254 (1970).

NATURE OF CASE: Appeal from judgment invalidating welfare termination procedure.

FACT SUMMARY: New York welfare recipients of Aid to Families with Dependent Children (AFDC) (P) sued New York State (D) for refusal to adopt a pretermination hearing procedure prior to termination of benefits.

🏛 **RULE OF LAW**
The Due Process Clause of the Fourteenth Amendment to the U.S. Constitution requires that an AFDC recipient be afforded an evidentiary hearing prior to termination of benefits.

FACTS: New York welfare recipients of AFDC (P) sued New York State (D), alleging that New York officials were about to terminate such aid without prior notice and hearing, thereby denying them due process of law. At the time the suits were filed, however, there was no requirement of prior notice or hearing of any kind before termination of financial aid.

ISSUE: Does the Due Process Clause of the Fourteenth Amendment require that an AFDC recipient be afforded an evidentiary hearing before termination of benefits?

HOLDING AND DECISION: (Brennan, J.) Yes. When welfare is discontinued, only a pretermination evidentiary hearing provides the recipient with procedural due process, because for qualified recipients, welfare provides the means to obtain essential food, clothing, housing, and medical care. Thus, the crucial factor in this context is that termination of aid pending resolution of a controversy over eligibility may deprive an eligible recipient of the very means by which to live while he or she waits. Because such persons lack independent resources, their situation becomes immediately desperate and, in turn, adversely affects their ability to seek redress from the welfare bureaucracy. Affirmed.

DISSENT: (Black, J.) As a matter of constitutional law, a pretermination evidentiary hearing for recipients of state-funded welfare payments finds no precedent in the American legal system. The Fourteenth Amendment should not be given such an unnecessarily broad construction. New experiments in carrying out a welfare program should not be frozen into our constitutional structure. They should be left to the legislative branch to determine.

▶ *ANALYSIS*

The Court noted that an AFDC pretermination hearing need not take the form of a judicial or quasi-judicial trial and that a "fair hearing" will provide the recipient with a full administrative review. Hence, a complete record and a comprehensive opinion need not be provided at the pretermination stage and "minimum procedural safeguards" are justified. At the very least, however, the affected individual must have an opportunity to state his or her case orally to an impartial decision maker.

■━■

Quicknotes

EVIDENTIARY HEARING Hearing pertaining to the evidence of the case.

FOURTEENTH AMENDMENT No person shall be deprived of life, liberty, or property without the due process of law.

FOURTEENTH AMENDMENT DUE PROCESS CLAUSE Provides that protections mandated by the Constitution and observed by the federal government are equally applicable, and therefore must be observed by the States.

PROCEDURAL DUE PROCESS The constitutional mandate that if the state or federal government acts so as to deny a citizen of a life, liberty, or property interest the individual is first entitled to notice and the right to be heard.

QUASI-JUDICIAL Function of administrative officers to hear and determine matters.

■━■

Mathews, Secretary of Health, Education and Welfare v. Eldridge

Secretary of Health, Education and Welfare (D) v. Social Security disability recipient (P)

424 U.S. 319 (1976).

NATURE OF CASE: Appeal from judgment declaring unconstitutional administrative procedures established by the Secretary of Health, Education and Welfare (HEW) for discontinuing federally funded disability payments.

FACT SUMMARY: Eldridge (P) challenged the constitutional validity of the administrative procedures established by HEW (D) for assessing whether there exists a continuing disability entitling him to Social Security payments.

🏛 **RULE OF LAW**
The Due Process Clause of the Fifth Amendment to the U.S. Constitution does not require that the recipient be afforded an opportunity for an evidentiary hearing prior to termination of Social Security disability benefit payments.

FACTS: After obtaining medical reports, the state agency charged with monitoring his medical condition notified Eldridge (P) that it had made a tentative decision that his disability had ceased, advising him that he could request additional time to seek reconsideration. Instead of requesting reconsideration, Eldridge (P) commenced suit challenging the constitutional validity of the administrative procedures established by HEW (D) for assessing whether there exists a continuing disability, specifically contending that a pretermination hearing was required.

ISSUE: Does the Due Process Clause of the Fifth Amendment require that the recipient be afforded an opportunity for an evidentiary hearing prior to termination of Social Security disability benefit payments?

HOLDING AND DECISION: (Powell, J.) No. The disabled worker's need for uninterrupted payments is likely to be less than that of a welfare recipient. In addition to the possibility of access to private resources, other forms of government assistance will become available if the termination of disability benefits places a worker or his or her family below the subsistence level. In addition, the existing pretermination procedures are fair and comparatively reliable, involving the more sharply focused and easily documented evaluation of a recipient's medical condition, rather than the more vague matter of his or her financial need. Hence, there is less reason here than in some other situations to depart from the ordinary principle that something less than an evidentiary hearing is sufficient prior to adverse administrative action. Experience with the constitutionalizing of governmental procedures suggests

that the ultimate additional cost in terms of money and administrative burden would be substantial. Reversed.

DISSENT: (Brennan, J.) The Court's consideration that a discontinuance of disability benefits causes a recipient only limited deprivation is not argument but speculation.

▶ *ANALYSIS*

The Supreme Court points out that the specific dictates of due process require consideration of three factors: (1) private interests affected; (2) risk of erroneous deprivation of such interests through the procedures used and the probative value of additional or substitute procedural safeguards; and (3) the government's interest, including the function involved and the fiscal and administrative burdens that the additional or substitute procedural requirement would entail.

■═■

Quicknotes

DUE PROCESS CLAUSE Clauses, found in the Fifth and Fourteenth Amendments to the United States Constitution, providing that no person shall be deprived of "life, liberty, or property, without due process of law."

EVIDENTIARY HEARING Hearing pertaining to the evidence of the case.

FIFTH AMENDMENT Provides that no person shall be compelled to serve as a witness against himself, or be subject to trial for the same offense twice, or be deprived of life, liberty, or property without due process of law.

PRETERMINATION HEARING A hearing held prior to the termination of a property interest.

■═■

Hamdi v. Rumsfeld

Alleged enemy combatant (P) v. Federal government/U.S. Secretary of Defense (D)

542 U.S. 507 (2004).

NATURE OF CASE: Habeas petition from designation and detention as an enemy combatant.

FACT SUMMARY: Hamdi (P) was charged as an enemy combatant and detained by the U.S. military. He challenged his status and the constitutionality of holding him without formal charges or proceedings.

🏛 RULE OF LAW
A United States citizen designated and detained as an enemy combatant has a due process right to challenge the underlying factual support for that designation before a neutral arbitrator.

FACTS: On September 11, 2001, al Qaeda terrorists attacked the United States and caused the deaths of 3,000 American citizens. In response, the President, authorized by Congress, sent military troops to Afghanistan to locate and subdue the terrorists and the Taliban regime supporting them. Yaser Esam Hamdi (P) was born in America but had lived most of his life in Saudi Arabia. He was captured by allied troops while fighting with the Taliban and turned over to the U.S. military. The Government (D) classified Hamdi (P) as an "enemy combatant" and decided to hold him indefinitely without formal charges or proceedings. Hamdi (P) challenged this designation as unconstitutional. The Fourth Circuit held that no further hearing was required and the U.S. Supreme Court granted certiorari.

ISSUE: Does a United States citizen designated and detained as an enemy combatant have a due process right to challenge the underlying factual support for that designation before a neutral arbitrator?

HOLDING AND DECISION: (O'Connor, J.) Yes. A United States citizen designated and detained as an enemy combatant has a due process right to challenge the underlying factual support for that designation before a neutral arbitrator. This Court finds that Congress did in fact authorize the detention of persons such as Hamdi (P) because Hamdi (P) was detained pursuant to an Act of Congress. Contrary to the Fourth Circuit's holding, it is not undisputed that Hamdi (P) was captured in a combat zone because all that is certain is that Hamdi (P) resided in that area. Hamdi (P) has thus not made any concessions abdicating his rights, if any, to further hearing. The Government (D) next argues that the Court should only consider whether broader authorization existed for the detention and not whether an individual detainee is entitled to further proceedings. A citizen, however, has a right to be free from unlawful detention without due process of law. The Court must weigh the governmental interest in confining enemy combatants against the individual liberty rights of the detainee. After due consideration, it is not necessary to provide initial due process hearings for captures, but those who must be detained further are entitled to further proceedings. The detainee must have an opportunity to demonstrate that the Government's (D) factual assertions are untrue. Vacated and remanded.

CONCURRENCE AND DISSENT: (Souter, J.) The plurality's judgment is correct insofar as it rejects the limits asserted by the Government (D) on the exercise of jurisdiction. But, the congressional Authorization for Use of Military Force did not allow for Hamdi's (P) detention, and the plurality's judgment on that issue is incorrect. In addition, the Government (D) cannot claim an evidentiary presumption, placing the burden of rebuttal on Hamdi (P).

DISSENT: (Scalia, J.) How the law is applied to the facts of this case must take into consideration the special nature of the offending activity. Hamdi (P) was detained by the Government (D) because the Government (D) suspected that he participated in waging war against the United States (D). The relevant question is whether there is a different, special procedure for imprisonment of a citizen accused of wrongdoing by aiding the enemy in wartime. Justice O'Connor argued that captured enemy combatants (other than those suspected of war crimes) have traditionally been detained until the cessation of hostilities and then released. That may be an accurate description of wartime practice with respect to enemy aliens, but the tradition with respect to American citizens has been different. Citizens aiding the enemy have been treated as traitors subject to the criminal process. The Government (D) must prosecute for treason or another crime in federal court unless wartime allows for the enactment of the Suspension Clause. As no one contends this is a Suspension Clause situation, nothing allows for the detention of this man without due process proceedings. This is especially true given that this man is a U.S. citizen and not a foreign-born captive.

DISSENT: (Thomas, J.) We have held in prior cases that legislative authority to detain enemy combatants, is unnecessary. Due process requires only a good faith determination by the executive branch whether or not to detain an individual during wartime. The executive branch, acting pursuant to both statutory and constitutional authority, may unilaterally decide to detain an individual if the executive makes a determination that the detention

Continued on next page.

will protect the public. Judicial second guessing of such a determination should not be allowed. Moreover, allowing hearings on Hamdi's (P) detention may harm the intelligence gathering process and may even force the government to divulge classified material.

▶ ANALYSIS

While the Court did not directly address presidential authority to designate and detain enemy combatants, it did temper the government's attempts to unilaterally control wartime captures as they related to American citizens. Although many supported the President's actions after the terrorist attacks of 2001, many more recognized the danger in vesting too much power in the executive branch even in wartime. Mistakes can be made and captured U.S. citizens should be entitled to place their case before an objective party.

■■■■

Quicknotes

CERTIORARI A discretionary writ issued by a superior court to an inferior court in order to review the lower court's decisions; the Supreme Court's writ ordering such review.

DUE PROCESS The constitutional mandate requiring the courts to protect and enforce individuals' rights and liberties consistent with prevailing principles of fairness and justice and prohibiting the federal and state governments from such activities that deprive its citizens of life, liberty, or property interest.

HABEAS CORPUS A proceeding in which a defendant brings a writ to compel a judicial determination of whether he is lawfully being held in custody.

■■■■

Connecticut v. Doehr

State (D) and Tort claimant (D) v. Tortfeasor (P)

501 U.S. 1 (1991).

NATURE OF CASE: Review of order quashing attachment levied on real estate.

FACT SUMMARY: Connecticut (D) law permitted ex parte prejudgment attachment of real estate without a showing of exigent circumstances.

🏛 RULE OF LAW
A state may not allow ex parte prejudgment attachment of property without a showing of exigent circumstances.

FACTS: DiGiovanni (D), a tort claimant against Doehr (P), utilized Connecticut's (D) prejudgment attachment procedure. Ex parte, he filed a declaration setting forth the nature of his claim against Doehr (P). State law required no showing of exigent circumstances necessitating prejudgment attachment. The court issued an attachment order. Doehr (P) responded with a federal suit challenging the constitutionality of the procedure. The district court upheld the procedure's validity, but the Second Circuit reversed. The U.S. Supreme Court granted review.

ISSUE: May a state allow an ex parte prejudgment attachment of real estate without a showing of exigent circumstances?

HOLDING AND DECISION: (White, J.) No. A state may not allow ex parte prejudgment attachment of property without a showing of exigent circumstances. In the context of suits between private parties, the analysis for the validity of prejudgment remedies involves (1) consideration of the private interest involved, (2) the risk of erroneous deprivation of that interest, and (3) the interest of the party seeking the prejudgment remedy. Here, Connecticut's (D) statutory attachment procedure clearly fails under this analysis. First, the owner of the attached property has an obvious interest in his property, and attachment places a severe restriction on the property's alienability and encumberability. The ex parte nature of the proceeding presents serious risk of erroneous deprivation, as a self-serving declaration will suffice to allow the attachment. Finally, if the party seeking attachment has no reason to fear that the property may be secreted, his interest is not all that compelling. For these reasons, absent exigent circumstances, an ex parte application is insufficient to warrant attachment of real estate. Affirmed and remanded.

▶ ANALYSIS

The analysis used by the Court was devised in *Mathews v. Eldridge*, 424 U.S. 319 (1976). That case involved deprivation by government as opposed to a private litigant. The Court, in adopting the analysis, believed the basic considerations to be the same without regard to the public or private status of the litigant.

■■■

Quicknotes

EXIGENT CIRCUMSTANCES Circumstances requiring an extraordinary or immediate response; an exception to the prohibition on a warrantless arrest or search when police officers believe probable cause to exist and there is no time for obtaining a warrant.

EX PARTE A proceeding commenced by one party.

■■■

Boddie v. Connecticut

Indigent married couples (P) v. State (D)

401 U.S. 371 (1971).

NATURE OF CASE: Appeal from dismissal of complaint challenging constitutionality of fee requirements for commencement of litigation.

FACT SUMMARY: Indigent married couples (P) sued the state (D), arguing that to require indigents to pay fees for access to courts in marital dissolution proceedings violates due process.

🏛 RULE OF LAW
Due process prohibits a state from denying, solely because of inability to pay, access to its courts to individuals who seek judicial dissolution of their marriages.

FACTS: Indigent married couples (P) sued the state (D) in a class action challenging certain state procedures for commencement of litigation, including requirements for payment of court fees and costs for service of process, which allegedly restricted their access to the courts in their efforts to bring an action for divorce.

ISSUE: Does due process prohibit a state from denying, solely because of inability to pay, access to its courts to individuals who seek judicial dissolution of their marriages?

HOLDING AND DECISION: (Harlan, J.) Yes. Given the basic position of the marriage relationship in American society's hierarchy of values and the concomitant state monopolization of the means for legally dissolving this relationship, due process does prohibit a state from denying, solely because of inability to pay, access to its courts to individuals seeking marital dissolution. Marriage involves interests of basic importance in American society, and in the instant case, meaningful opportunity to be heard, within the limits of practicality, must be protected against denial by particular laws, such as here, that operate to jeopardize it for particular individuals. Reversed.

DISSENT: (Black, J.) Absent some specific federal constitutional or statutory provision, marriage and divorce in America are completely under state control. In determining applicability of the due process clause, civil lawsuits are not like criminal prosecutions, and the government is not usually involved as an actual party; hence, there is no deprivation of life, liberty, or property.

▎ *ANALYSIS*

In concluding that the due process clause requires an indigent applicant an opportunity to go into court to obtain a divorce even if such person cannot afford to pay the court fees, the Court emphasized that it went no further than necessary to dispose of the case before it and did not decide that access for all individuals to the courts is a right that is, in all circumstances, guaranteed by the Due Process Clause.

▪══▪

Quicknotes

DUE PROCESS CLAUSE Clauses, found in the Fifth and Fourteenth Amendments to the United States Constitution, providing that no person shall be deprived of "life, liberty, or property, without due process of law."

INDIGENT A person who is poor and thus is unable to obtain counsel to defend himself in a criminal proceeding and for whom counsel must be appointed.

MARITAL DISSOLUTION Legal termination of the marital relationship.

▪══▪

Lassiter v. Department of Social Services of Durham County, North Carolina

Parent (D) v. State agency (P)

452 U.S. 18 (1981).

NATURE OF CASE: Appeal from a termination of parental rights.

FACT SUMMARY: Lassiter (D) contended she was entitled to the appointment of counsel in a procedure to terminate her parental rights.

⚖ RULE OF LAW
There is no constitutional right to appoint counsel, unless the indigent litigant, if he loses, may be deprived of his physical liberty.

FACTS: Lassiter (D) lost custody of her infant son, William, after a trial court found she had neglected him and failed to provide him with adequate medical care. Following this, Lassiter (D) was charged with murder and convicted and sentenced to 25 to 40 years of imprisonment. The Department of Social Services (P) brought a proceeding to terminate her parental rights. At the hearing, Lassiter (D) was not represented by counsel, and she did not indicate that she was indigent. Following the taking of testimony, her parental rights were terminated. Lassiter (D) appealed, contending that she was in fact indigent and that she was entitled to appointed counsel prior to the termination of her parental rights. The Supreme Court of North Carolina denied the asserted right to appointed counsel, and the U.S. Supreme Court granted review.

ISSUE: Is there a right to appointed counsel, unless the party, if she loses, may be deprived of physical liberty?

HOLDING AND DECISION: (Stewart, J.) No. There is no right to appointed counsel, unless the party, if she loses, may be deprived of her physical liberty. The basis for Lassiter's (D) assertion of a right to counsel is based upon the Due Process Clause of the Fourteenth Amendment. This clause has been interpreted on many occasions as requiring only appointed counsel where the right to personal liberty is in jeopardy. These situations almost always involve criminal proceedings. The result of the termination of parental rights is not one that encompasses the possibility of a deprivation of personal liberty. As a result, there is no right to appointed counsel, and no abuse of discretion was displayed by the trial court in failing to supply such counsel. As a result, the holding of the North Carolina Supreme Court must be affirmed.

DISSENT: (Blackmun, J.) The case at issue involves the interest of a parent in the companionship, care, custody, and management of his or her children. A more fundamental right cannot be imagined, and the deprivation

of such right clearly approaches, if not exceeds, the right to personal liberty. As a result, the right to appointment of counsel must be recognized in this situation in order to uphold the policy behind maintaining the family unit. Without such counsel, she has been deprived of an opportunity to be meaningfully heard prior to the termination of her fundamental right as a parent.

▶ ANALYSIS

The seminal case in due process discussions of the type illustrated in this case is that found in *Mathews v. Eldridge*, 424 U.S. 319 (1976). In that case, a formula involving three elements was developed, and courts were required to evaluate such elements in deciding the requirements of due process. Those three elements include the private interests at stake, the government's interests, and the risk that the procedures used will lead to erroneous decisions. The use of these factors in this case allows the Court to conclude that while a parent has an extremely high private interest in maintaining the parental rights, the government's interests and the risk of the procedures used leading to an erroneous decision simply outweighed those rights in this case. The procedure by which the rights were terminated was found to be adequate, and the governmental interest in protecting the child was found to be paramount. As a result, it was found that due process was not violated in this case.

■■■

Quicknotes

DUE PROCESS CLAUSE Clauses, found in the Fifth and Fourteenth Amendments to the United States Constitution, providing that no person shall be deprived of "life, liberty, or property, without due process of law."

FOURTEENTH AMENDMENT DUE PROCESS CLAUSE Provides that protections mandated by the Constitution and observed by the federal government are equally applicable, and therefore must be observed by the States.

INDIGENT A person who is poor and thus is unable to obtain counsel to defend himself in a criminal proceeding and for whom counsel must be appointed.

■■■

Turner v. Rogers

Deadbeat Dad (D) v. Government (P)

131 S. Ct. 2507 (2011).

NATURE OF CASE: Writ of certiorari.

FACT SUMMARY: South Carolina's Family Court enforces its child support orders by threatening with incarceration for civil contempt those who are (1) subject to a child support order, (2) able to comply with that order, but (3) fail to do so. Michael Turner (D), an indigent non-custodial parent who fell behind in child-support payments, was sentenced for civil contempt to 12 months in prison. He was not asked whether he was able to pay the child support prior to incarceration. Turner (D) appealed to the state supreme court, which affirmed, and he then sought certiorari to the U.S. Supreme Court.

🏛 RULE OF LAW
(1) The Due Process Clause does not automatically require the provision of counsel at civil contempt proceedings to an indigent individual who is subject to a child support order.
(2) A state must provide safeguards to reduce the risk of erroneous deprivation of liberty in civil contempt cases.

FACTS: South Carolina's Family Court enforces its child support orders by threatening with incarceration for civil contempt those who are (1) subject to a child support order, (2) able to comply with that order, but (3) fail to do so. Michael Turner (D), an indigent non-custodial parent, fell behind in child-support payments several times over a period of three years, and was incarcerated for civil contempt several times, each time for several months. He remained in arrears for a little over $5,000 after his release, and in 2008 was sentenced for civil contempt to 12 months in prison. He was not asked whether he was able to pay the child support prior to incarceration, and the court made no finding about Turner's (D) ability to pay. Turner (D) appealed to the state supreme court, arguing the U.S. Constitution guaranteed him a right to counsel for his civil contempt hearing. The court affirmed the lower court ruling, rejecting Turner's (D) right-to-counsel argument, pointing out that the same constitutional protections available in criminal contempt proceedings are not available in civil contempt proceedings. Turner (D) then sought certiorari to the U.S. Supreme Court.

ISSUE:
(1) Does the Due Process Clause automatically require the provision of counsel at civil contempt proceedings to an indigent individual who is subject to a child support order?

(2) Must a state provide safeguards to reduce the risk of erroneous deprivation of liberty in civil contempt cases?

HOLDING AND DECISION: (Breyer, J.)
(1) No. The Due Process Clause does not automatically require the provision of counsel at civil contempt proceedings to an indigent individual who is subject to a child support order. The Sixth Amendment right to counsel applies to criminal contempt proceedings where incarceration is possible, but it does not apply to civil proceedings, where the point is not punishment, but coercion to comply with court orders. Where civil contempt is at issue, the Fourteenth Amendment Due Process Clause permits a state to provide fewer procedural safeguards than in criminal matters. Precedent directly addressing a right to counsel in civil matters is sparse (*In re Gault*, 387 U.S. 1 (1967); *Vitek v. Jones*, 445 U.S. 480 (1980); *Lassiter v. Department of Social Services of Durham County*, 452 U.S. 18 (1981); *Gagnon v. Scarpelli*, 411 U.S. 778 (1973)), and none of the cases clearly deals with the facts set forth in this case.

(2) Yes. A state must provide safeguards to reduce the risk of erroneous deprivation of liberty in civil contempt cases. What specific safeguards the Constitution's Due Process Clause requires in order to make a civil proceeding fundamentally fair are determined by *Mathews v. Eldridge*, 424 U.S. 319, 335 (1976) (considering fairness of an administrative proceeding). Those factors include (1) the nature of the private interest that will be affected, (2) the comparative risk of an erroneous deprivation of that interest with and without additional or substitute procedural safeguards, and (3) the nature and magnitude of any countervailing interest in not providing additional or substitute procedural requirements. The private interest at stake is Turner's (D) liberty. With respect to the risks of erroneous deprivation of liberty, and the countervailing interest in not providing additional or substitute procedural requirements, three considerations are informative. First, ability to pay—the issue that must be considered prior to incarcerating an individual for civil contempt—could be determined by measures that don't require counsel, and making that determination would lower the risk of erroneous incarceration. Second, this civil contempt hearing was primarily for the benefit of the custodial parent who was unrepresented by counsel, and providing Turner (D) with counsel might have made the proceedings unfair to the custodial parent or delay the proceedings unnecessarily. Third, there is available a

Continued on next page.

set of procedural safeguards that, if employed, could reduce the risk of an erroneous deprivation of the right to liberty. Those safeguards might include (1) notice to the defendant that his "ability to pay" is a critical issue in the contempt proceeding; (2) the use of a form (or the equivalent) to uncover relevant financial information; (3) an opportunity at the hearing for the defendant to respond to statements and questions about his financial status (for example, those triggered by his responses on the form); and (4) an express finding by the court that the defendant has the ability to pay. Imposing a categorical right to counsel in proceedings of the kind in this case would carry with it disadvantages (in the form of unfairness and delay) that, in terms of ultimate fairness, would deprive it of significant superiority over the alternatives listed here. In particular, that Due Process Clause does not require the provision of counsel where the opposing parent or other custodian (to whom support funds are owed) is not represented by counsel and the State provides alternative procedural safeguards, such as adequate notice of the importance of ability to pay, fair opportunity to present, and to dispute, relevant information, and court findings. In this case, though Turner's (D) right-to-counsel argument is rejected, he was not afforded the kinds of procedural safeguards to ensure protection of his right to liberty in a civil context. Therefore, the judgment of the state supreme court is vacated and remanded.

DISSENT: (Thomas, J.) The Due Process Clause of the Fourteenth Amendment does not provide a right to appointed counsel for indigent defendants facing incarceration in civil contempt proceedings, and the state court judgment should be affirmed. The majority agrees with that holding, but nevertheless vacates the judgment of the South Carolina Supreme Court on a different ground, namely that Turner's (D) contempt proceeding violated due process because it did not include "alternative procedural safeguards." For two reasons, that is the wrong conclusion. First, this question should not be reached because Turner (D) did not raise this question in his brief. The question therefore was not before the court and should not have been considered. Second, the *Mathews v. Eldridge* balancing test, applied by the majority, should not have been applied, because it weighs an individual's interest against that of the Government. It does not account for the interests of the child and custodial parent, who is usually the child's mother, and their interests are the very reason for the child support obligation and the civil contempt proceedings that enforce it.

▶ *ANALYSIS*

According to the majority, the year-long incarceration of Turner (D) for failure to pay child support violated the Constitution because adequate safeguards had not been

in place to ensure that his failure to pay was willful. But the majority also ruled—and the dissent agreed—that parents facing jail time for failure to pay child support do not have a categorical right to a court-appointed attorney when the other parent is unrepresented. The ruling was explicitly confined to cases in which an unrepresented custodial parent brings a petition for civil contempt. The Court did not address the question of whether counsel is required in cases involving state agencies seeking to collect past due child support, which have a right to collect from recipients of welfare benefits.

Quicknotes

CERTIORARI A discretionary writ issued by a superior court to an inferior court in order to review the lower court's decisions; the Supreme Court's writ ordering such review.

CIVIL LAW RULE Rule of law pertaining to an individual's private rights; rule based on statutory law rather than upon court decisions.

RIGHT TO COUNSEL Right conferred by the Sixth Amendment that the accused shall be provided effective legal assistance in a criminal proceeding.

SIXTH AMENDMENT Provides the right to a speedy and public trial by impartial jury, the right to be informed of the accusation, the right to confront witnesses, and the right to have the assistance of counsel in all criminal prosecutions.

Remedies and Stakes

Quick Reference Rules of Law

United States v. New York Times Co., et al.

Government (P) v. Newspaper (D)

328 F. Supp. 324 (S.D.N.Y. 1971).

NATURE OF CASE: Motion for preliminary injunction.

FACT SUMMARY: The New York Times (D) published summaries and excerpts from the Pentagon Papers. The U.S. government (P) sought a preliminary injunction against publication and an order directing the Times (D) to return the documents in its possession. The trial court issued a temporary restraining order against the Times (D) until the hearing on the preliminary injunction.

🏛 RULE OF LAW
A court may not issue a preliminary injunction where the party seeking the injunction cannot show irreparable harm and the probability of success in litigation.

FACTS: The New York Times ("the Times") (D) published summaries and excerpts from a 1968 study of the history of the Vietnam conflict and the Tonkin Gulf Study, collectively commonly known as "the Pentagon Papers." The United States (P) sought to enjoin the Times (D) from "further dissemination, disclosure or divulgence" of materials contained in the documents and for the court to order the Times (D) to furnish to the court all the documents involved so that they could be impounded pending a determination. The trial court entered a temporary restraining order against the Times (D) preventing further publication until a determination by the court on the merits of the Government's (P) application for a preliminary injunction. The court at that time, in the absence of any evidence, refused to require the documents to be impounded. At the hearing on the motion for preliminary injunction, the Government (P) argued that the documents still unpublished and in the possession of the Times (D) involved a serious breach of the security of the United States (P) and would compromise the national defense. Because the case possibly involved issues concerning national security, the hearing on the motion was held in camera.

ISSUE: May a court issue a preliminary injunction where the party seeking the injunction cannot irreparable harm and the probability of success in litigation?

HOLDING AND DECISION: (Gurfein, J.) No. A court may not issue a preliminary injunction where the party seeking the injunction cannot show irreparable harm and the probability of success in litigation. While the right of the Government (P) to injunctive relief against a newspaper that is about to publish information or documents absolutely vital to current national security is not in doubt, the facts of this case do not suggest that the documents contain information absolutely vital to national security. Purely as a matter of fact, the in camera proceedings did not show that the publication of these historical documents would seriously breach the national security. It is true that any breach of security would alarm U.S. security agencies and possibly foreign governments who deal with us. But to sustain a preliminary injunction the Government (P) would have to establish not only irreparable injury, but also the probability of success in the litigation itself. No cogent reasons were advanced as to why these documents except in the general framework of embarrassment previously mentioned, would vitally affect the security of the country. There is no reasonable likelihood of the Government (P) successfully proving that the actions of the Times (D) were not in good faith, nor is there irreparable injury to the Government (P). Further, the First Amendment generally prohibits prior restraint, and while these protections are not absolute, the facts in this case present no vital security interest of the country that might have justified the abrogation of the compelling constitutional doctrine against prior restraint that might.

▌ANALYSIS

This was a case of first impression for the court. It was an important decision and the precursor to the U.S. Supreme Court's landmark First Amendment decision *New York Times v. United States*, 403 U.S. 713 (1971), which affirmed the lower court rulings. That case was cited most recently in context of the case against a U.S. army private, Pfc. Bradley Manning, who leaked sensitive documents to *WikiLeaks* publisher, Julian Assange.

■=■

Quicknotes

IN CAMERA In private chambers.

PRELIMINARY INJUNCTION A judicial mandate issued to require or restrain a party from certain conduct; used to preserve a trial's subject matter or to prevent threatened injury.

TEMPORARY RESTRAINING ORDER A court order preserving the status quo pending a hearing regarding injunctive relief.

■=■

Walgreen Co. v. Sara Creek Property Co.

Retail tenant (D) v. Owner of shopping center (P)

966 F.2d 273 (7th Cir. 1992).

NATURE OF CASE: Appeal from grant of permanent injunction against owner of shopping center.

FACT SUMMARY: Walgreen Co. (D) brought suit for permanent injunction against Sara Creek Property Co. (Sara Creek) (P), the owner of shopping center, to prevent Sara Creek from breaching its lease by renting space to a competing pharmacy. Injunction was granted to Walgreen (D), and Sara Creek (D) appealed.

🏛 RULE OF LAW
Where damages would be a costly and inadequate remedy, injunctive relief is appropriate.

FACTS: Walgreen Co. (P) leased retail space from Sara Creek Property Co. (Sara Creek) (D) in a shopping mall and ran a pharmacy in the leased space. Walgreen (P) brought a diversity suit for breach of contract against Sara Creek (D) when it learned that, in violation of a lease provision, Sara Creek (D) was about to rent space to a second pharmacy within a few hundred feet of Walgreen's pharmacy (P). Walgreen (P) also requested an injunction against Sara Creek (D) to prevent it from leasing space to the competing drugstore.

ISSUE: Should injunctive relief be granted where damages would be a costly and inadequate remedy?

HOLDING AND DECISION: (Posner, J.) Yes. Injunctive relief should be granted where damages would be a costly and inadequate remedy. The choice between remedies requires a balancing of the costs and benefits of the alternatives. Here, the effect of upholding the injunction would be to substitute for the costly processes of forensic fact determination the less costly processes of private negotiation. In other words, it would cost society less to grant the injunction and allow the parties to work out in private negotiations just how much compensation the plaintiff drugstore, Walgreen (P), would be willing to take to dissolve the injunction, than it would cost to bring the apparatus of the state to bear in a trial to determine the amount in money damages that would compensate Walgreen (P) for its losses if Sara Creek (D) breaks the lease and allows a competing pharmacy to open in the same shopping center. Here, there were 10 years left on Walgreen's (P) lease, and determining its revenues that far into the future, discounted by the effects of the competing pharmacy on its business and adjusting for present value, would be fraught with uncertainty. The Court was satisfied that the analytical approach of the trial judge did not exceed the bounds of reasonable judgment in concluding that the costs (including forgone benefits) of the damages remedy would exceed the costs (including forgone benefits) of an injunction. Affirmed.

▶ ANALYSIS

The court noted that a plaintiff who seeks an injunction has the burden of persuasion. Because damages are the norm, the plaintiff must show why his or her case is "abnormal."

■━■

Quicknotes

BREACH OF CONTRACT Unlawful failure by a party to perform its obligations pursuant to contract.

INJUNCTION A court order requiring a person to do or prohibiting that person from doing a specific act.

INJUNCTIVE RELIEF A court order issued as a remedy, requiring a person to do, or prohibiting that person from doing, a specific act.

■━■

Carey v. Piphus

School officials (D) v. Suspended student (P)

435 U.S. 247 (1978).

NATURE OF CASE: Appeal of award of damages for civil violations.

FACT SUMMARY: Damages in excess of a nominal amount were awarded in absence of proof of injury.

🏛 RULE OF LAW
In an action based on denial of procedural due process, only nominal damages may be awarded in the absence of actual injury.

FACTS: Piphus (P) was suspended from school for several days. He was reinstated but brought an action under 28 U.S.C. § 1983, contending he was denied procedural due process. The district court found no actual injury and dismissed. The court of appeals reversed, holding that Piphus (P) was entitled to injunctive relief and also that denial of procedural due process was compensable even in the absence of actual injury. The U.S. Supreme Court accepted renewal of the latter portion of the appellate court's holding.

ISSUE: In an action based on denial of procedural due process, may damages in excess of a nominal amount be awarded in the absence of proof of injury?

HOLDING AND DECISION: (Powell, J.) No. In an action based on denial of procedural due process, only nominal damages may be awarded. The basic purpose of § 1983 is to compensate individuals for injuries caused by the deprivation of constitutional rights. The structure under which this is done borrows from tort law. Just as tort law requires injury for compensation to be merited, so does § 1983. It cannot be assumed that denial of procedural due process, in itself, is an injury. Many will suffer no distress when such denial leads to no injury, and in such cases compensation would be inappropriate. It is injury caused by deprivation, not the deprivation itself, which is compensable. Here, no evidence on the issue of injury was put forth, so actual damages would be inappropriate. Reversed and remanded.

▶ ANALYSIS

The decision was apparently rather purposefully limited in scope. The Court always limited its terms to procedural due process. Substantive due process was not mentioned.

Also, the Court said in a footnote that punitive damages might be awarded in the absence of actual injury.

■▬■

Quicknotes

INJUNCTIVE RELIEF A court order issued as a remedy, requiring a person to do, or prohibiting that person from doing, a specific act.

NOMINAL DAMAGES A small sum awarded to a plaintiff in order to recognize that he sustained an injury that is either slight or incapable of being established.

PROCEDURAL DUE PROCESS The constitutional mandate that if the state or federal government acts so as to deny a citizen of a life, liberty or property interest the individual is first entitled to notice and the right to be heard.

PUNITIVE DAMAGES Damages exceeding the actual injury suffered for the purposes of punishment, deterrence and comfort to plaintiff.

■▬■

Marek v. Chesny

Offeror (D) v. Settlement offeree (P)

473 U.S. 1 (1985).

NATURE OF CASE: Appeal of denial of award of attorney fees.

FACT SUMMARY: Chesny (P) refused a settlement offer in a § 1983 action and was awarded less in trial.

🏛 RULE OF LAW
Attorney fees incurred by a plaintiff subsequent to an offer of settlement will not be paid when the plaintiff recovers less than the offer.

FACTS: Chesny (P) sued Marek (D) under 42 U.S.C. § 1983. Prior to trial, Marek (D) and the other defendants offered $100,000 to settle. Chesny (P) refused and was awarded $60,000 at trial. The court awarded Chesny (P) $32,000 in costs and fees incurred before the offer but refused to award costs and fees subsequent to the offer, per Fed. R. Civ. P. 68, which shifts to the plaintiff all costs incurred subsequent to an offer of judgment not exceeded by the ultimate recovery. The district court held that fees recoverable by a plaintiff in a § 1983 action were considered costs for purposes of Fed. R. Civ. P. 68. The Seventh Circuit disagreed and reversed. The U.S. Supreme Court granted certiorari.

ISSUE: Will attorney fees incurred by a plaintiff subsequent to an offer of settlement be paid when the plaintiff recovers less than the offer?

HOLDING AND DECISION: (Burger, C.J.) No. Attorney fees incurred by a plaintiff subsequent to an offer of settlement will not be paid when the plaintiff recovers less than the offer. Legislative history shows when Fed. R. Civ. P. 68 was drafted attorney fees were considered part of costs. When 42 U.S.C. § 1988 was enacted, enabling successful plaintiffs to recover costs and fees, Congress was aware that Fed. R. Civ. P. 68 included fees in its operation, and it could have exempted plaintiffs in § 1983 actions from the force of Fed. R. Civ. P. 68, but it did not do so. In the absence of this, the salutary effect of Fed. R. Civ. P. 68, the encouragement of settlements, should not be hindered. Reversed.

DISSENT: (Brennan, J.) The Court's reasoning is wholly inconsistent with the history and structure of the Federal Rules. Its application to the over 100 attorney fees statutes enacted by Congress will produce absurd variations in Rule 68's operation among the statutes. This is contrary to the purpose of the Federal Rules, which is a uniform procedure in federal courts.

▶ ANALYSIS

42 U.S.C. § 1988 was enacted in 1976. As the Court states, it provides that prevailing plaintiffs in § 1983 actions will be awarded costs and fees. The purpose of the section was to ensure that civil rights plaintiffs obtained effective access to the judicial process.

Quicknotes

42 U.S.C. § 1983 Provides that every person, who under color of state law subjects or causes to be subjected any citizen of the United States or person within its jurisdiction to be deprived of rights, privileges and immunities guaranteed by the federal constitution and laws, is liable to the injured party at law or in equity.

42 U.S.C. § 1988 Allows for attorney fees to be awarded the prevailing party in an action pursuant to § 1983.

CERTIORARI A discretionary writ issued by a superior court to an inferior court in order to review the lower court's decisions; the Supreme Court's writ ordering such review.

SETTLEMENT OFFER An offer made by one party to a lawsuit to the other agreeing upon the determination of rights and issues between them, thus disposing of the need for judicial determination.

City of Riverside v. Rivera

City (D) v. Individuals (P)

477 U.S. 561 (1986).

NATURE OF CASE: Appeal from judgment affirming award of attorneys' fees in federal civil rights suit.

FACT SUMMARY: Individuals (P) sued City of Riverside (D) for civil rights violations under 42 U.S.C. § 1983 for using "unnecessary physical force" in breaking up a party.

🏛 RULE OF LAW
An award of attorneys' fees under 42 U.S.C. § 1988 is not per se "unreasonable" within the meaning of the statute if it exceeds the amount of damages recovered by the plaintiff in the underlying civil rights action.

FACTS: Individuals (P) sued City of Riverside (D) for civil rights violations under 42 U.S.C. § 1983 for using "unnecessary physical force" in breaking up a party. Upon trial, the individuals (P) were awarded $33,350 for their claims. The individuals (P) also sought attorneys' fees under 42 U.S.C. § 1988 for 1,946.75 hours expended by their two attorneys and were awarded $245,456.25 as attorneys' fees.

ISSUE: Is an award of attorneys' fees under 42 U.S.C. § 1988 per se "unreasonable" within the meaning of the statute if it exceeds the amount of damages recovered by the plaintiff in the underlying civil rights action?

HOLDING AND DECISION: (Brennan, J.) No. The district court had carefully considered the results obtained by the attorneys and properly concluded that the attorneys were entitled to recover for all hours expended on the litigation because the amount of time reflected sound legal judgment under the circumstances and counsels' excellent performances entitled them to be compensated at prevailing market rates, even though they were relatively young when the litigation began. It would have been inappropriate to adjust the fee downward to account for the fact that the attorneys had prevailed only on some on their claims and against only some of the defendants. The relatively small size of the actual damages award did not imply that the attorneys' success was limited. Furthermore, the district court paid particular attention to the fact that the case presented complex and interrelated issues of fact and law and that a fee award in this civil rights action would advance the public interest. Affirmed.

CONCURRENCE: (Powell, J.) Affirmance is required by the district court's detailed findings of fact, that were approved by the court of appeals. Although there is no basis to reject those findings, the fee award seems unreasonable.

DISSENT: (Burger, C.J.) The fee award is unreasonable and constitutes a grave abuse of discretion. The attorneys' level of experience did not justify the fee.

DISSENT: (Rehnquist, J.) It was patently unreasonable for the attorneys to have spent 1,946.75 hours in light of the fact that they ultimately prevailed against only the City (D) and five police officers, no restraining orders or injunctions were ever issued, and the City (D) was never compelled to change a single practice or policy as a result of the suit.

▶ ANALYSIS

Although the amount of damages a plaintiff recovers is relevant to the amount of attorneys' fees to be awarded under 42 U.S.C. § 1988, the Supreme Court made clear that it is only one of many factors that a court should consider. Furthermore, the Court emphasized that unlike most private tort litigants, a civil rights plaintiff seeks to vindicate important civil and constitutional rights that cannot be valued solely in monetary terms.

■=■

Quicknotes

42 U.S.C. § 1983 Provides that every person, who under color of state law subjects or causes to be subjected any citizen of the United States or person within its jurisdiction to be deprived of rights, privileges and immunities guaranteed by the federal constitution and laws, is liable to the injured party at law or in equity.

42 U.S.C. § 1988 Allows for attorney fees to be awarded the prevailing party in an action pursuant to § 1983.

INJUNCTION A court order requiring a person to do or prohibiting that person from doing a specific act.

RESTRAINING ORDER An order prohibiting a defendant from certain activities until a hearing regarding an injunction on such activities may be conducted.

■=■

Walker v. City of Birmingham

Protester (D) v. City (P)

388 U.S. 307 (1967).

NATURE OF CASE: Certiorari to resolve constitutional questions arising out of sanctions for criminal contempt for the violation of a court order.

FACT SUMMARY: After a temporary restraining order was issued at City of Birmingham's (P) request preventing demonstrations without a permit, Walker (D) and Dr. Martin Luther King went ahead with a demonstration without appealing the court order or following the local ordinance it enforced. Walker (D) and Dr. King were cited for contempt and attempted to defend their convictions by alleging the unconstitutionality of the ordinance.

🏛 RULE OF LAW

A contempt citation for violation of a court order may properly issue from a court with proper jurisdiction upon a showing of such violation where the order was not challenged in a court proceeding and the underlying law the order sought to protect was not followed.

FACTS: Walker (D) and Dr. Martin Luther King organized a protest demonstration. A city commissioner of the City of Birmingham (P) refused twice to issue a permit for the demonstration, but no formal application to the full commission was made as stipulated by the permit ordinance. The court issued an ex parte temporary injunction against the demonstration. Walker (D) and Dr. King defied the injunction and were cited for criminal contempt. The judge refused to consider the unconstitutionality of application of the permit ordinance as a defense since there had been no attempt to comply with the permit ordinance or to dissolve the injunction. The court upheld the contempt convictions, holding that the only issues were jurisdiction of the court and knowing violation. Affirmed on appeal. Certiorari granted.

ISSUE: Did the court err in refusing to consider the underlying ordinance's constitutionality?

HOLDING AND DECISION: (Stewart, J.) No. The state court had sufficient jurisdiction to issue the injunction in upholding the permit ordinance. Walker (D) and Dr. King did not attempt to apply to the state courts for an authoritative construction of the ordinance. They did not attempt to modify or dissolve the injunction after it was granted. It cannot be presumed that the state courts would have ignored constitutional claims. As such, this Court cannot hold that Walker (D) and Dr. King were constitutionally free to ignore the procedures of law, and, when they did so, they were properly held in contempt. Affirmed.

DISSENT: (Warren, C.J.) The facts do not lend support to the conclusion that Walker (D) and Dr. King disregarded the judicial process. It shows no disrespect to violate a statute on the ground that it is unconstitutional. The ordinance violated was unconstitutional on its face as against the rights preserved by the First Amendment in that it was shown that a permit would not be granted under any circumstances. Also, the ex parte injunction in this case may have been used to subvert judicial process. This case involves an entirely different situation and is distinguishable from the *Mine Workers'* case, 330 U.S. 258 (1947).

DISSENT: (Douglas, J.) The Court should make sure state tribunals work within the Constitution. Here, the state court has flouted the First Amendment. There is a right to defy an unconstitutional statute.

▌ ANALYSIS

The ordinance that Walker (D) and Dr. King were prohibited by the temporary restraining order from violating was later overturned as unconstitutional. However, the rationale of this case, that the proper procedure to subvert an injunction is to subject it to review and not to disobey it, remains legally strong whatever its moral weaknesses.

■=■

Quicknotes

CERTIORARI A discretionary writ issued by a superior court to an inferior court in order to review the lower court's decisions; the Supreme Court's writ ordering such review.

CRIMINAL CONTEMPT CITATION Conduct by a party to a proceeding intended to obstruct the court's effective administration of justice or to otherwise disrespect its authority.

EX PARTE A proceeding commenced by one party without providing any opposing parties with notice or that is uncontested by an adverse party.

FIRST AMENDMENT Prohibits Congress from enacting any law respecting an establishment of religion, prohibiting the free exercise of religion, abridging freedom of speech or the press, the right of peaceful assembly and the right to petition for a redress of grievances.

Continued on next page.

INJUNCTION A court order requiring a person to do or prohibiting that person from doing a specific act.

ORDINANCE Law or statute usually enacted by a municipal government.

RESTRAINING ORDER An order prohibiting a defendant from certain activities until a hearing regarding an injunction on such activities may be conducted.

■═■

Thinking Like a Trial Lawyer, Pleadings, and Simple Joinder

Quick Reference Rules of Law

Conley v. Gibson

Union members (P) v. Labor union (D)

355 U.S. 41 (1957).

NATURE OF CASE: Appeal from dismissal of complaint alleging that labor union failed fairly to represent black union members.

FACT SUMMARY: Black union members brought class action against their labor union alleging that, because they were black, the union failed to represent them fairly in negotiations between them and their employer in seniority and other job protection matters.

> ### RULE OF LAW
> The Federal Rules of Civil Procedure do not require a complaint to set out in detail the facts upon which the claim is based.

FACTS: A labor contract existed between a railroad and a union that gave the employees certain protections from discharge and loss of seniority rights. Black union members (P), arguing violation of these rights, brought a class action against their labor union (D) alleging that, because they were black, the union (D) failed to represent them fairly in negotiations between them and the railroad as to these seniority and other job protection matters.

ISSUE: Do the Federal Rules of Civil Procedure require a complaint to set out in detail the facts upon which the claim is based?

HOLDING AND DECISION: (Black, J.) No. The Federal Rules of Civil Procedure do not require a complaint to set out in detail the facts upon which the claim is based. All the Rules require is "a short and plain statement of the claim" that will give the defendant fair notice of what the plaintiff's claim is and the grounds upon which it rests. Here, the complaint sufficiently alleged that the black union members (P) were discharged wrongfully by their railroad employer and that their union (D), acting according to plan, refused to protect their jobs as it did those of white employees, or to help them with their grievances, all because they were black. Reversed and remanded.

▶ ANALYSIS

The Court noted that simplified "notice pleading," as in this case, is made possible by the liberal opportunity for discovery and other pretrial procedures established by the Federal Rules of Civil Procedure to disclose more precisely the basis of both claim and defense and to define more narrowly the disputed facts and issues.

Quicknotes

CLAIM The demand for a right to payment or equitable relief; the fact or facts giving rise to such demand.

PLEADING A statement setting forth the plaintiff's cause of action or the defendant's defenses to the plaintiff's claims.

Ashcroft v. Iqbal

Former U.S. Attorney General (D) v. Pakistani citizen (P)

556 U.S. 662 (2009).

NATURE OF CASE: Certiorari to determine complaint sufficiency in constitutional claim.

FACT SUMMARY: Javaid Iqbal (P), a Pakistani citizen, was arrested in the United States on criminal charges and detained by federal officials soon after the 9/11 terrorist attacks. He claimed his confinement conditions violated his constitutional rights. The federal official defendants moved to dismiss Iqbal's (P) complaint as facially insufficient.

🏛 RULE OF LAW
A well-pleaded complaint requires nonconclusory, plausible, factual pleadings.

FACTS: United States officials arrested Javaid Iqbal (P), a Pakistani citizen and Muslim, on criminal charges and detained him after the 9/11 terrorist attacks. Iqbal (P) filed a federal complaint alleging he was deprived of certain constitutional rights while confined. He alleged the deprivations occurred because of his race, religion, or national origin. He named former U.S. Attorney General John Ashcroft (D) and FBI Director Robert Mueller (D) in addition to several others. Ashcroft (D) and Mueller (D) moved to dismiss the complaint as facially insufficient and raised the defense of qualified immunity based on their official status at the time of the confinement. The district court denied the motion and Ashcroft (D) and Mueller (D) took an interlocutory appeal to the Second Circuit Court of 7 Appeals. The Second Circuit affirmed, and the U.S. Supreme Court granted certiorari.

ISSUE: Does a well-pleaded complaint require nonconclusory, plausible, factual pleadings?

HOLDING AND DECISION: (Kennedy, J.) Yes. A well-pleaded complaint requires nonconclusory, plausible, factual pleadings. Iqbal's (P) complaint alleges the federal government had a policy of detaining Arab Muslims after the 9/11 attacks until the individuals were "cleared" by the FBI. Iqbal (P) claimed Ashcroft (D) was the "architect" of this policy and Mueller (D) was instrumental in its "adoption, promulgation, and implementation." This Court held in *Bell Atlantic Corp. v. Twombly*, 550 U.S. 544 (2007), that pleadings required factual content that allows the court to draw the reasonable inference that the defendant is liable for the alleged misconduct. The plausibility standard did not rise to a probability but requires more than conclusions of misconduct. *Twombly* supported the principles that a court accepts factual allegations as true but need not accept conclusory allegations as true. Fed. R. Civ. P. 8 may now permit more flexibility but it does not permit mere conclusions. Further, only a complaint that states a plausible claim survives a motion to dismiss. The courts may begin their analysis with determining which pleadings include factual allegations that will be entitled to a presumption of truth. Here, Iqbal (P) states only conclusory allegations that Ashcroft (D) was the principal architect and Mueller (D) was the principal implementer of the policies. These conclusory allegations are not entitled to a presumption of truth. Iqbal (P) fails to include factual allegations supporting his conclusions that Ashcroft (D) and Mueller (D) knew of the federal officials' behavior regarding his confinement. The consideration then becomes whether the complaint suggests an entitlement to relief. It does not. Iqbal (P) was plausibly held for reasons other than race, religion, or national origin. Detaining such suspects until cleared does not violate constitutional protections. Iqbal (P) argues *Twombly* should be limited to antitrust pleadings, but nothing supports this theory. *Twomby* is the pleading standard for all civil actions. Iqbal (P) finally argues Fed. R. Civ. P. 9(b) permits him "general" rather than "specific" pleading for an alleged constitutional violation. Rule 9(b) does not override the factual pleading requirements of Rule 8 but merely requires even greater specificity for the enumerated claims. Reversed and remanded.

DISSENT: (Souter, J.) Consistent with *Twombly*, nonconclusory allegations should be taken as true unless they are "sufficiently fantastic to defy reality." The key allegations here are not conclusory and the complaint was facially sufficient.

DISSENT: (Breyer, J.) The lower court expressly rejected minimally intrusive discovery in favor of dismissal. That would have been appropriate because the discovery could have been in anticipation of a summary judgment motion.

▶ ANALYSIS

Pleading requirements have become stricter so general notice is no longer sufficient. The defendant is not merely put on notice of the plaintiff's claim but is entitled to factual allegations informing it of the support for the claim. Some analysts were concerned about the future of litigation because of a fear that pleadings would have to be so specific that most plaintiffs would not be able to proceed. Most courts, however, have required factual pleading for a long time and did not become more stringent after

Continued on next page.

Iqbal. The rule stated in *Iqbal* is "plausibility" not "probability" so the allegations do not have to be proven on the face of the complaint but the facts alleged must be plausible and permit a reasonable inference of defendant's misconduct.

■══■

Quicknotes

INTERLOCUTORY APPEAL The appeal of an issue that does not resolve the disposition of the case but is essential to a determination of the parties' legal rights.

■══■

Bower v. Weisman

Former partner (P) v. Former partner (D)

639 F. Supp. 532 (S.D.N.Y. 1986).

NATURE OF CASE:
Motions for a more definite statement, to dismiss for failure to state claim with particularity, and to dismiss for failure to state a claim upon which relief can be granted.

FACT SUMMARY:
After her fifteen-year relationship with Weisman (D) ended, Bower (P) sought to enforce an agreement under which Weisman (D) agreed to continue to provide her and her daughter with financial security. He allegedly breached the agreement, and she filed a seven-count claim against him. He filed three motions with respect to each count of the claim.

🏛 RULE OF LAW
A complaint is deficient if it either (1) fails to clearly identify which defendant it refers to, where there are multiple defendants; (2) only generally states that three defendants intentionally misrepresented and defrauded by making promises and representations, without stating specifics; or (3) fails to set forth facts to support a claim.

FACTS:
After her fifteen-year relationship with Weisman (D) ended, Bower (P) sought to enforce an agreement under which Weisman (D) agreed to continue to provide her and her daughter with financial security and a home, provided she didn't remarry or move from the country. Weisman (D) allegedly breached the agreement, and Bower (P) filed a seven-count claim against him. Count one asserted a tort and contract claim for money damages for breach of the agreement; count two asserted claims of fraud, misrepresentation, and deceit in connection with the agreement; count three alleged breach of contract and conversion concerning Weisman's (D) attempt to remove Bower (P) from a townhouse he owned, and his alleged conversion of art and furniture; counts four and five charged Weisman (D) and his two companies (D) with trespass and false imprisonment in connection with his dispatch of armed guards at the house, allowing access to only Bower (P), her daughter, and medical personnel; and counts six and seven claimed intentional infliction of emotional distress and private nuisance, also in connection with Weisman's (D) action to recover the townhouse. Weisman (D) filed three motions with respect to several counts of the complaint. He moved for a more definite statement under Rule 12(e) with respect to which of the three defendants is charged with each act; to dismiss for failure to state fraud with particularity under Rule 9(b); and to dismiss for failure to state a claim upon which relief can be granted under Rule 12(b)(6).

ISSUE:
Is a complaint deficient if it either (1) fails to clearly identify which defendant it refers to, where there are multiple defendants; (2) only generally states that three defendants intentionally misrepresented and defrauded by making promises and representations, without stating specifics; or (3) fails to set forth facts to support a claim?

HOLDING AND DECISION:
(Sweet, J.) Yes. A complaint is deficient if it either (1) fails to clearly identify which defendant it refers to, where there are multiple defendants; (2) only generally states that three defendants intentionally misrepresented and defrauded by making promises and representations, without stating specifics; or (3) fails to set forth facts to support a claim. First, Bower's (P) claim fails to distinguish between Weisman (D) and his two co-defendants, both of which are companies he owns. The essence of a complaint is to inform the defendant as to the general nature of the action to allow him to effectively respond. Bower (P) had to identify which defendant is referred to in each charge, or Weisman (D) would not be able to effectively respond to Bower's (P) complaint. In addition, Bower's (P) pleadings are vague and fail to provide the specificity required by Rule 9(b) with respect to her second claim for misrepresentation, fraud and deceit. The second claim is therefore dismissed. Finally, Bower's (P) fifth claim for false imprisonment is dismissed because she failed to set forth any facts that would support her claim that she was confined at the townhouse. Bower's (P) seventh claim for private nuisance is also dismissed, because she failed to show that there was a substantial and unreasonable interference with her property rights, which are required for the claim of nuisance.

▶ ANALYSIS
Though this case has a very fact-specific holding, it illustrates the slight tension between Rule 8(a)(2), which requires only a short and plain statement of the claim showing that the pleader is entitled to relief, and other Rules requiring some level of specificity. The Rules, as so stated by the court, have to be read in conjunction with each other, which in practice can sometimes lead to confusion.

■◼■

Quicknotes
COMPLAINT The initial pleading commencing litigation that sets forth a claim for relief.

Continued on next page.

NUISANCE An unlawful use of property that interferes with the lawful use of another's property.

PLEADING A statement setting forth the plaintiff's cause of action or the defendant's defenses to the plaintiff's claims.

■━■

Doe v. United Services Life Insurance Company

Applicant for life insurance (P) v. Life insurance company (D)

123 F.R.D. 437 (S.D.N.Y. 1988).

NATURE OF CASE: Motion of plaintiff for order permitting him to prosecute suit under pseudonym.

FACT SUMMARY: Doe (P), a life insurance applicant, requested the court permit him to initiate a lawsuit under a pseudonym based on fear that he might be identified as a homosexual.

🏛 RULE OF LAW
A litigant may use a fictitious name in exceptional cases to protect privacy.

FACTS: Doe (P) applied for a policy with United Services Life Insurance Company (United Services) (D). As part of the application process, he was caused by United Services (D) to undergo additional medical testing because United Services (D) considered him (P) to fit a homosexual profile and hence to entail extra risks for insurance. When Doe (P) brought suit against United Services (D) for discrimination, Doe (P) asserted that use of a pseudonym (Doe) was necessary to protect his privacy.

ISSUE: May a litigant remain anonymous in exceptional cases to protect privacy?

HOLDING AND DECISION: (Sweet, J.) Yes. A litigant may remain anonymous in exceptional cases to protect privacy. Although generally lawsuits are public events and the public has a legitimate interest in knowing pertinent facts, such as the parties' real names, under special and exceptional circumstances courts allow parties to remain anonymous to protect their privacy in regard to intimate matters, such as, for example, abortion, transsexuality, mental illness, and illegitimacy. Cases such as this, where a party risks public identification as a homosexual, also raise privacy concerns that support an exception to the general rule of disclosure. The court's decision to permit this claimant to proceed with a fictitious name reflects the court's concern for his public identification as a homosexual, not a concern for his employment status as a law clerk to a federal judge. Motion granted.

▶ ANALYSIS

The court made clear that courts should not permit a party to proceed anonymously with a fictitious name simply to protect the party's professional or economic life.

■═■

Quicknotes

RIGHT TO PRIVACY An individual's right to be protected against unwarranted interference in his personal affairs, falling into one of four categories: (1) appropriating the individual's likeness or name for commercial benefit; (2) intrusion into the individual's seclusion; (3) public disclosure of private facts regarding the individual; and (4) disclosure of facts placing the individual in a false light.

■═■

Singletary v. Pennsylvania Department of Corrections

Mother of inmate (P) v. Prison and prison employees (D)

266 F.3d 186 (3d Cir. 2001).

NATURE OF CASE: Appeal from denial of a motion to amend a complaint to add a defendant.

FACT SUMMARY: Subsequent to filing suit and after the running of the limitations period, Dorothy Singletary (P) sought to add a newly named defendant under the "relation back" doctrine.

🏛 **RULE OF LAW**
After the statute of limitations has run, a new party may not be added to a suit under the "relation back" doctrine unless such party received notice of the institution of the action within 120 days of the filing of the original complaint.

FACTS: On October 6, 1996, Edward Singletary committed suicide while incarcerated at SCI-Rockview. On October 6, 1998, Dorothy Singletary (P), Edward's mother, filed a civil rights lawsuit under 42 U.S.C. § 1983, naming as defendants Pennsylvania Department of Corrections (PADOC) (D), SCI-Rockview (D), Joseph Mazurkiewicz (former Superintendent of SCI-Rockview) (D), and "Unknown Corrections Officers" (D). On July 28, 2000, nearly two years after the statute of limitations had run, Dorothy Singletary (P) moved for leave to amend her original complaint to substitute Robert Regan, a psychologist at SCI-Rockview (D), for "Unknown Corrections Officers." She also moved to have the amended complaint relate back to her original complaint under Fed. R. Civ. P. 15(c)(3). The district court denied Dorothy Singletary's (P) motion to amend her complaint to add Regan as a defendant on the grounds that that claim would be barred by the statute of limitations because it did not meet the conditions for "relation back" under Fed. R. Civ. P. 15(c)(3). The district court also granted summary judgment in favor of PADOC (D), SCI-Rockview (D), and Joseph Mazurkiewicz (D).

ISSUE: After the statute of limitations has run, may a new party be added to a suit under the "relation back" doctrine where such party did not receive notice of the institution of the action within 120 days of the filing of the original complaint?

HOLDING AND DECISION: (Becker, C.J.) No. After the statute of limitations has run, a new party may not be added to a suit under the "relation back" doctrine unless such party received notice of the institution of the action within 120 days of the filing of the original complaint. In order for an amended complaint that substitutes newly named defendants to successfully relate back under Fed. R. Civ. P. 15(c)(3), three conditions must be met. Fed. R. Civ. P. 15(c)(3)(A) states that one of the three

conditions is that the newly named party must have received notice of the institution of the action (a) within 120 days after the filing of the original complaint, and (b) the notice is sufficient that the defendant is not prejudiced in maintaining his defense. In the context of Fed. R. Civ. P. 15(c), "notice" does not require actual service of process on the party sought to be added to the complaint. Notice concerning the institution of an action may be actual, constructive, or imputed. Constructive or implied notice can be by two methods: (a) the shared attorney method or (b) the identity of interest method. Notice can be implied under the shared attorney method where the attorney's later relationship with the newly named defendant gives rise to the inference that the attorney, within the 120-day period, had some communication or relationship with, and thus gave notice of the action to, the newly named defendant. Notice can be implied under the identity of interest method where the parties are so closely related in their business operations or other activities that the institution of an action against one serves to provide notice of the litigation to the other. Dorothy Singletary (P) argues that Regan received timely notice under the shared attorney method because he shared his attorney with SCI-Rockview (D), an originally named party. Dorothy Singletary (P) also argues that Regan received timely notice under the identity of interest method because he had an identity of interest with SCI-Rockview (D). The facts do not support Dorothy Singletary's (P) contention that Regan shared an attorney with the other defendants. The attorney who represented the defendants through the 120-day period following the filing of the original complaint never represented Regan. That attorney was replaced by another. The attorney who took over after the 120-day period, and who had connection with Regan and the defendants, did not become attorney for the defendants until well after the relevant 120-day period. The facts also do not support Dorothy Singletary's (P) contention that Regan received constructive or implied notice by way of the identity of interest method. Regan was a staff-level employee at SCI-Rockview (D) with no administrative or supervisory duties. His position alone cannot serve as a basis for finding an identity of interest with his employer because he was not highly enough placed in the prison hierarchy to support a conclusion that his interests as an employee were identical to the prison's interests. Absent other circumstances that permit the inference that notice was actually received, a non-management employee like Regan does not share a sufficient nexus of interests with his or her employer so that notice

Continued on next page.

given to the employer can be imputed to the employee for Fed. R. Civ. P. 15(c)(3) purposes. Because Regan did not receive actual, constructive, or implied notice of the institution of the action within 120 days of the filing of the original complaint, the district court correctly denied Dorothy Singletary's (P) motion for leave to amend her complaint. Affirmed.

▶ ANALYSIS

The issue whether the facts satisfy the second requirement for relating back an amendment under Fed. R. Civ. P. 15(c)(3)(B) was not resolved by the court because the first condition, dealing with notice, was not met, and the case was disposed of on that issue alone. The court does note that the language of Fed. R. Civ. P. 15(c)(3)(B) is unclear. Specifically, there is a division in authority as to whether not knowing the identity of a potential defendant is the same as mistaking the identity of a defendant. Most courts seem to take the position that not knowing the identity of a defendant is not a mistake concerning the defendant's identity. Therefore, "the bulk of authority from other courts of appeals takes the position that the amendment of a 'John Doe' complaint, i.e., the substituting of real names for 'John Does' or 'Unknown Persons' named in an original complaint, does not meet the 'but for a mistake' requirement in 15(c)(3)(B)." While the court notes that it is bound by a case that held that not knowing the identity of a defendant can be a mistake under Fed. R. Civ. P. 15(c)(3)(B), the court expressed concern over the state of the law on Fed. R. Civ. P. 15(c)(3), and, in particular, other Circuits' interpretation of the "mistake" requirement. The court recommended to the Advisory Rules Committee a modification of Fed. R. Civ. P. 15(c)(3) to bring the Rule into accord with the prevailing opinion about it.

■══■

Quicknotes

42 U.S.C. § 1983 Provides that every person, who under color of state law subjects or causes to be subjected any citizen of the United States or person within its jurisdiction to be deprived of rights, privileges and immunities guaranteed by the federal Constitution and laws, is liable to the injured party at law or in equity.

ACTUAL NOTICE Direct communication of information that would cause an ordinary person of average prudence to inquire as to its truth.

COMPLAINT The initial pleading commencing litigation that sets forth a claim for relief.

CONSTRUCTIVE NOTICE Knowledge of a fact that is imputed to an individual who was under a duty to inquire and who could have learned of the fact through the exercise of reasonable prudence.

RELATION BACK DOCTRINE Doctrine that holds that a party may not amend its pleading to set forth a new or

different claim or defense unless it involves the subject matter of the original pleading; under Fed. R. Civ. P. 15, if a party amends its pleading as a matter of course before a responsive pleading is served, such amendment is said to relate back to the original pleading if it involves the subject matter of the original pleading.

STATUTE OF LIMITATIONS A law prescribing the period in which a legal action may be commenced.

■══■

Krupski v. Costa Crociere S.P.A.

Cruise ship passenger (P) v. Cruise owner (D)

130 S. Ct. 2485 (2010).

NATURE OF CASE: Appeal of circuit court judgment.

FACT SUMMARY: Wanda Krupski (P) injured herself while on a cruise. She brought suit against the wrong party, and sought to amend a complaint to name the proper defendant after the limitations period lapsed. The Court of Appeals for the Eleventh Circuit held that the amended complaint did not relate back because she should have known the identity of the proper defendant.

RULE OF LAW

Federal Rule of Civil Procedure 15(c) permits an amended complaint to relate back to a previously filed complaint if the proper defendant knew or should have known within the time of service that but for a mistake in identity, the plaintiff would have asserted the claims against the proper defendant.

FACTS: Wanda Krupski (P) was injured while a passenger on the cruise ship Costa Magica. She sued Costa Cruise S.P.A. (D), the business through which she had booked her cruise and which had sent her travel documents. In its answer to the complaint, Costa Cruise (D) stated that it was only the North American sales and booking agent for the ship operator, Costa Crociere (D), which was the proper defendant. Krupski (P) amended her complaint to add Costa Crociere (D) as a party. But Costa Crociere (D), which was represented by the same attorney as Costa Cruise (D), argued that the expiration of the contractual one-year limitations period had expired. The Court of Appeals for the Eleventh Circuit held that Federal Rule of Civil Procedure 15(c) was not satisfied because Krupski (P) knew or should have known the identity of the proper defendant before the expiration of the limitations period, and that because she chose not to sue Costa Crociere (D), she didn't make the type of mistake about the identity of the defendant that Rule 15(c) contemplated. The court also held that relation back was not appropriate because the plaintiff had unduly delayed in seeking to amend.

ISSUE: Does Federal Rule of Civil Procedure 15(c) permit an amended complaint to relate back to a previously filed complaint if the proper defendant knew or should have known within the time of service that but for a mistake in identity, the plaintiff would have asserted the claims against the proper defendant?

HOLDING AND DECISION: (Sotomayor, J.) Yes. Federal Rule of Civil Procedure 15(c) permits an amended complaint to relate back to a previously filed complaint if the proper defendant knew or should have known within the time of service that but for a mistake in identity, the plaintiff would have asserted the claims against the proper defendant. Whether an amendment relates back under Rule 15(c)(1)(C) depends on what the party to be added knew or should have known, not on the amending party's knowledge or timeliness in seeking to amend the pleading. Rule 15 asks what the prospective defendant "knew or should have known," not what the plaintiff "knew or should have known," as was understood by the Eleventh Circuit. Costa Crociere (D) should have known that Krupski's (P) failure to name it as a defendant was due to a mistake concerning the proper party's identity. Reversed.

CONCURRENCE: (Scalia, J.) The Court reached the correct decision, but its use of the Notes of the Advisory Committee to the Federal Rules of Civil Procedure in reaching its decision was inappropriate.

ANALYSIS

This decision illustrates a very basic fact about being human: People can make mistakes even when they know all of the facts. The Eleventh Circuit found that because Krupski (P) knew about the existence of Costa Crociere (D), and that the company was the owner of the ship, she could not have made a mistake when she chose to sue Costa Cruise (D). But Rule 15(c) does not require that the mistake of the plaintiff be reasonable. It requires only that a mistake was made.

■■■

Quicknotes

FED. R. CIV. P. 15(c) Provides that a claim or defense arising out of the conduct or occurrence set forth in the original pleading will relate back to the date of the original pleading.

■■■

Chaplin v. Du Pont Advance Fiber Systems

Seven employees (P) v. Employer (D)

303 F. Supp. 2d 766 (E.D. Va. 2004), *aff'd*, 124 Fed. Appx. 771 (4th Cir. 2005).

NATURE OF CASE: Motion for Rule 11 sanctions.

FACT SUMMARY: Seven Du Pont employees (P), who are white, Christian, and Confederate Southern Americans, brought an action under Title VII of the 1964 Civil Rights Act, alleging employment discrimination based on national origin, religion, and race. Du Pont (D) sought sanctions under Rule 11(b)(1) for filing a complaint for an improper purpose, under Rule 11(b)(2) for stating claims without sufficient basis in law, and under Rule 11(b)(3) for stating claims without sufficient basis in fact.

🏛 RULE OF LAW
(1) Sanctions for filing a complaint with improper purpose are not necessarily warranted where the complaint "creatively" pursues a new legal theory.
(2) Sanctions for filing a complaint containing claims that lack legal authority are not necessarily warranted where there is no authoritative precedent precluding the claims.
(3) Sanctions for filing a complaint containing claims that lack factual basis are necessarily warranted where there is no factual basis whatsoever to support the complaint's allegations.

FACTS: Du Pont Advance Fiber Systems, Du Pont Spruance, and Du Pont Textiles & Interiors, Inc. (collectively, "Du Pont") (D) instituted in 2000 a policy banning the display of offensive symbols on Du Pont (D) property. The policy included a ban on the display of the Confederate battle flag, specifically on the wearing or displaying of Confederate symbols on clothing, newspapers, pictures, photographs, and bumper stickers. Seven Du Pont employees (P), who are white, Christian, and Confederate Southern Americans, brought an action under Title VII of the 1964 Civil Rights Act, alleging employment discrimination based on national origin, religion, and race. One plaintiff had been ordered to discontinue wearing clothing bearing the Confederate symbols, another plaintiff had been told "it was not a good idea" to wear his Confederate belt buckle, two plaintiffs had been ordered to remove bumper stickers from their vehicles, and another plaintiff had been told to stop wearing a Confederate t-shirt or risk a reprimand and he had been ordered to sit in the back of the room during an off-site, Du Pont-sponsored multicultural workshop because he had worn such a shirt. Du Pont (D) sought sanctions under Rule 11(b)(1) for filing a complaint for an improper purpose, under Rule 11(b)(2)

for stating claims without sufficient basis in law, and under Rule 11(b)(3) for stating claims without sufficient basis in fact.

ISSUE:
(1) Are sanctions for filing a complaint with improper purpose necessarily warranted where the complaint "creatively" pursues a new legal theory?
(2) Are sanctions for filing a complaint containing claims that lack legal authority necessarily warranted where there is no authoritative precedent precluding the claims?
(3) Are sanctions for filing a complaint containing claims that lack factual basis necessarily warranted where there is no factual basis whatsoever to support the complaint's allegations?

HOLDING AND DECISION: (Hudson, J.)
(1) No. Sanctions for filing a complaint with improper purpose are not necessarily warranted where the complaint "creatively" pursues a new legal theory. The purpose of Rule 11 is not to thwart an attorney's enthusiasm or creativity in pursuing factual or legal theories. Regardless of the merits of the claims, the attorney's purpose in filing the lawsuit was not to harass Du Pont (D) but to broaden the interpretation of "national origin" protection under Title VII. Therefore, the motion for sanctions under Rule 11(b)(1) is denied.
(2) No. Sanctions for filing a complaint containing claims that lack legal authority are not necessarily warranted where there is no authoritative precedent precluding the claims. Where an argument has absolutely no chance of success under existing authoritative precedent, it may be sanctionable. While there is no authoritative case law anywhere in the country to support the claim of national origin discrimination in this case, there also is no binding case to the contrary. Therefore, the motion for sanctions under Rule 11(b)(2) is denied.
(3) Yes. Sanctions for filing a complaint containing claims that lack factual basis are necessarily warranted where there is no factual basis whatsoever to support the complaint's allegations. The complaint lists many facts, both supported and unsupported, backing their national origin discrimination claim, and whether they have merit or not, they satisfy Rule 11(b)(3). However, there is absolutely no evidence that Du Pont (D) denied them a religious accommodation that they requested, or that Du Pont's (D) policy discriminates against Caucasians. Therefore, with respect to counts alleging religious and

Continued on next page.

race discrimination, the complaint is frivolous and un-warranted, and the motion for sanctions is granted.

▶ *ANALYSIS*

It would seem easiest to comply with Rule 11(b)(3), as compared with Rules 11(b)(1) and (b)(2); the complaint simply has to have a factual basis. Sanctions for Rule 11(b)(3) violations are, therefore, easier to pursue. On the other hand, if a complaint is arguably proper and arguably based on the law, or on some extended legal theory, the Rule is satisfied.

■══■

Quicknotes

SANCTIONS A penalty imposed in order to ensure compliance with a statute or regulation.

■══■

Lopez v. City of Irvington

Thieves (P) v. Police department (D)

2008 WL 565776 (D.N.J. Feb. 28, 2008).

NATURE OF CASE: Motion for separate trials.

FACT SUMMARY: After the Irvington police department's (D) K-9 unit allegedly mauled them, four thieves (P) claimed in a lawsuit that they were the victims of excessive police force. The four plaintiffs were arrested at different times for different crimes, and the city (D) moved to sever their trials.

🏛 RULE OF LAW
(1) When deciding whether joinder of parties is permissible under Fed. R. Civ. P. 20, it must be shown that (a) the joined parties assert a right to relief jointly, severally, or that their claim arises out of the same transaction and (b) there are questions of law or facts common to all parties sought to be joined.
(2) When considering a motion to sever, courts may also consider (a) whether the issues sought to be tried separately are significantly different from one another, (b) whether the separable issues require the testimony of different witnesses and different documentary proof, (c) whether the party opposing the severance will be prejudiced if it is granted, and (d) whether the party requesting the severance will be prejudiced if it is not granted.

FACTS: Plaintiffs Jaime Lopez (P), Arnold Daniels (P), Willie McKenzie (P), and Hilbert Gresham (P), filed a civil lawsuit against the city of Irvington (D), the Irvington police department (D), and officers Alfredo Aleman (D) and Christopher Burrell (D) (among others not listed), claiming that the department (D) failed to properly supervise the department's K-9 unit, and specifically officers Aleman (D) and Burrell (D) and their dog, Bullet. Aleman (D) was the dog's handler. The plaintiffs were each arrested at different times and for different crimes. Lopez (P) was arrested on May 2, 2004, while he was engaged in a burglary, and he claims that during the arrest Aleman (D) kicked Lopez (D) in the ribs, and held him down on the floor while Bullet bit him and tore flesh from his left arm. Daniels (P) was arrested on June 29, 2005, also in the process of burglarizing a home, and claims that despite not resisting arrest, he was thrown to the ground by Aleman (D) and mauled by Bullet at Aleman's (D) command even after being handcuffed. On Aug. 24, 2005, McKenzie (P) was arrested when he was seen exiting a stolen vehicle. He also claims to have been mauled by Bullet at Aleman's (D) command after being handcuffed. On Aug. 25, 2005, Gresham (P) was arrested after running

from the officers (D), and once handcuffed, was attacked by Bullet. Defendants filed a motion to sever seeking to separate the trial of each plaintiff, arguing that the trials should be severed because plaintiffs' claims did not arise out of the same transaction or occurrence, and joinder of the plaintiffs would subject the defendants to prejudice, since the plaintiffs could join forces and parrot each other's story.

ISSUE:
(1) When deciding whether joinder of parties is permissible under Fed. R. Civ. P. 20, must it be shown that (a) the joined parties assert a right to relief jointly, severally, or that their claim arises out of the same transaction and (b) there are questions of law or facts common to all parties sought to be joined?
(2) When considering a motion to sever, may courts also consider (a) whether the issues sought to be tried separately are significantly different from one another, (b) whether the separable issues require the testimony of different witnesses and different documentary proof, (c) whether the party opposing the severance will be prejudiced if it is granted, and (d) whether the party requesting the severance will be prejudiced if it is not granted?

HOLDING AND DECISION: (Greenaway, Jr., J.) Yes.
(1) When deciding whether joinder of parties is permissible under Fed. R. Civ. P. 20, it must be shown that (a) the joined parties assert a right to relief jointly, severally, or that their claim arises out of the same transaction and (b) there are questions of law or facts common to all parties sought to be joined. Both elements—the transaction element and the question of law or fact element—must be proved to support joinder. First, defendants argue that plaintiffs should not have been joined because the each arrest was based on a separate set of facts, and the plaintiffs were arrested on different days at different locations by different officers. But the plaintiffs' argument is more persuasive. They claim that the city (D) and police department (D) failed to properly supervise and monitor its K-9 Unit, and as a result of such failure, permitted a pattern or practice of excessive force to exist among the police officers of the K-9 unit. Each plaintiff's example of excessive force is alleged to have resulted from this pattern or practice. Other courts have found the common transaction element met when the plaintiffs alleged that a pattern or practice of discrimination existed. Therefore the

Continued on next page.

allegations in the complaint are found to arise from the same transaction, occurrence, or series of transactions or occurrences. Similarly, there exists a common question of law or fact. Although plaintiffs allegedly suffered different incidents of force, by different police officers and at different times and locations, the allegation of a pattern or practice of excessive force is a common question of fact central to each claim. Second, defendants argue that they will be seriously prejudiced if the court does not sever plaintiffs' claims. But they do not offer any persuasive indication of prejudice.

(2) When considering a motion to sever, courts may also consider (a) whether the issues sought to be tried separately are significantly different from one another, (b) whether the separable issues require the testimony of different witnesses and different documentary proof, (c) whether the party opposing the severance will be prejudiced if it is granted, and (d) whether the party requesting the severance will be prejudiced if it is not granted. These factors weigh in favor of denying the motion. The first factor, regarding the issues that would be tried separately, has been discussed above. Next, several witnesses are common to each plaintiff's claim, including the defendants. Finally, plaintiffs will be prejudiced if the motion is granted, while defendants will not be prejudiced if the motion is denied. Plaintiffs alleged a pattern or practice of excessive force, and they will therefore need to provide the jury with sufficient evidence to meet their burden that a pattern or practice actually existed. If there were separate trials, this would be difficult if not impossible. On the other hand, defendants have offered no support for their allegation of prejudice.

Defendants' motion is denied.

▶ ANALYSIS

Strictly speaking, there was not a common transaction, occurrence, or series of transactions or occurrences. Each arrest was based on a distinct set of facts, and each arrest occurred on a different day. There's no evidence that the four plaintiffs were working together. The court points to the fact that the plaintiffs' claim was that there was a pattern or practice of excessive force that was overlooked or encouraged by the police department, but the court's rationale for allowing that to form the basis of the transaction element is that "other courts" had found a common transaction where there was a claim of a pattern or practice. It might be difficult to show a pattern or practice if the parties were not joined, but that difficulty does not support joinder.

■■■

Quicknotes

JOINDER OF PARTIES The joining of parties in one lawsuit.

JOINT AND SEVERAL LIABILITY Liability amongst tortfeasors allowing the injured party to bring suit against any of the defendants, individually or collectively, and to recover from each up to the total amount of damages awarded.

SEVERANCE Dividing or separating; setting aside one or more claims in a lawsuit to be tried separately.

■■■

Podhorn v. Paragon Group, Inc.

Tenant (P) v. Landlord (D)

606 F. Supp. 185 (D. Mo. 1985).

NATURE OF CASE: Motion to dismiss.

FACT SUMMARY: A landlord (D) sued tenants in state court for failure to pay rent. The tenants did not counterclaim, but later filed a federal claim against the landlord (D) that was based on the same tenancy that gave rise to the state court claim.

🏛 RULE OF LAW
A claim arising out of the transaction that is the subject matter of the opposing party's claim, and which does not require for its adjudication the presence of third parties over whom the court does not have jurisdiction, must be stated as a counterclaim, even where the counterclaim may not have been triable in the court where the original pleading was filed.

FACTS: Paragon Group, Inc. (D), which owned the apartment building in which Paul, Liana, and Renata Podhorn (P) lived, sued them in state court for failure to pay rent. The Podhorns (P) did not file a counterclaim, and default judgment was entered. [The Podhorns (P) then filed suit against Paragon Group (D), alleging constructive eviction, breach of implied warranty of habitability, false swearing, false credit report, breach of implied covenant of quiet enjoyment, negligence, abuse of process, tort, conversion, and malicious prosecution.] Paragon Group (D) moved to dismiss the claim on grounds that it should have been filed as a compulsory counterclaim in the state court action, because it arose from the same tenancy that gave rise to the state court claim.

ISSUE: Must a claim arising out of the transaction that is the subject matter of the opposing party's claim, and which does not require for its adjudication the presence of third parties over whom the court does not have jurisdiction, be stated as a counterclaim, even where the counterclaim may not have been triable in the court where the original pleading was filed?

HOLDING AND DECISION: (Hungate, J.) Yes. A claim arising out of the transaction that is the subject matter of the opposing party's claim, and which does not require for its adjudication the presence of third parties over whom the court does not have jurisdiction, must be stated as a counterclaim, even where the counterclaim may not have been triable in the court where the original pleading was filed. The Podhorns' (P) claim arose out of the transaction that gave rise to Paragon Group's (D) rent action in the state court case, and the Podhorns (P) were therefore required to file their federal court claims as compulsory counterclaims. Their failure to do so bars them from having those claims heard. The fact that the state court was without jurisdiction to hear their counterclaim if filed, because the claim exceeded the statutory limit, does not relieve the Podhorns (P) of their obligation to file it. The issue of jurisdiction would have been resolved through assignment to a judge who could hear the claim. Motion to dismiss granted.

▶ ANALYSIS

Though the opinion lists very little in the way of facts, one might imagine a claim that might not have arisen from the same transaction or occurrence as the landlord's nonpayment of rent claim, such as breaking and entering by the landlord, and it becomes clear that the holding may be too broad in scope. The court seems to say that any issue arising during a tenancy that is based on any action by the landlord must be pled as a counterclaim, whether related to the landlord-tenant relationship or not.

■■■

Quicknotes

CLAIM The demand for a right to payment or equitable relief; the fact or facts giving rise to such demand.

COUNTERCLAIM An independent cause of action brought by a defendant to a lawsuit in order to oppose or deduct from the plaintiff's claim.

■■■

Gross v. Hanover Insurance Co.

Insured (P) v. Insurer (D)

138 F.R.D. 53 (S.D.N.Y. 1991).

NATURE OF CASE: Motion under Federal Rule of Civil Procedure 14(a) to implead third-party defendants.

FACT SUMMARY: Gross (P) brought claim against Hanover Insurance Co. (Hanover) (D), his insurer, for theft of jewelry consigned to a retail jewelry store. Hanover (D) sought to implead Joseph Rizzo and Anthony Rizzo, an employee and owner of the store at the time of the theft.

🏛 RULE OF LAW
A third-party defendant may be impleaded under Fed. R. Civ. P. 14(a), in the sound discretion of the court, when such third party is purportedly liable to the defendant for all or part of the defendant's liability to the plaintiff.

FACTS: Gross (P) consigned jewelry to a store from which the jewelry was stolen and brought suit against Hanover Insurance Co. (Hanover) (D), his insurer. Hanover (D), under Rule 14(a), sought to implead the owner of the jewelry store and the owner's brother, who worked there, on evidence that the brother had been involved in the theft and, hence, that the owner and brother would be liable to reimburse the insurer (D) for the stolen goods.

ISSUE: May a defendant implead a third party under Fed. R. Civ. P. 14(a) when it appears that the third party will be liable to the defendant for all or part of the defendant's liability to the plaintiff?

HOLDING AND DECISION: (Leisure, J.) Yes. A third-party defendant may be impleaded under Fed. R. Civ. P. 14(a), in the sound discretion of the court, when such third party is purportedly liable to the defendant for all or part of the defendant's liability to the plaintiff. The interest in judicial economy is served by permitting Hanover (D) to implead the store owner and his brother. Any prejudice felt by Gross (P), the insured, due to the need for additional discovery, was sufficiently outweighed by the benefits of more efficient litigation to be gained by permitting impleader. Furthermore, federal and state court decisions both hold that third-party impleader practice encompasses, as here, subrogation claims. Motion to implead granted.

▶ ANALYSIS

The court emphasized that the district court has considerable discretion in deciding whether to permit a third-party complaint.

Quicknotes

DISCOVERY Pretrial procedure during which one party makes certain information available to the other.

IMPLEADER Procedure by which a third party, who may be liable for all or part of liability, is joined to an action so that all issues may be resolved in a single suit.

SUBROGATION The substitution of one party for another in assuming the first party's rights or obligations.

THIRD-PARTY COMPLAINT A complaint filed by the defendant against a party not yet involved in a lawsuit, alleging liability on the part of the third party for all or part of the damages being sought by the plaintiff.

Temple v. Synthes Corporation, Ltd.

Patient (P) v. Medical device manufacturer (D)

498 U.S. 1042 (1991).

NATURE OF CASE: Appeal of dismissal with prejudice of action for damages for products liability, medical malpractice, and negligence.

FACT SUMMARY: Temple's (P) federal suit against Synthes (D), the manufacturer of a plate implanted in Temple's (P) back, was dismissed when Temple (P) failed to join the doctor and the hospital responsible for installing the plate.

🏛 RULE OF LAW
Joint tortfeasors are not necessary parties under Federal Rule of Civil Procedure 19.

FACTS: A plate and screw device implanted in Temple's (P) back malfunctioned. Temple (P) filed a federal court products liability action against Synthes (D), the manufacturer of the device. Temple (P) also filed a state court medical malpractice and negligence action against the doctor who implanted the device and the hospital where the operation was performed. Synthes (D) filed a motion to dismiss the federal lawsuit under Fed. R. Civ. P. 19 for Temple's (P) failure to join necessary parties. The district court agreed that the doctor and the hospital were necessary parties and gave Temple (P) twenty days to join them. When Temple (P) did not, the court dismissed the suit with prejudice. The court of appeals affirmed, finding that Rule 19 allowed the district court to order joinder in the interest of complete, consistent, and efficient settlement of controversies. It further found that overlapping, separate lawsuits would have prejudiced Synthes (D) because Synthes (D) might claim the device was not defective but that the doctor and the hospital were negligent, and the doctor and the hospital might claim the opposite. Temple (P) appealed, arguing that joint tortfeasors are not necessary parties under Rule 19.

ISSUE: Are joint tortfeasors necessary parties under Federal Rule of Civil Procedure 19?

HOLDING AND DECISION: (Per curiam) No. Joint tortfeasors are not necessary parties under Federal Rule of Civil Procedure 19. It has long been the rule that joint tortfeasors need not be named as defendants in a single lawsuit. Rule 19 does not change that principle. The Advisory Committee Notes to Rule 19(a) state that a tortfeasor with the usual joint and several liability is merely a permissive party. There is a public interest in avoiding multiple lawsuits. However, since the threshold requirements of Rule 19(a) have not been met, the district court had no authority to order dismissal. Reversed and remanded.

▶ ANALYSIS

The function of compulsory joinder as codified in Federal Rule of Civil Procedure 19 is to bring all affected parties into the same lawsuit. Joinder is often required where the suit involves jointly held rights or liabilities, where more than one party claims the same property, or where granting relief necessarily would affect the rights of parties not in the lawsuit. Though there is a strong interest in "complete, consistent, and efficient settlement of controversies," compulsory joinder is limited. There is a strong tradition of allowing the parties themselves to determine who shall be a party, what claims shall be litigated, and what litigation strategies shall be followed.

■══■

Quicknotes

COMPULSORY JOINDER The joining of parties to a lawsuit that is mandatory if complete relief cannot be afforded to the parties in his absence or his absence will result in injustice.

INDISPENSABLE PARTY Parties whose joining in a lawsuit is essential for the adequate disposition of the action and without whom the action cannot proceed.

JOINDER The joining of claims or parties in one lawsuit.

JOINT TORTFEASORS Two or more parties that either in concert, or whose individual acts combine to cause a single injury, rendering them jointly and severally liable for damages incurred.

MEDICAL MALPRACTICE Conduct on the part of a doctor falling below that demonstrated by other doctors of ordinary skill and competency under the circumstances, resulting in damages.

PREJUDICE A preference of the court toward one party prior to litigation.

■══■

Daynard v. Ness, Motley, Loadholdt, Richardon & Poole, P.A.

Law professor (P) v. Law firms litigating against big tobacco (D)

184 F. Supp. 2d 55 (D. Mass. 2001).

NATURE OF CASE: Breach of contract.

FACT SUMMARY: A South Carolina law firm (D) argued that the breach of contract action brought by Daynard (P) should be dismissed for failure to join an indispensable party, a Mississippi law firm (D).

🏛 RULE OF LAW
A jointly and severally liable co-obligor under a verbal contract is not an indispensable party.

FACTS: Daynard (P), a law professor, was an advisor to two law firms that represented the state government in litigation against the tobacco industry (the State Tobacco Litigation). The defendant firms are Ness, Motley, Loadholdt, Richardson & Poole, P.A. from South Carolina (South Carolina defendants) (D) and Scruggs, Milette, Bozeman & Dent, P.A. from Mississippi (Mississippi defendants) (D). There was no written contract between Daynard (P) and either defendant, but Daynard (P) alleged that he and one of the partners from the Mississippi defendants (D) shook hands on a deal that would have paid Daynard (P) five percent of any attorneys' fees paid to either of the defendants. The Mississippi defendants (D) moved to dismiss for lack of personal jurisdiction, and the motion was granted. The South Carolina defendants (D) argued that the case should not proceed without the Mississippi defendants (D) because it was allegedly that firm that made the deal with Daynard (P). Daynard (P) argued that the two firms together agreed that he would be paid for his services, even though the handshake was with the partner of only one, and that under a theory of joint and several liability, only one defendant need be named in the complaint.

ISSUE: Is a jointly and severally liable co-obligor under a verbal contract an indispensable party?

HOLDING AND DECISION: (Young, C.J.) No. A jointly and severally liable co-obligor under a verbal contract is not an indispensable party. Determination of whether a party is "indispensable" requires two steps. The first step is to determine whether the party is "necessary" under Fed. R. Civ. P. 19(a). The second step is to determine whether the party is, in addition to being "necessary," also "indispensable" under Fed. R. Civ. P. 19(b). It is important to note that "indispensable" is a subset of "necessary," not a mutually exclusive category. A "necessary" party is one that should be joined to effect a just adjudication, while an "indispensable" party under Rule 19 (b) is a "necessary" party under Rule 19(a) who cannot be made a party and without whom the court determines the action cannot

proceed. Under Rule 19(a)(1) and (2), the Mississippi defendants (D) are not a "necessary" party. First, the Mississippi defendants (D) are not "necessary" under Rule 19(a)(1). Since the South Carolina defendants (D) bear the burden of persuasion on their motion to dismiss, the court must draw inferences in Daynard's (P) favor and assume that the defendants are jointly and severally liable. Second, the Mississippi defendants (D) are not "necessary" under Rule 19(a)(2)(i). Any judgment against the South Carolina defendants (D) will not be binding against the Mississippi defendants (D), and any such judgment would not be "persuasive precedent" and thus impair the Mississippi defendants' (D) ability to protect their interests. Third, the possibility that the South Carolina defendants (D) may bear the entire bill unless the Mississippi defendants (D) are joined does not make the Mississippi defendants (D) "necessary" under 19(a)(2)(ii) because under the theory of joint and several liability, Daynard (P) has the right to satisfy his whole judgment by execution against any one of the multiple defendants who are liable to him. Fourth, under the traditional rule of thumb co-obligees are "indispensable" parties while co-obligors might not even be "necessary," the South Carolina defendants (D) tried to cast themselves as co-obligees under the alleged contract. The South Carolina defendants (D) argued that Daynard (P) still owes legal research and advice to them, even though the State Tobacco Litigation already settled. The facts do not support the conclusion that Daynard (P) still owes services to the South Carolina defendants (D). Finally, the South Carolina defendants (D) argued that a mutual release to which Daynard (P) allegedly agreed puts the validity and enforceability of the alleged contract into question, and thus requires joinder of all parties to the alleged contract, but this argument twists the traditional rule of thumb, which is that an action in equity to determine the rights under a contract requires joinder of all parties to the contract. This case concerns only money damages and does not concern rescission or specific performance. Thus, the traditional rule of thumb that rescission requires joinder of all parties must give way to the traditional rule of thumb that a plaintiff need not name all co-obligors as defendants. Therefore, it is not necessary for Daynard (P) to join the Mississippi defendants (D) in this action because they are jointly and severally liable as co-obligors. Since the Mississippi defendants (D) are not a "necessary" party under Rule 19(a), then by definition, they cannot be "indispensable" under Rule 19(b).

Continued on next page.

▶ *ANALYSIS*

The court notes that since the Mississippi defendants (D) are not a "necessary" party, they cannot be "indispensable." That fact resolves the issue in the case. But the court went on to consider the South Carolina defendants' (D) arguments under Rule 19(b) anyway. The four factors to consider under Rule 19(b), which overlap with the factors enumerated in Rule 19(a), are: (1) To what extent might a judgment rendered in the person's absence be prejudicial to the person or those already parties? The court rejected the South Carolina defendants' (D) argument here, stating that (a) joint and several liability by definition includes the possibility that one defendant ends up footing the entire bill, (b) "persuasive precedent" alone cannot, as a practical matter, impair or impede the Mississippi defendants' (D) ability to defend themselves, and (c) Rule 19 is concerned with the risk of inconsistent obligations, not inconsistent adjudications. (2) To what extent can the prejudice be lessened or avoided by protective provisions in the judgment, by shaping of relief, of other measures? (3) Would a judgment rendered in the person's absence be adequate? (4) Would the plaintiff have an adequate remedy if the action is dismissed for non-joinder? The court found that the first and third factors favor Daynard (P), the second factor is not relevant, and the fourth factor favors the South Carolina defendants (D). Even if the Mississippi defendants (D) were regarded as "necessary" parties, the court would allow the action to proceed against the South Carolina defendants (D). Given the significant overlap between the four factors in parts (a) and (b) of Fed. R. Civ. P. 19, the difference between "necessary" and "indispensable" is that an "indispensable" party is also "necessary," whereas a "necessary" party is not always "indispensable." Where a "necessary" party cannot, for whatever reason, be made a party, the case must be dismissed. Note that if the Mississippi defendants had not been granted their motion to dismiss for lack of personal jurisdiction, they would have been able to be made party to the lawsuit, and therefore may have been found to be "necessary." The court went on to show that even if that had been the case, they would not have been deemed "indispensable." The court probably dealt with the issue of "indispensable" in order to not have to deal with the issue in future litigation—the grant of the motion to dismiss was on appeal at the time of this decision.

■═■

Quicknotes

BREACH OF CONTRACT Unlawful failure by a party to perform its obligations pursuant to contract.

COMPLAINT The initial pleading commencing litigation that sets forth a claim for relief.

EXECUTION The full performance of an agreement's obligations.

INDISPENSABLE PARTY Party, whose joining in a lawsuit is essential for the adequate disposition of the action and without whom the action cannot proceed.

JOINDER The joining of claims or parties in one lawsuit.

JOINT AND SEVERAL LIABILITY Liability amongst tortfeasors allowing the injured party to bring suit against any of the defendants, individually or collectively, and to recover from each up to the total amount of damages awarded.

PERSONAL JURISDICTION The court's authority over a person or parties to a lawsuit.

RESCISSION The canceling of an agreement and the return of the parties to their positions prior to the formation of the contract.

SPECIFIC PERFORMANCE An equitable remedy whereby the court requires the parties to perform their obligations pursuant to a contract.

■═■

United States v. Northern Indiana Public Service Co., et al.

Federal government (P) v. Landowner (D)

100 F.R.D. 78 (N.D. Ind. 1983).

NATURE OF CASE: Motion to intervene in a condemnation proceeding.

FACT SUMMARY: The Government (P) filed notice of condemnation against Northern Indiana Public Service Company (D). Save the Dunes Council (Council) filed a motion to intervene.

🏛 RULE OF LAW
A motion to intervene under Fed. R. Civ. P. 24(a)(2) must be denied where any of the four conditions of the rule are absent.

FACTS: The Government (P) filed its notice of condemnation affecting almost 40 acres of land owned by Northern Indiana Public Service Co. (NIPSCO) (D) on August 7, 1978. NIPSCO (D) filed objections to the notice on September 25, 1978. A hearing on NIPSCO's (D) objections was scheduled for February 8, 1982. The hearing was removed from the calendar on January 22, 1982. On April 4, 1982, the Save the Dunes Council (Council) filed a motion to intervene as a plaintiff under Fed. R. Civ. P. 24. NIPSCO (D) filed a motion to strike. On September 7, 1983, the United States (P) and NIPSCO (D) settled the case. Briefs were then filed on the issue of intervention.

ISSUE: Must a motion to intervene under Fed. R. Civ. P. 24(a)(2) be denied where any of the four conditions of the rule are absent?

HOLDING AND DECISION: (Sharp, C.J.) Yes. A motion to intervene under Fed. R. Civ. P. 24(a)(2) must be denied where any of the four conditions of the rule are absent. Fed. R. Civ. P. 24(a)(2) requires that four conditions be met by the proposed intervenor: (1) timely application, (2) an interest relating to the property or transaction that is the subject of the case, (3) that the disposition of the action may as a practical matter impair or impede his ability to protect that interest, and (4) that the interest is not adequately represented by existing parties. Council satisfied the first condition by moving to intervene promptly after knowing or having reason to know its interest may be adversely affected by the outcome of the litigation. NIPSCO (D) argued that the Council should have moved to intervene prior to the time of the original parties' settlement. The case history shows that the first reference to a settlement was on January 12, 1982, and the Council filed its motion to intervene on April 2, 1982. The original parties did not settle and file to dismiss until over a year later. Additionally, from the institution of the action until early 1983, Council had no reason to believe that intervention would be required, since Congress had

expressed intent to preserve the land in question, which would have protected the Council's perceived interest. Thus, the timeliness condition is met. As to the second condition, the Council does not have an interest relating to the property. There is no consensus in case law as to what constitutes a litigable interest for purposes of intervention. However, cases in this circuit emphasize an interest that is legally protectable. NIPSCO (D) is the only party with a legal interest, as it is the sole owner of the property. The Council worked to preserve the development of the national lake shore, but is essentially a private citizen with no interest in the property. The Council's motion to intervene is denied.

▶ ANALYSIS

Although the court expressly stated in the opinion the Council's motion fails on the second condition of Fed. R. Civ. P. 24(a), the language of the last paragraph of the opinion seems to imply that the court could have ruled in the Council's favor, notwithstanding its failure to meet the second condition of the rule. This is perhaps in response to Rule 24's language allowing intervention by discretion of the court.

■=■

Quicknotes

CONDEMNATION The taking of private property for public use so long as just compensation is paid therefor.

MOTION TO INTERVENE The method by which a party, not an initial party to the action, is admitted to the action, in order to assert an interest in the subject matter of a lawsuit.

■=■

Discovery

Quick Reference Rules of Law

Hickman v. Taylor

Representative (P) v. Tug owner (D)

329 U.S. 495 (1947).

NATURE OF CASE: Action for damages for wrongful death.

FACT SUMMARY: Five crew members drowned when a tug sank. In anticipation of litigation, the attorney for Taylor (D), the tug owner, interviewed the survivors. Hickman (P), as representative of one of the deceased, brought this action and tried by means of discovery to obtain copies of the statements Taylor's (D) attorney obtained from the survivors.

> ## 🏛 RULE OF LAW
> Material obtained by counsel in preparation of litigation is the work product of the lawyer, and while such material is not protected by the attorney-client privilege, it is not discoverable on mere demand without a showing of necessity or justification.

FACTS: Five of the nine crew members drowned when a tug sank. A public hearing was held at which the four survivors were examined. Their testimony was recorded and was made available to all interested parties. A short time later, the attorney for Taylor (D), the tug owner, interviewed the survivors in preparation for possible litigation. He also interviewed other persons believed to have information on the accident. Ultimately, claims were brought by representatives of all five of the deceased. Four were settled. Hickman (P), the fifth claimant, brought this action. He filed interrogatories asking for any statements taken from crew members, as well as any oral or written statements, records, reports, or other memoranda made concerning any salvaging and repair of the tug and the death of the deceased. Taylor (D) refused to summarize or set forth the material on the ground that it was protected by the attorney-client privilege.

ISSUE: Does a party seeking to discover material obtained by an adverse party's counsel in preparation for possible litigation have a burden to show a justification for such production?

HOLDING AND DECISION: (Murphy, J.) Yes. The deposition-discovery rules are to be accorded a broad and liberal treatment, since mutual knowledge of all the relevant facts gathered by both parties is essential to proper litigation. But discovery does have ultimate and necessary boundaries. Limitations arise upon a showing of bad faith or harassment or when the inquiry seeks material that is irrelevant or privileged. In this case, the material sought by Hickman (P) is not protected by the attorney-client privilege. However, such material as that sought here does constitute the work product of the lawyer. The general policy against invading the privacy of an attorney in performing his various duties is so well recognized and so essential to the orderly working of our legal system that the party seeking work-product material has a burden to show reasons to justify such production. Interviews, statements, memoranda, correspondence, briefs, mental impressions, etc., obtained in the course of preparation for possible or anticipated litigation fall within the work product. Such material is not free from discovery in all cases. Where relevant and nonprivileged facts remain hidden in an attorney's file and where production of those facts is essential to the preparation of one's case, discovery may be had. But there must be a showing of necessity and justification. In this case, Hickman (P) seeks discovery of oral and written statements of witnesses whose identity is well known and whose availability to Hickman (P) appears unimpaired. Here, no attempt was made to show why it was necessary for Taylor's (D) attorney to produce the material. No reasons were given to justify this invasion of the attorney's privacy. Hickman's (P) counsel admitted that he wanted the statements only to help him prepare for trial. That is insufficient to warrant an exception to the policy of protecting the privacy of an attorney's professional activities. Affirmed.

CONCURRENCE: (Jackson, J.) The primary effect of the practice advocated would be to require attorneys to act as witnesses.

▶ *ANALYSIS*

The *Hickman* decision left open a number of questions as to the scope of the work product doctrine and the showing needed to discover work product material. In 1970, Federal Rule 26(b)(3) was added to deal with the discovery of work product. It provides that documents and tangible things that were prepared in anticipation of litigation or for trial are discoverable only upon a showing that the party seeking such materials has substantial need of them and that he is unable without undue hardship to obtain the substantial equivalent of the materials by other means. The rule states that mental impressions, conclusions, opinions, or legal theories of an attorney or other representative of a party, are to be protected against disclosure.

■═■

Quicknotes

ATTORNEY-CLIENT PRIVILEGE A doctrine precluding the admission into evidence of confidential communications

Continued on next page.

between an attorney and his client made in the course of obtaining professional assistance.

DEPOSITION A pretrial discovery procedure whereby oral or written questions are asked by one party of a witness of the opposing party under oath in preparation for litigation.

DISCOVERY Pretrial procedure during which one party makes certain information available to the other.

INTERROGATORIES A method of pretrial discovery in which written questions are provided by one party to another who must respond in writing under oath.

WORK PRODUCT Work performed by an attorney in preparation of litigation that is not subject to discovery.

WORK PRODUCT RULE A doctrine excluding from discovery work performed by an attorney in preparation of litigation.

WRONGFUL DEATH An action brought by the beneficiaries of a deceased person, claiming that the deceased's death was the result of wrongful conduct by the defendant.

■═■

Moss v. Blue Cross and Blue Shield of Kansas, Inc.

Employer (D) v. Former employee (P)

241 F.R.D. 683 (D. Kan. 2007).

NATURE OF CASE: Objections to discovery requests.

FACT SUMMARY: Michele Moss (P) sued Blue Cross and Blue Shield (BCBS) (D) under the Family and Medical Leave Act (FMLA) for allegedly interfering with her FMLA rights. BCBS (D) objected to several interrogatories and requests for production of documents.

🏛 RULE OF LAW

(1) When discovery sought appears relevant, the party resisting discovery has the burden of establishing the lack of relevance.

(2) The party resisting discovery on grounds that it is overly broad and unduly burdensome has the burden of demonstrating that the time or expense involved in responding to the requested discovery is unduly burdensome, unless the discovery request is unduly burdensome on its face.

FACTS: Michele Moss (P) sued Blue Cross and Blue Shield (BCBS) (D) under the Family and Medical Leave Act (FMLA) for allegedly interfering with her FMLA rights. BCBS (D) objected to several interrogatories and requests for production of documents. Interrogatories 8 and 9 asked BCBS (D) to list any and all employees in the last 10 years who had been terminated or disciplined, reprimanded, or suffered any type of adverse employment action for violating the FMLA leave policy, or for failing to "call in" for two consecutive days of absence, in violation of company policy. Document Requests 2 and 3 asked for any and all correspondence of any kind either to or from Moss (P), and any documents bearing Moss's (P) name. Document Requests 7 and 20 asked for any and all documents from the previous five years relating to any legal action concerning discrimination of any kind that BCBS (D) was involved in, and any and all confidential settlement agreements arising out of any discrimination claims against BCBS (D).

ISSUE:

(1) When discovery sought appears relevant, does the party resisting discovery have the burden of establishing the lack of relevance?

(2) Does the party resisting discovery on grounds that it is overly broad and unduly burdensome have the burden of demonstrating that the time or expense involved in responding to the requested discovery is unduly burdensome, unless the discovery request is unduly burdensome on its face?

HOLDING AND DECISION: (Sebelius, J.)

(1) Yes. When discovery sought appears relevant, the party resisting discovery has the burden of establishing the lack of relevance. When relevancy is not readily apparent, the party seeking discovery has the burden of showing the relevancy. Interrogatories 8 and 9 are relevant, as Moss (P) argued, because an employer's general practices and operations are relevant even if the plaintiff is asserting an individual employment violation. In addition, answers to the two interrogatories could lead to evidence regarding BCBS's (D) application of its FMLA or attendance "call in" policies, and whether that application was uniform. Document Requests 7 and 20 are irrelevant, because they are not reasonably calculated to lead to the discovery of admissible evidence. People with whom BCBS (D) entered into settlement agreements have no bearing on the present case. On the basis of relevance, BCBS's (D) objection to Interrogatories 8 and 9 is overruled, however, BCBS's objection to Document Requests 7 and 20 on the basis of relevance is sustained.

(2) Yes. The party resisting discovery on grounds that it is overly broad and unduly burdensome has the burden of demonstrating that the time or expense involved in responding to the requested discovery is unduly burdensome, unless the discovery request is unduly burdensome on its face. BCBS (D) also failed to meet its obligation to support its claim that Interrogatories 8 and 9 were overly broad and unduly burdensome, but because some parts of the interrogatories are overly broad and unduly burdensome on their face, the objection will be sustained as to those parts. Specifically, to determine "any type of adverse employment action" would require BCBS (D) to "engage in mental gymnastics in order to determine what might be remotely responsive" as to the interrogatories at issue, and the lack of a time frame for Interrogatory 9 is facially overbroad. But to locate any employee who has suffered any type of adverse employment action due to violation of the FMLA or "call in" attendance policy would require review of 1800 personnel files, which is not necessarily overly broad or unduly burdensome on its face, because FMLA leave and termination for attendance is coded and searchable by computer. Therefore, BCBS (D) must respond to Interrogatory 9 to the extent it seeks information about those employees who have been terminated or disciplined in writing for violating BCBS's (D)

Continued on next page.

FMLA policy, and to respond to Interrogatory 9 to the extent it seeks information regarding documented instances of employee termination for attendance within the past five years.

Document Requests 2 and 3 are overly broad and unduly burdensome on their face because Moss's (P) five years of employment required her to extensively communicate with providers in BCBS's (D) network. BCBS's (D) objection to Requests 2 and 3 are sustained because they are overly broad and unduly burdensome, and adequate guidance as to what extent the requests are not objectionable cannot be provided. Finally, Request 7 is overly broad and unduly burdensome on its face, because to answer it would require BCBS (D) to "engage in mental gymnastics to determine what information may or may not be remotely responsive." As no reasonable guidance exists to define the extent to which Request 7 is not objectionable, BCBS's (D) objection is sustained.

▶ ANALYSIS

Before the Federal Rules of Civil Procedure were amended in 2000, Rule 26 allowed discovery into "any matter, not privileged, which is relevant to the subject matter involved in the pending action." The 2000 amendment focused the discovery on the "claim or defense" of any party.

■══■

Quicknotes

DISCOVERY Pretrial procedure during which one party makes certain information available to the other.

INTERROGATORIES A method of pretrial discovery in which written questions are provided by one party to another who must respond in writing under oath.

■══■

Teague v. Target Corp.

Former employee (P) v. Employer (D)

2007 WL 1041191 (W.D.N.C. 2007).

NATURE OF CASE: Motion for sanctions for spoliation of evidence.

FACT SUMMARY: A Target employee (P) who brought a wrongful termination action against the company discarded a computer containing files that purported to show her job search efforts. Target (D) filed a motion to dismiss her claim for back pay due to spoliation.

🏛 RULE OF LAW
A court may issue jury instructions that permit the jury to draw an adverse inference from a party's destruction of evidence that is relevant to claims and defenses in the case, if the party has an obligation to preserve the evidence and destroys it with a "culpable state of mind."

FACTS: Teague (P), a Target employee, was fired from her job. She filed an action charging that she was wrongfully terminated on the basis of her gender and intentional infliction of emotional distress. She sought lost wages, benefits, and compensatory and punitive damages. Target (D) claimed she failed to mitigate her damages, among other things. Teague (P) claimed that she conducted her entire online job search after leaving Target (D) on a computer that "crashed," and that she subsequently discarded. The computer was discarded approximately one year after she had retained counsel regarding her claims against Target (D) and after filing her charge of discrimination with the EEOC. The only documented evidence of Teague's (P) post-termination job search are work search records she submitted to the North Carolina unemployment benefits office. Target (D) filed a motion to dismiss her claim for back pay due to spoliation.

ISSUE: May a court issue jury instructions that permit the jury to draw an adverse inference from a party's destruction of evidence that is relevant to claims and defenses in the case, if the party has an obligation to preserve the evidence and destroys it with a "culpable state of mind?"

HOLDING AND DECISION: (Mullen, J.) Yes. A court may issue jury instructions that permit the jury to draw an adverse inference from a party's destruction of evidence that is relevant to claims and defenses in the case, if the party has an obligation to preserve the evidence and destroys it with a "culpable state of mind." A plaintiff has an obligation to preserve evidence relating to her claims and her efforts to mitigate her damages, and the affirmative duty to preserve material evidence arises long before the filing of an initial pleading. The sanction for spoliation should be tailored to serve the prophylactic, punitive, and remedial rationales underlying the spoliation doctrine. One possible sanction is the issuance of jury instructions permitting the jury to draw an adverse inference from a party's destruction of evidence, and a court may order such a sanction where a party destroys relevant evidence despite an obligation to preserve the evidence with a "culpable state of mind." A "culpable state of mind" could include bad faith/knowing destruction, gross negligence, and ordinary negligence. Because Teague (P) had an obligation to preserve her computer, discarded it despite the fact that it contained electronic evidence relating to her claims against Target (D) and her efforts to mitigate her damages, and after she hired counsel and filed an Equal Employment Opportunity Commission (EEOC) charge, it is reasonable to conclude that she discarded the computer with a "culpable state of mind." An adverse inference instruction to the jury is warranted and appropriate. Motions for sanctions granted in part and denied in part.

▶ ANALYSIS

This case is straightforward in terms of its rule of law, but implementing the rule could prove difficult, because the exact instruction could be crafted in a way that is either too severe or too lenient. If drafted severely, it could doom a plaintiff's case. It is difficult to see a difference between such an instruction and simply dismissing a case for spoliation, though the latter is generally not authorized absent bad faith conduct.

■■■

Quicknotes

BAD FAITH Conduct that is intentionally misleading or deceptive.

GROSS NEGLIGENCE The intentional failure to perform a duty with reckless disregard of the consequences.

PUNITIVE DAMAGES Damages exceeding the actual injury suffered for the purposes of punishment of the defendant, deterrence of the wrongful behavior or comfort to the plaintiff.

SPOLIATION The destruction or material alteration of evidence or the failure to preserve property for another's use as evidence in pending or reasonably foreseeable litigation.

WRONGFUL TERMINATION Unlawful termination of an individual's employment.

■■■

Helmert v. Butterball, LLC

Former employees (P) v. Former employer (D)

2010 WL 2179180 (E.D. Ark. 2010).

NATURE OF CASE: Motion to compel production of electronic evidence.

FACT SUMMARY: Sheila Helmert (P), Wilma Brown (P), and Lori West (P) filed suit on behalf of themselves and others similarly situated against their former employer, Butterball, LLC (D), under the Fair Labor Standards Act (FLSA) and Arkansas law. The plaintiffs claimed that Butterball (D) refused to conduct a meaningful search of its electronically stored information (ESI), and they filed a motion to compel under to Fed. R. Civ. P. 37(a). Butterball (D) argued that, while the plaintiffs were entitled to more documents than those it received, the scope of the plaintiffs' request is too broad. Butterball (D) also argued that cost should be shifted to the plaintiffs.

🏛 RULE OF LAW
Discovery of relevant, nonprivileged electronically stored information (ESI) is limited if the party from whom discovery is sought establishes that it is unreasonably cumulative or duplicative or that the burden or expense of the proposed discovery outweighs its likely benefit.

FACTS: Sheila Helmert (P), Wilma Brown (P), and Lori West (P) sued their former employer, Butterball, LLC (D), for alleged violations of the Fair Labor Standards Act (FLSA) and Arkansas law. They and other hourly production employees at Butterball's (D) Huntsville, Ozark, and Jonesboro plants argue they were not fully compensated for time spent donning, doffing, and sanitizing protective gear and equipment. The plaintiffs' requests for production of documents included all documents, correspondence, e-mail, or other written materials related to employee donning and doffing of personal protective equipment, safety equipment, tools, uniforms, and/or other gear or clothing; all documents showing communications amongst and between employees, management or otherwise, that concern payment of wages for time spent donning, doffing, walking, sanitizing, or waiting in any production facility; and all documents related to Butterball's (D) payroll and punch-clock procedures. Butterball (D) produced 800 documents, including 87 emails. Plaintiffs sought to compel Butterball (D) to conduct additional searches. Butterball (D) objected to the number of proposed search terms and custodians and, despite several attempts, the parties failed to reach an agreement on the scope of discovery. Eventually, the plaintiffs sought to compel Butterball (D) to search for additional information "from all possible sources of electronically stored information (ESI) belonging to 43 custodians" using 70 separate terms. Butterball (D) consented to searching the active and archived email folders of 33 custodians using 12 previously proposed terms and argued any additional searching would be unreasonably duplicative, would impose significant burden, and would require searching locations deemed "not reasonably accessible."

ISSUE: Is discovery of relevant, nonprivileged ESI limited if the party from whom discovery is sought establishes that it is unreasonably cumulative or duplicative or that the burden or expense of the proposed discovery outweighs its likely benefit?

HOLDING AND DECISION: (Holmes, J.) Yes. Discovery of relevant, nonprivileged ESI is limited if the party from whom discovery is sought establishes that it is unreasonably cumulative or duplicative or that the burden or expense of the proposed discovery outweighs its likely benefit. As a general rule, Federal Rule of Civil Procedure 26 (b) permits parties to obtain discovery regarding any nonprivileged matter that is relevant to any party's claim or defense. A request for discovery should be allowed unless it is clear that the information sought can have no possible bearing on the claim or defense of a party. But discovery of relevant, nonprivileged ESI is limited if the party from whom discovery is sought establishes that it is unreasonably cumulative or duplicative or that the burden or expense of the proposed discovery outweighs its likely benefit. Under these rules, the plaintiff's motion was granted in part and denied in part, as follows: First, the plaintiffs proposed an expanded list of search terms that included 70 terms from four categories: terms related to donning and doffing cases against Smithfield Foods—one of Butterball's (D) owners—and its subsidiaries; terms related to Supreme Court and seminal donning and doffing cases; terms related to individuals, law firms, and industry organizations; and terms related to Butterball (D) compensation practices. With the exception of terms related to individuals, law firms, and industry organizations, the categories of search terms are approved because they are relevant to the issues in this case, and Butterball (D) failed to show that the estimated costs of the searches was too burdensome. With respect to those terms related to individuals, law firms, and industry organizations, they may lead to the production of relevant information, but that information will merely duplicate information that could be produced by searching other, more specific terms. Second, the plaintiffs proposed an expanded list of custodians. Some of plaintiffs' proposals for expanding the number of

Continued on next page.

custodians are approved, including the search of certain "non-Butterball (D) ESI sources," such as the personal and professional email accounts of upper management who were not on Butterball's (D) email system during the relevant time period. But Butterball (D) will not be ordered to conduct searches of custodial sources unlikely to contain responsive material and sources deemed not reasonably accessible, including backup tapes. Third, the plaintiffs sought to require Butterball (D) to search backup tapes, in addition to active and archived emails. Butterball (D) had argued that the backup tapes were not reasonably accessible, because to conduct such a search, Butterball (D) would need to recover the emails stored on the tapes, build a server, install new software, and restore "an entire post office." The hardware to restore the post office alone was estimated to cost $10,000. All of this was necessary before any searching could be conducted. Thus, the backup tapes are not reasonably accessible. The plaintiffs' argument that the search should nonetheless be compelled because they had good cause to obtain the information on the backup tapes is rejected. Each of the seven factors identified for consideration by the advisory committee notes to Rule 26(b)(2) suggest that Butterball (D) should not be compelled to search backup tapes. The plaintiffs have no idea what, if any, discoverable information may be obtained by rebuilding a server post office and searching the emails of the listed persons that are stored on the backup tapes. The slim likelihood that new and relevant information may be discovered does not outweigh the substantial burden and expense required to retrieve the information from the backup tapes. Fourth, the plaintiffs sought to determine whether or not Butterball (D) has a good faith or non-willful defense under the FLSA, and for that reason, it is important to discover what Butterball (D), its employees, and its management knew or believed about donning-and-doffing-related compensation. The plaintiffs suggested that, if Butterball (D) participated in the Labor Department's surveys and investigations into FLSA compliance, then it might have believed that it was in violation of the FLSA and lack a good faith defense. But the plaintiffs offer no evidence at this point that Butterball (D) participated in a Labor Department survey or investigation or any other discussions regarding donning and doffing prior to 2005. Therefore, a search of ESI prior to 2005 may not result in the discovery of information relevant to a claim or defense that has been presented, and it is therefore denied. Because the court did not compel discovery of any ESI that was not readily accessible, the court found cost shifting was inappropriate.

▶ ANALYSIS

Arguments that e-discovery is "impossible" or that it would cause "undue burden" are becoming implausible as more software is created that allows for cost-efficient wide-scope searches. Whether this court's findings of impossibility and undue burden are justified is questionable, since the case is only two years old and e-discovery methods were not, at that time, in their infancy.

■══■

Quicknotes

DISCOVERY Pretrial procedure during which one party makes certain information available to the other.

■══■

Société Nationale Industrielle Aérospatiale v. United States District Court

[Parties not identified.]

482 U.S. 522 (1987).

NATURE OF CASE: Motion for a protective order.

FACT SUMMARY: [Facts not stated in casebook excerpt.]

🏛 RULE OF LAW
(1) The Hague Convention does not set out exclusive and mandatory procedures for conducting pretrial discovery.
(2) Comity does not require that in all cases the Hague Convention be used as a matter of first resort for issues related to discovery, but does require a particularized analysis of the interests of the foreign and requesting nations prior to resort to the Hague Convention.

FACTS: [Facts not stated in casebook excerpt.]

ISSUE:
(1) Does the Hague Convention set out exclusive and mandatory procedures for conducting pretrial discovery?
(2) Does comity not require that in all cases the Hague Convention be used as a matter of first resort for issues related to discovery, but does require a particularized analysis of the interests of the foreign and requesting nations prior to resort to the Hague Convention?

HOLDING AND DECISION: (Stevens, J.)
(1) No. The Hague Convention does not set out exclusive and mandatory procedures for conducting pretrial discovery. The Convention does not speak in mandatory terms about procedures to be followed for all permissible transnational-discovery, and exclude all other practices, such as those under the Federal Rules of Civil Procedure. Rather, the Convention was intended as a permissive supplement, not a preemptive replacement, for other means of obtaining evidence. The Convention therefore does not deprive a federal court of the jurisdiction it otherwise possesses to order a foreign national party before it to produce evidence physically located outside the United States.
(2) Yes. Comity does not require that in all cases the Hague Convention be used as a matter of first resort for issues related to discovery, but does require a particularized analysis of the interests of the foreign and requesting nations prior to resort to the Hague Convention. Judicial supervision of discovery, especially when it seeks evidence abroad, should aim to minimize cost and inconvenience, and to prevent improper use of discovery requests.

▶ ANALYSIS

The Supreme Court affirmed a ruling by the court of appeals, which in turn affirmed the district court. The ruling does not curb the relatively broad scope of American discovery, but the Court does not think it needs to, reasoning that foreign tribunals will respect the notion that final decisions regarding evidence to be used in American courts must be made by American courts.

■══■

Quicknotes

COMITY A rule pursuant to which courts in one state give deference to the statutes and judicial decisions of the court of another state.

DISCOVERY Pretrial procedure during which one party makes certain information available to the other.

HAGUE CONVENTION Multilateral treaty governing service of process in foreign jurisdictions.

■══■

The Right to Jury Trial and Judicial Control of Results

Quick Reference Rules of Law

Chauffeurs, Teamsters and Helpers, Local No. 391 v. Terry

Union (D) v. Union members (P)

494 U.S. 558 (1990).

NATURE OF CASE: Review of denial of motion to strike jury demand in action for breach of the duty of fair representation.

FACT SUMMARY: The Teamsters Union (D), subject to a suit for breach of fair representation, contended that Terry and others (P) were not entitled to a jury.

🏛 **RULE OF LAW**
A plaintiff in an action against a union for breach of duty of fair representation is entitled to a jury.

FACTS: Terry and other various members (P) of the Teamsters Union, Local 391 ("the Union") (D) brought an action against the Union (D), contending that it did not represent them fairly in a grievance claim seeking back pay. The plaintiffs requested a jury. The Union (D) moved to strike the jury demand. The district court denied the motion and the Fourth Circuit affirmed. The U.S. Supreme Court granted certiorari.

ISSUE: Is a plaintiff in an action against a union for breach of a duty of fair representation entitled to a jury?

HOLDING AND DECISION: (Marshall, J.) Yes. A plaintiff in an action against a union for breach of representation is entitled to a jury. The Seventh Amendment guarantees a civil party a right to trial by jury in actions at law. Consequently, any decision as to whether a party is entitled to a jury depends on whether the issue being tried is legal or equitable, and whether the remedy sought is legal or equitable. Here, the action at issue is similar to an action for breach of fiduciary duty, an equitable action. At the same time, the action has elements of breach of contract, as the plaintiffs must show that their employer breached the collective bargaining agreement. Thus, the issue being tried is both legal and equitable. However, the remedy sought, damages, is wholly legal. This being so, the action is more legal than equitable, and the right to a jury therefore exists. Affirmed.

CONCURRENCE: (Brennan, J.) The right to a jury should be determined only with reference to the remedy sought.

DISSENT: (Kennedy, J.) The action is most analogous to breach of fiduciary duty, an equitable action.

▶ *ANALYSIS*

At common law, equity and law were separate. Their merger came after adoption of the Seventh Amendment. The radical transformation of forms of action since then has made Seventh Amendment jurisprudence an often confusing field.

■══■

Quicknotes

BREACH OF CONTRACT Unlawful failure by a party to perform its obligations pursuant to contract.

BREACH OF FIDUCIARY DUTY The failure of a fiduciary to observe the standard of care exercised by professionals of similar education and experience.

CERTIORARI A discretionary writ issued by a superior court to an inferior court in order to review the lower court's decisions; the Supreme Court's writ ordering such review.

COLLECTIVE BARGAINING Negotiations between an employer and employee that are mediated by a specified third party.

EQUITY Fairness; justice; the determination of a matter consistent with principles of fairness and not in strict compliance with rules of law.

SEVENTH AMENDMENT Provides that no fact tried by a jury shall be otherwise re-examined in any court of the United States, other than according to the rules of the common law.

■══■

Adickes v. S.H. Kress & Co.

Restaurant patron (P) v. Restaurant owner (D)

398 U.S. 144 (1970).

NATURE OF CASE: Appeal of summary judgment denying damages for civil rights violation.

FACT SUMMARY: In a civil rights action in which a conspiracy between the police and a S.H. Kress & Co. (D) was alleged, summary judgment was granted when Adickes (P) could not produce evidence to support a conspiracy.

🏛 RULE OF LAW
In an action based on conspiracy, summary judgment may not be granted unless a defendant can show that no evidence thereof exists.

FACTS: Adickes (P) was refused service at a restaurant owned by S.H. Kress & Co. (Kress) (D) and arrested for loitering. She then brought an action seeking damages under § 1983, alleging a conspiracy between Kress (D) and the police. Under the circumstances of the case, a conspiracy could have existed only if police had been present at the store before the arrest. When Adickes (P) could not show that police had earlier been present, Kress (D) moved for summary judgment. This was granted and affirmed on appeal. Adickes (P) appealed to the U.S. Supreme Court.

ISSUE: In an action based on conspiracy, may summary judgment be granted if a defendant has not shown that no evidence thereof exists?

HOLDING AND DECISION: (Harlan, J.) No. In an action based on conspiracy, summary judgment may not be granted unless a defendant can show that no evidence thereof exists. In a motion for summary judgment, the burden is on the moving party to affirmatively show the absence of a genuine issue as to any material fact. The fact that the burden would be on the other party on the same fact at trial is of no matter. Here, while at trial, Adickes (P) would have to prove the presence of police earlier in the day; at the summary judgment level, the burden was on Kress (D) to prove they were not. This it did not do. Reversed.

▶ ANALYSIS

The present case's rule was modified by the Court 16 years later in *Celotex Corp. v. Catrett*, 477 U.S. 317 (1986). The Court in *Celotex* liberalized the burden on a moving party, holding that such a party, on an issue the opposing party has the ultimate burden of proving, could prevail on the basis that the nonmoving party could not produce evidence on the issue. This has made summary judgment a much easier procedure to obtain in federal courts than in most state courts, as most states' procedural rules are similar to that announced in the present action.

■=■

Quicknotes

42 U.S.C. § 1983 Provides that every person, who under color of state law subjects or causes to be subjected any citizen of the United States or person within its jurisdiction to be deprived of rights, privileges and immunities guaranteed by the federal Constitution and laws, is liable to the injured party at law or in equity.

BURDEN OF PROOF The duty of a party to introduce evidence to support a fact that is in dispute in an action.

CONSPIRACY Concerted action by two or more persons to accomplish some unlawful purpose.

MATERIAL FACT A fact without the existence of which a contract would not have been entered.

SUMMARY JUDGMENT Judgment rendered by a court in response to a motion by one of the parties, claiming that the lack of a question of material fact in respect to an issue warrants disposition of the issue without consideration by the jury.

■=■

Celotex Corp. v. Catrett

Asbestos manufacturer (D) v. Widow (P)

477 U.S. 317 (1986).

NATURE OF CASE: Appeal from reversal of grant of summary judgment.

FACT SUMMARY: The court of appeals reversed summary judgment in favor of Celotex Corp. (D) on the basis that Celotex (D) had not offered sufficient evidence rebutting Catrett's (P) allegations.

🏛 RULE OF LAW
Summary judgment must be entered against a party who fails to make a showing sufficient to establish the existence of an element essential to this case and on which he bears the burden of proof at trial.

FACTS: Catrett's (P) husband died, and she sued several asbestos manufacturers, claiming the death resulted from exposure to their products. Celotex Corp. (D), one of the manufacturers, moved for summary judgment on the basis that no evidence existed that the decedent had been exposed to Celotex's (D) products. The district court granted the motion, and the court of appeals reversed, holding that Celotex (D) had not offered sufficient evidence to rebut Catrett's (P) allegations. The U.S. Supreme Court granted certiorari.

ISSUE: Must summary judgment be entered against a party who fails to meet his burden of proof on any essential element of the cause of action?

HOLDING AND DECISION: (Rehnquist, J.) Yes. Summary judgment must be entered against a party who fails to make a showing sufficient to establish the existence of an element essential to his case and on which he has the burden of proof at trial. Catrett (P) had the burden of showing that Celotex (D) had some level of culpability in order to go forward on her claim. She thus bore the burden of proof on this issue. Her failure to meet this burden and thus establish a genuine issue of material fact justified entry of summary judgment. Reversed and remanded.

CONCURRENCE: (White, J.) The party moving for summary judgment must meet the burden placed upon him by the Federal Rules of Civil Procedure.

DISSENT: (Brennan, J.) Celotex (D) failed to meet its burden of production, and summary judgment was therefore improper. The party moving for summary judgment has the burden of establishing the nonexistence of a "genuine issue." This burden has two distinct components: an initial burden of production, which shifts to the nonmoving party if satisfied by the moving party; and an ultimate burden of persuasion, which always remains on the moving party. Here, Celotex (D) failed to discharge its initial burden of production. It chose to base its motion on the argument that there was no evidence in the record to support plaintiff's claim, and therefore was not free to ignore supporting evidence that the record clearly contained. Rather, Celotex (D) was required, as an initial matter, to attack the adequacy of this evidence. Celotex's (D) failure to fulfill this simple requirement constituted a failure to discharge its initial burden of production under Rule 56, and thereby rendered summary judgment improper.

▶ ANALYSIS

Summary judgment is a radical judicial tool that completely disposes of a case or issue prior to trial. The basis for the motion is the absence of a genuine issue of material fact. When such occurs, the only questions remaining are legal questions that are determined by the court. Because the result of a successful motion is the end of a case, the court exercises great restraint in granting them.

■=■

Quicknotes

BURDEN OF PROOF The duty of a party to introduce evidence to support a fact that is in dispute in an action.

CAUSE OF ACTION A fact or set of facts the occurrence of which entitle a party to seek judicial relief.

CERTIORARI A discretionary writ issued by a superior court to an inferior court in order to review the lower court's decisions; the Supreme Court's writ ordering such review.

ISSUE OF MATERIAL FACT A fact that is disputed between two or more parties to litigation that is essential to proving an element of the cause of action or a defense asserted or would otherwise affect the outcome of the proceeding.

SUMMARY JUDGMENT Judgment rendered by a court in response to a motion by one of the parties, claiming that the lack of a question of material fact in respect to an issue warrants disposition of the issue without consideration by the jury.

■=■

Scott v. Harris

Police officer (D) v. Injured suspect (P)

127 S. Ct. 1769 (2007).

NATURE OF CASE: Appeal of judgment for suspect injured while fleeing.

FACT SUMMARY: Victor Harris (P) was seriously injured when a police officer, Timothy Scott (D), rammed his car with the police cruiser to stop a high-speed chase. Harris (P) claimed he used excessive force.

🏛 RULE OF LAW

A police officer who stops a high-speed chase by ramming a fleeing suspect's car does not violate the Fourth Amendment's protection against unreasonable seizure.

FACTS: After a police officer attempted to pull him over for speeding, Victor Harris (P) fled in his vehicle, which began a high-speed car chase. Attempting to end the chase, the police officer, Timothy Scott (D), rammed Harris's (P) vehicle with his police cruiser. Harris (P) crashed and became a quadriplegic. Harris (P) sued Scott (D) in federal district court, alleging that Scott (D) had violated his Fourth Amendment rights by using excessive force that resulted in an unreasonable seizure. Scott (D) claimed qualified immunity as a government official acting in his official capacity, but the district court rejected the claim. The U.S. Court of Appeals for the Eleventh Circuit affirmed, holding that Scott's (D) actions constituted an unreasonable seizure in violation of the Fourth Amendment. Harris (P) remained in control of his vehicle and the roads were relatively empty, there was no imminent threat, and Scott's (D) use of deadly force was therefore unconstitutional.

ISSUE: Does a police officer who stops a high-speed chase by ramming a fleeing suspect's car violate the Fourth Amendment's protection against unreasonable seizure?

HOLDING AND DECISION: (Scalia, J.) No. A police officer who stops a high-speed chase by ramming a fleeing suspect's car does not violate the Fourth Amendment's protection against unreasonable seizure. Scott's (D) actions were reasonable under the Fourth Amendment. A videotape of the car chase contradicted Harris's (P) claim that he was driving responsibly even while being pursued by the police. It is clear from the videotape that Harris (P) posed an actual and imminent threat to the lives of any pedestrians who might have been present, to other civilian motorists, and to the officers involved in the chase. The need to prevent the harm Harris (P) could have caused must be balanced against the high probability that Harris (P) himself would be harmed by Scott's (D) use of force, and Harris (P) started the chase in the first place. It is

reasonable for a police officer to use deadly force to prevent harm to innocent bystanders, even to the point of putting the fleeing motorist at serious risk of injury or death. Reversed.

DISSENT: (Stevens, J.) The videotape was not as definitive as the majority made it out to be, and a jury should make the determination on the justifiability of deadly force.

▶ ANALYSIS

Consider that summary judgment is only to be granted where there are no issues of fact. Central to the Court's conclusions was the videotape that directly contradicted Harris's (P) version of the story. That in itself creates a factual issue, one might argue, warranting a trial, and making summary judgment inappropriate.

■■■

Quicknotes

DEADLY FORCE That degree of force that is likely to result in death or great bodily injury.

FOURTH AMENDMENT Provides that persons be secure as to their person and private belongings against unreasonable searches and seizures.

QUALIFIED IMMUNITY An affirmative defense relieving officials from civil liability for the performance of activities within their discretion so long as such conduct is not in violation of an individual's rights pursuant to law as determined by a reasonable person standard.

■■■

Galloway v. United States

Disabled veteran (P) v. Federal government (D)

319 U.S. 372 (1943).

NATURE OF CASE: Action to recover disability benefits under a government insurance policy.

FACT SUMMARY: Galloway (P) sued to prove that he was eligible for insurance benefits due to permanent disability that began before the date that his G.I. insurance policy lapsed. The lower court granted the Government's (D) motion for a directed verdict on the ground that the evidence introduced by Galloway (P) was legally insufficient to sustain a verdict in Galloway's (P) favor.

🏛 RULE OF LAW
The power of a judge to direct a verdict, thereby preventing the evidence from going to the jury, does not violate the constitutional guarantee of "trial by jury."

FACTS: In order to collect liability benefits under his G.I. policy, Galloway (P) had to prove that he had been totally and permanently disabled due to insanity since May 31, 1919, the date on which his policy lapsed for nonpayment of premiums. As supporting evidence, Galloway (P) introduced testimony of two fellow soldiers that he had done two "crazy" acts while on active duty in 1920, the testimony of an old friend that he was a "wreck" in 1919 to 1922, the testimony of a chaplain that a soldier with the same name as Galloway (P) was insane in 1920, the testimony of Galloway's (P) commanding officers that he had alternating periods of gaiety and depression in 1920 to 1922, a 1930 examination that showed permanent insanity, and expert testimony by a physician who first examined Galloway (P) in 1938, that he had been insane since 1918. Galloway (P) introduced no evidence covering the period from 1925 to 1930, and gave no reason for this lack of evidence. In order to collect benefits, he had to prove that his disability began in 1919 and continued until the date of the trial. The lower court granted the Government's (D) request for a directed verdict because the evidence submitted by Galloway (P) was not sufficient to prove total and continuous disability from 1919.

ISSUE: Does power of a judge to direct a verdict, thereby preventing the evidence from going to the jury, violate the constitutional right of a trial by jury?

HOLDING AND DECISION: (Rutledge, J.) No. The power of a judge to direct a verdict, thereby preventing the evidence from going to the jury, does not violate the constitutional guarantee of "trial by jury." The Seventh Amendment guarantees the right of trial by jury "in suits at common law," but this right does not prevent a court from relieving a jury of its function by directing it to return a verdict for one of the parties. Galloway (P) argues that since the directed verdict was not known at the time of the enactment of the Seventh Amendment, the procedure is therefore unconstitutional. This argument fails, because the Seventh Amendment served to preserve only the most fundamental elements of the institution of a jury trial and not all the procedural elements of a jury trial that existed at the time of its enactment. Also, even at the time of the adoption of the amendment, the judge could remove a case from jury consideration by the devices of a demurrer to the evidence or a motion for a new trial. By a demurrer to the evidence a party had to admit all the facts that his opponent sought to prove, and the judge would make final judgment on these facts; if the demurring party lost he could not attempt to disprove the facts admitting by the demurrer. By a motion for a new trial after a verdict, the moving party was given another chance to prove his case in a second trial. Since these two devices produced such contradictory results (the demurrer ending all litigation without the demurring party being allowed to prove his case, and the motion for new trial allowing relitigation of all facts in dispute), it is obvious that the amendment did not enact any one specific device to allow a judge to remove a case from the jury. Therefore, courts have the power to direct a verdict for insufficiency of the evidence. The standard for determining whether proof is sufficient to allow submission of the evidence to the jury is that "mere speculation" can't take the place of probative facts, after making allowance for all reasonable inferences in the favor of the party whose case is attacked. Here, Galloway's (P) case failed, since he introduced no facts, only speculation, his condition continued for the entire period in question. Affirmed.

DISSENT: (Black, J.) Granting a motion for a directed verdict is not appropriate in this case. The jury is the best judge of disputed facts. The majority's statement that a directed verdict serves the same function as a demurrer to the evidence is misleading. In the demurrer, the moving party undertook a great risk in admitting the facts that the opposing party's evidence tends to prove, so the device was not commonly used. There is no such risk in a directed verdict because if the motion is denied, the case then goes to the jury. The directed verdict is frequently used, and to prevent abuse of the procedure that would allow judges to decide cases that should go to the jury, it should be used only where there is no room in the evidence for an honest difference of opinion. There is in this case sufficient

Continued on next page.

evidence for dispute and the case should have gone to the jury.

▶ *ANALYSIS*

The federal rules allow either party to move for a directed verdict after the presentation of the other party's evidence, and if the motion is denied, that party can still present his own evidence in rebuttal and the case will go to the jury. The device is used to test the sufficiency of the other party's evidence to prove a cause of action, and the judge must evaluate the evidence to see if it tends to prove the elements alleged by the party against whom the motion is made. The motion for directed verdict is granted if there is an absence of evidence or a defect of proof of a crucial element of the challenged claim or defense.

■══■

Quicknotes

CAUSE OF ACTION A fact or set of facts the occurrence of which entitle a party to seek judicial relief.

DEMURRER The assertion that the opposing party's pleadings are insufficient and that the demurring party should not be made to answer.

DIRECTED VERDICT A verdict ordered by the court in a jury trial.

PROBATIVE Tending to establish proof.

RIGHT TO TRIAL BY JURY The right guaranteed by the Sixth Amendment to the federal constitution that in all criminal prosecutions the accused has a right to a trial by an impartial jury of the state and district in which the crime was allegedly committed.

SEVENTH AMENDMENT Provides that no fact tried by a jury shall be otherwise re-examined in any court of the United States, other than according to the rules of the common law.

■══■

Brandon v. Chicago Board of Education

Disabled claimant (P) v. Board of Education (D)

143 F.3d 293 (7th Cir. 1998).

NATURE OF CASE: Action for relief from judgment for failure to prosecute.

FACT SUMMARY: A series of errors by the Clerk of the district court and by Brandon's (P) attorney resulted in judgment against Brandon (P) for failure to prosecute. Brandon (P) moved for relief from judgment under Fed. R. Civ. P. 60(b)(6).

🏛 RULE OF LAW
Federal Rule of Civil Procedure 60(b)(1) applies to errors by both the district court clerk and the parties' attorneys.

FACTS: Brandon (P) filed an Americans with Disabilities action against the Chicago Board of Education (the Board) (D). Due to repeated errors by the office of the Clerk of the United States District Court, Brandon's (P) attorneys did not receive notice of two different status hearings and failed to appear in court on Brandon's (P) behalf. After the second hearing, the court dismissed the case for want of prosecution. The order dismissing the case was sent to the wrong address. One year and three days after the dismissal, Brandon's (P) attorney filed a Rule 60 motion to vacate the judgment. Before the hearing, Brandon's (P) attorney received notice from the court that the motion was granted. As a courtesy, Brandon's (P) attorney sent to the Board's (D) attorney a letter stating that the motion had been granted, and that no appearance was necessary on the date set for hearing the motion. But the Board's (D) attorney appeared in court on the day of the hearing anyway, and persuaded the court to vacate its order granting Rule 60 relief. After briefing on the motion, the court denied Rule 60 relief.

ISSUE: Does Federal Rule of Civil Procedure 60(b)(1) apply to errors by both the district court clerk and the parties' attorneys?

HOLDING AND DECISION: (Rovner, J.) Yes. Federal Rule of Civil Procedure 60(b)(1) applies to errors by the district court clerk and the parties' attorneys. Under Rule 60(b), the motion to vacate judgment pursuant to Rule 60(b)(1) must be brought within one year of the judgment. Here, the motion was brought by Brandon's (P) attorney one year and three days after judgment. The district court determined that Brandon's (P) attorney demonstrated a lack of due diligence that was not excusable neglect under Rule 60(b)(1) by failing to bring the motion in a timely fashion, and therefore denied Brandon's (P) motion. A trial court's denial of a Rule 60(b) motion cannot be reversed absent an abuse of discretion, and no abuse of discretion was found here. Since Rule 60(b)(1) applies, Rule 60(b)(6) does not. Therefore, the motion was correctly denied. Affirmed.

▶ ANALYSIS

The district court narrowly construed the language of Rule 60(b). If the Clerk's errors did not occur, Brandon's (P) attorney's failure to bring the motion on time would undoubtedly be considered inexcusable neglect. Under the circumstances, however, Brandon's (P) attorney's neglect could be construed as excusable within the meaning of the Rule. The Clerk's errors continued, even after the attorney who was confused with Brandon's (P) attorney wrote to the Clerk to clear up the issue. The multiple errors by the Clerk could be construed as mitigating the error committed by Brandon's (P) attorney, thus making it excusable within the meaning of Rule 60(b)(1).

Quicknotes

ABUSE OF DISCRETION A determination by an appellate court that a lower court's decision was based on an error of law.

AMERICANS WITH DISABILITIES ACT Prohibits discrimination in employment, housing, transportation and other services on the basis of an individual's physical or mental disabilities.

DUE DILIGENCE The standard of care as would be taken by a reasonable person in accordance with the attendant facts and circumstances.

WANT OF PROSECUTION Dismissal of an action where the prosecution fails to further the case toward final disposition or trial.

Questioning and Taming the Current System

Quick Reference Rules of Law

Brown v. Plata

Prisoners (P) v. State (D)

131 S. Ct. 1910 (2011).

NATURE OF CASE: Appeal from district court order.

FACT SUMMARY: A three-judge panel ordered the state of California (D) to reduce its prison population to 137.5 percent of the prisons' design capacity within two years. Assuming the state (D) does not increase capacity through new construction, the order requires a population reduction of 38,000 to 46,000 persons. Because the state (D) probably cannot complete sufficient construction to comply fully with the order, the prison population will have to be reduced to at least some extent. The state (D) appealed.

🏛 RULE OF LAW

A remedial order issued by a three-judge panel that requires a state to address unconstitutional prison conditions by reducing prison population to 137.5 percent of the prison's design capacity within two years is consistent with requirements and procedures set forth in the Prison Litigation Reform Act of 1995.

FACTS: In 1990, prisoners (P) incarcerated in California state prisons brought suit against the state of California (D) in *Coleman v. Brown*, arguing that the prison system did not provide adequate medical care to mentally ill inmates. In 1995, after a 39-day trial, the *Coleman* district court found overwhelming evidence of systematic failure to deliver necessary care to mentally ill inmates in California prisons. The court appointed a special master to oversee development and implementation of a remedial plan of action. Twelve years after his appointment, the special master filed a report stating that, after years of slow improvement at the beginning of his tenure, the state of mental health care in California's prisons was again deteriorating. The special master attributed this change to increased overcrowding. The prisons had retained more mental health staff, but the expansion hadn't matched the increased demand. In 2001, this lawsuit was filed by California state prisoners (P) alleging inadequate prison medical care for inmates with serious medical conditions. During a hearing in the case, California (D) conceded that the deficiencies in medical care constituted violation of prisoners' Eighth Amendment protection against cruel and unusual punishment. The state (D) stipulated to a remedial injunction, but failed to comply with it, and in 2005 the district court appointed a receiver to oversee remedial efforts. In 2008, three years after the district court's decision, the receiver described continuing deficiencies in health care. According to the receiver, overcrowding had increased the incidence of infectious disease,

and had led to rising prison violence and greater reliance by custodial staff on lockdowns, which in turn inhibited the delivery of medical care. The *Coleman* and *Plata* plaintiffs moved their respective district courts to convene a three-judge court empowered under the Prison Litigation Reform Act to order reductions in the prison population. After a hearing, the three-judge court ordered California (D) to reduce its prison population to 137.5 percent of the prisons' design capacity within two years. Assuming the state (D) does not increase capacity through new construction, the order requires a population reduction of 38,000 to 46,000 persons. Because the state (D) probably cannot complete sufficient construction to comply fully with the order, the prison population will have to be reduced to at least some extent. The court did not order the state (D) to achieve this reduction in any particular manner. Instead, the court ordered the state (D) to formulate a plan for compliance and submit its plan for approval by the court. The state (D) appealed.

ISSUE: Is a remedial order issued by a three-judge panel that requires a state to address unconstitutional prison conditions by reducing prison population to 137.5 percent of the prison's design capacity within two years consistent with requirements and procedures set forth in the Prison Litigation Reform Act of 1995?

HOLDING AND DECISION: (Kennedy, J.) Yes. A remedial order issued by a three-judge panel that requires a state to address unconstitutional prison conditions by reducing prison population to 137.5 percent of the prison's design capacity within two years is consistent with requirements and procedures set forth in the Prison Litigation Reform Act of 1995. Under the PLRA, only a three-judge court may enter an order limiting a prison population. [To issue an order limiting the prison population, the three-judge court was required to find (1) crowding is the primary cause of the deprivation of a federal right, (2) no other relief will remedy the violation, (3) the relief must extend no further than necessary to correct the violation, and in making the determination the court must (4) give substantial weight to any adverse impact on public safety or the operation of the criminal justice system caused by the relief.] The three-judge court acknowledged that the violations were caused by factors in addition to overcrowding and that reducing crowding in the prisons would not entirely cure the violations. But it also found that overcrowding was the primary cause of the constitutional violations, and such a finding was permissible, despite

Continued on next page.

a finding that other factors had to be addressed. The three-judge court was also required to find by clear and convincing evidence that "no other relief will remedy the violation of the federal right." The state (D) argued that the violation could have been remedied through a combination of new construction, transfers of prisoners out of state, hiring of medical personnel, and continued efforts by the *Plata* receiver and *Coleman* special master. The order expressly permits the state (D) to comply with the population limit by transferring prisoners to county facilities or facilities in other states, or by constructing new facilities to raise the prisons' design capacity. And the order does not bar the state (D) from undertaking any other remedial efforts. If the state (D) does find an adequate remedy other than a population limit, it may seek modification or termination of the order on that basis. But the evidence at trial supports the three-judge court's conclusion that an order limited to other remedies would not provide effective relief. California's legislature had not been willing or able to allocate the resources necessary to meet the crisis absent a reduction in overcrowding, and there is no reason to believe it will begin to do so at this point, when the state (D) is facing a budgetary shortfall. Without a reduction in overcrowding, there will be no remedy for the unconstitutional condition of the prisons. The PLRA also states that no relief can be issued with respect to prison conditions unless it is narrowly drawn, extends no further than necessary to correct the violation of a federal right, and is the least intrusive means necessary to correct the violation. When determining whether these requirements are met, courts must "give substantial weight to any adverse impact on public safety or the operation of a criminal justice system." The scope of the remedy must be proportional to the scope of the violation, and the order must extend no further than necessary to remedy the violation. The order is narrowly drawn: it does not dictate to the state (D) which prisoners should be released, or which institutions the released prisoners must come from, and it does not constrict the state's (D) authority to run its prisons. The state (D) is free to relieve overcrowding either through increased capacity or reductions in population, and if the latter, it may choose which prisons to release prisoners from, and which prisoners to release. The PLRA's requirement a court give "substantial weight" to public safety, does not require the court to certify that its order has no possible adverse impact on the public. The three-judge court credited substantial evidence that prison populations can be reduced in a manner that does not increase crime to a significant degree, and some evidence indicated that reducing overcrowding in California's prisons could even improve public safety. Expert witnesses produced statistical evidence that prison populations had been lowered without adversely affecting public safety in a number of other jurisdictions. Establishing the population at which the state (D) could begin to provide constitutionally adequate medical and mental health care and the appropriate time frame within which to achieve the necessary reduction requires a degree

of judgment, and courts have substantial flexibility when making these judgments. Nevertheless, the PLRA requires a court to adopt a remedy that is "narrowly tailored" to the constitutional violation and that gives "substantial weight" to public safety. When a court is imposing a population limit, this means the court must set the limit at the highest population consistent with a remedy. The court must also order the population reduction achieved in the shortest period of time reasonably consistent with public safety. The three-judge court concluded that the population of California's (D) prisons should be capped at 137.5 percent of design capacity. The record supports this conclusion. Some evidence supported a limit as low as 100 percent of design capacity. This weighing of the evidence was not clearly erroneous. In light of substantial evidence supporting an even more drastic remedy, the three-judge court complied with the requirement of the PLRA in this case. Affirmed.

DISSENT: (Scalia, J.) First, the plaintiffs have not established that there has been a systemwide violation of the Eighth Amendment. The vast majority of inmates have not been adversely affected by deficient medical care in the prison system, and yet a substantial portion of that majority will be released under this order. Second, even if they had established that there was a systemwide violation of the Eighth Amendment, the order is a structural injunction, which essentially turns the court into an administrator of an institution, like a prison, a role that is outside the scope of authority of an Article III court. Structural injunctions allow courts to become, essentially, policymakers, and policy is almost always based in part on one's personal beliefs. Thus, the judge moves outside its role as objective fact-finder to subjective policymaker. This order actually expands the scope of a structural injunction by holding that an entire system is unconstitutional, simply because it *may* produce constitutional violations—underscoring the point that one thing scarier than a policymaking judge is one who makes policy that applies to the prison system. District courts should not run prison systems.

▶ *ANALYSIS*

The California state prison system was designed to house just fewer than 80,000 inmates and at the time of this decision, the population was more than double that. It has substantially increased since the date of this decision. This is a landmark case. Its impact was not immediate, because the Court pointed the state of California (D) to several ways of dealing with the overpopulation problem that don't involve releasing prisoners, at least in the short term. But it is widely believed that by making the conditions in California prisons visible, the Court paved the way for prison reform. Kennedy stated that several states have successfully cut their prison populations without seeing

Continued on next page.

their crime rates escalate. Many criminologists point to research concluding that mass incarceration may actually increase the public rate of crime—incarceration obviously cuts inmates' ties to their jobs, families, and communities, it widens opportunities for connecting with other criminals, and it subjects inmates to overcrowded and abusive conditions.

■━■

Quicknotes

CRUEL AND UNUSUAL PUNISHMENT Punishment that is excessive or disproportionate to the offense committed and which is prohibited by the Eighth Amendment to the U.S. Constitution.

EIGHTH AMENDMENT The Eighth Amendment to the United States Constitution prohibits the imposition of excessive bail, fines, and cruel and unusual punishment.

■━■

Choice of an Appropriate Court: Personal Jurisdiction, Notice, and Venue

Quick Reference Rules of Law

Pennoyer v. Neff

Purchaser of property (D) v. Real property owner (P)

95 U.S. 714 (1877).

NATURE OF CASE: Action to recover possession of land.

FACT SUMMARY: Neff (P) alleged that Pennoyer's (D) deed from a sheriff's sale was invalid because the court ordering the sale had never obtained personal jurisdiction over Neff (P).

🏛 RULE OF LAW
Where the object of the action is to determine the personal rights and obligations of the parties, service by publication against nonresidents is ineffective to confer jurisdiction on the court.

FACTS: Neff (P) owned real property in Oregon. Mitchell brought suit in Oregon to recover legal fees allegedly owed him by Neff (P). Neff (P), a nonresident, was served by publication, and Mitchell obtained a default judgment. The court ordered Neff's (P) land sold at a sheriff's sale to satisfy the judgment. Pennoyer (D) purchased the property. Neff (P) subsequently learned of the sale and brought suit in Oregon to recover possession of his property. Neff (P) alleged that the court ordering the sale had never acquired in personam jurisdiction over him. Therefore, the court could not adjudicate the personal rights and obligations between Neff (P) and Mitchell, and the default judgment had been improperly entered.

ISSUE: Where an action involves the adjudication of personal rights and obligations of the parties, is service by publication against a nonresident sufficient to confer jurisdiction?

HOLDING AND DECISION: (Field, J.) No. Every state possesses exclusive jurisdiction and sovereignty over persons and property within its territory. Following from this, no state can exercise direct jurisdiction and authority over persons or property outside of its territory. These are two well-established principles of public law respecting the jurisdiction of an independent state over persons and property. However, the exercise of jurisdiction that every state possesses over persons and property within it will often affect persons and property outside of it. A state may compel persons domiciled within it to execute, in pursuance of their contracts respecting property situated elsewhere, instruments transferring title. Likewise, a state may subject property situated within it that is owned by nonresidents to the payment of the demands of its own citizens. Substituted service by publication or by other authorized means may be sufficient to inform the parties of the proceedings where the property is brought under the control of the court or where the judgment is sought as a means of reaching such property or effectuating some interest therein. That is, such service is effectual in proceedings in rem. The law assumes that property is always in the possession of its owner or an agent. It proceeds upon the theory that a seizure of the property will inform the owner that he must look to any proceedings upon such seizure for the property's condemnation or sale. But where the entire object of the action is to determine personal rights and obligations, the action is in personam, and service by publication is ineffectual to confer jurisdiction over the nonresident defendant upon the court. Process sent out of state to a nonresident is equally ineffective to confer personal jurisdiction. In an action to determine a defendant's personal liability, he must be brought within the court's jurisdiction by service of process within the state or by his voluntary appearance. Without jurisdiction, due process requirements are not satisfied. In the case herein, Neff (P) was not personally served and never appeared. Hence, the personal judgment obtained against Neff (P) was not valid, and the property could not be sold. Affirmed.

▶ ANALYSIS

This is the leading case on the extent of the court's power to compel a defendant's attendance. At common law the presence of the defendant within the jurisdiction plus service while there, were the indispensable ingredients for the acquisition of jurisdiction of the person of the defendant. It still remains the basic method of acquiring jurisdiction over the defendant. It does not matter how transient the defendant's presence is if she is served within the jurisdiction. One case held that service on a defendant while he was in an airplane passing over a state is sufficient. Of course, a voluntary appearance by a defendant also gives the court jurisdiction over her.

■━■

Quicknotes

DEED A signed writing transferring title to real property from one person to another.

DEFAULT JUDGMENT A judgment entered against a defendant due to his failure to appear in a court or defend himself against the allegations of the opposing party.

DUE PROCESS CLAUSE Clauses, found in the Fifth and Fourteenth Amendments to the United States Constitution, providing that no person shall be deprived of "life, liberty, or property, without due process of law."

Continued on next page.

IN PERSONAM JURISDICTION The jurisdiction of a court over a person as opposed to his interest in property.

IN REM JURISDICTION A court's authority over a thing so that its judgment is binding in respect to the rights and interests of all parties in that thing.

SERVICE OF PROCESS The communication of reasonable notice of a court proceeding to a defendant in order to provide him with an opportunity to be heard.

■▬■

Harris v. Balk

Debtor (D) v. Creditor (P)

198 U.S. 215 (1905).

NATURE OF CASE: Action to recover a debt.

FACT SUMMARY: In North Carolina, Harris (D) owed a debt to Balk (P), which was attached by Epstein in Maryland.

🏛 RULE OF LAW

A debtor's obligation to pay debt accompanies him wherever he goes, and the question of jurisdiction is not dependent on either the situs of the debt or the nature of the debtor's stay in a state.

FACTS: Harris (D) and Balk (P) were both North Carolina residents. Harris (D) owed Balk (P) $180. Balk (P) owed Epstein, a Maryland resident, $300. In 1896, while Harris (D) was temporarily in Maryland, Epstein brought suit and had issued a writ of attachment, attaching the debt Harris (D) owed Balk (P). Harris (D) did not contest the process issued to garnish the debt due Balk (P). Judgment was entered for Epstein for $180, which Harris (D) paid. One week later, Balk (P) brought this action against Harris (D) in North Carolina to recover the $180 owed him. Harris (D) answered with Epstein's recovery in Maryland. The lower court entered judgment for Balk (P) on the ground that the Maryland court obtained no jurisdiction to attach or garnish the debt due Balk (P) because Harris (D) was in Maryland only temporarily and the situs of the debt was in North Carolina.

ISSUE: Is the question of jurisdiction dependent upon either the situs of the debt or the nature of the debtor's stay in the state?

HOLDING AND DECISION: (Peckham, J.) No. Power over the person of the garnishee (or debtor) confers jurisdiction on the courts of the state where a writ of attachment issues. Jurisdiction is not dependent upon the original situs of the debt or upon the character of the garnishee's stay in the state where attachment is issued. As for the situs, the obligation of the debtor to pay the debt accompanies him wherever he goes. He is as much bound to pay the debt in a foreign state when sued there by a creditor as he is in the state where the debt was contracted. Balk (P) had a right to sue Harris (D) in Maryland since as a citizen of North Carolina he is entitled to all the privileges and immunities of citizens of all the states. If the garnishee is found in a state and process is personally served on him there, the court thereby acquires jurisdiction over him, and he can garnish the debt due from him and condemn it, provided the garnishee could be sued by his creditor in that state. Hence, the judgment against Harris (D) in Maryland was valid because the court had jurisdiction over Harris (D) by personal service. Further, Balk (P) obviously had notice of the Maryland suit because he sued Harris (D) a few days later. He could have contested it in Maryland but did not. Judgment for Balk (P) is reversed, and the case is remanded.

▶ ANALYSIS

This case demonstrates how a debt may be seized. Since, for the purposes of garnishment, a debt clings to the debtor, quasi-in-rem jurisdiction can be obtained over the debt by personal service of process on the debtor. The problem becomes more complex when the debtor goes into another state or country or is a corporation who might be sued in many states. In *Weitzel v. Weitzel*, 27 Ariz. 117, 230 P. 1106 (1924), the plaintiff had a judgment for alimony against her husband, who was working in Mexico for a railroad company. She served a garnishee summons on the railroad in Arizona to reach the debt it owed her husband in Mexico. The court did not allow the garnishment on the ground that it was probable the Mexican courts would not respect the quasi-in-rem judgment of the Arizona court.

■▬■

Quicknotes

ATTACHMENT The seizing of the property of one party in anticipation of, or in order to satisfy, a favorable judgment obtained by another party.

QUASI-IN-REM JURISDICTION A court's authority over the defendant's property within a specified geographical area.

SITUS Location; in community property, the location of an asset.

■▬■

Hess v. Pawloski

Nonresident driver (D) v. Accident victim (P)

274 U.S. 352 (1927).

NATURE OF CASE: Review of verdict in plaintiff's favor in action to recover damages for personal injuries.

FACT SUMMARY: A Massachusetts statute provided that nonresident motorists were deemed to have appointed a state official as their agent for service of process in cases growing out of accidents or collisions involving them. Pawloski (P) sued Hess (D), a nonresident, for damages due to an auto accident in Massachusetts.

RULE OF LAW
In advance of a nonresident's use of its highways, a state may require the nonresident to appoint one of the state's officials as his agent on whom process may be served in proceedings growing out of such highway use.

FACTS: Pawloski (P) alleged that Hess (D) negligently drove a car on a Massachusetts highway, thereby injuring Pawloski (P). Hess (D) was a nonresident of Massachusetts. No personal service was made on him, and no property belonging to him was attached. A Massachusetts statute provided that nonresident motorists were deemed to have appointed the registrar of motor vehicles as their agent for service of process in cases arising out of accidents or collisions in which nonresidents were involved. The statute also required that notice of such service and a copy of the process be sent by registered mail to the defendant. Hess (D) moved to dismiss on due process grounds, but the lower courts held the statute to be a valid exercise of the police power. The U.S. Supreme Court granted review.

ISSUE: Does a state statute by which nonresident motorists are deemed to have appointed a state official as their agent for service of process in cases arising out of accidents involving them, violate due process?

HOLDING AND DECISION: (Butler, J.) No. Motor vehicles are dangerous vehicles. In the public interest, the state may make and enforce regulations reasonably calculated to promote care on the part of all who use its highways. The statute involved in this case limits the nonresident's implied consent to proceedings growing out of accidents or collisions on a highway involving the nonresident. It requires that he receive notice of the service and a copy of the process. It makes no hostile discrimination against nonresidents. The state's power to regulate the use of its highways extends to its use by nonresidents as well as residents. In advance of the operation of a motor vehicle on its highway by a nonresident, the state may require him to appoint one of its officials as his agent on whom process

may be served in proceedings growing out of such use. Affirmed.

▶ ANALYSIS

Other states were quick to pass similar nonresident motorist statutes, and thus provide their citizens with local forums for injuries caused by nonresident motorists. Some passed statutes subjecting nonresident boat and airplane owners to local forums also. Under the reasoning of *Hess*, it was thought that in order to subject the nonresident to local jurisdiction the activity engaged in must be one subject to state regulations under its police power. Consequently, the first extensions of *Hess* were to such situations as the sale of securities, an industry subject to a high degree of regulation, and the ownership of local real estate.

■━■

Quicknotes

DUE PROCESS CLAUSE Clauses, found in the Fifth and Fourteenth Amendments to the United States Constitution, providing that no person shall be deprived of "life, liberty, or property, without due process of law."

IMPLIED CONSENT The manifestation by actions, or by the failure to act, of an agreement of the minds or of the acquiescence by one party to the will of another.

PLAINTIFF IN ERROR Appellant; a party that appeals from a lower court judgment.

POLICE POWERS The power of a state or local government to regulate private conduct for the health, safety and welfare of the general public.

SERVICE OF PROCESS The communication of reasonable notice of a court proceeding to a defendant in order to provide him with an opportunity to be heard.

STATUTE A law enacted pursuant to the legislature's power and consistent with specified procedure so that it regulates a particular activity.

■━■

International Shoe Co. v. State of Washington

Delaware corporation (D) v. State (P)

326 U.S. 310 (1945).

NATURE OF CASE: Proceedings to recover unemployment contributions.

FACT SUMMARY: A state statute authorized the mailing of notice of assessment of delinquent contributions for unemployment compensation to nonresident employers. International Shoe Co. (International) (D) is a nonresident corporation. Notice of assessment was served on one of its salespersons within the state and was mailed to International's (D) office.

🏛 RULE OF LAW

For a state to subject a nonresident defendant to in personam jurisdiction, due process requires that he have certain minimum contacts with it such that the maintenance of the suit does not offend traditional notions of fair play and substantial justice.

FACTS: A Washington statute set up a scheme of unemployment compensation that required contributions by employers. The statute authorized the commissioner, Washington (P), to issue an order and notice of assessment of delinquent contributions by mailing the notice to nonresident employers. International Shoe Co. (International) (D) was a Delaware corporation having its principal place of business in Missouri. International (D) employed 11 to 13 salespersons under the supervision of managers in Missouri. These salespeople resided in Washington and did most of their work there. They had no authority to enter into contracts or make collections. International (D) did not have any office in Washington and made no contracts there. Notice of assessment was served upon one of International's (D) Washington salespersons, and a copy of the notice was sent by registered mail to International's (D) Missouri address.

ISSUE: For a state to subject a nonresident defendant to in personam jurisdiction, does due process require only that he have certain minimum contacts with it, such that the maintenance of the suit does not offend notions of fair play and substantial justice?

HOLDING AND DECISION: (Stone, C.J.) Yes. Historically, the jurisdiction of courts to render judgment in personam is grounded on their power over the defendant's person, and his presence within the territorial jurisdiction of a court was necessary to a valid judgment. But now, due process requires only that in order to subject a defendant to a judgment in personam, if he is not present within the territorial jurisdiction, he must have certain minimum contacts with the territory such that the maintenance of the suit does not offend traditional notions of fair

play and substantial justice. The contacts must be such as to make it reasonable, in the context of our federal system, to require a defendant corporation to defend the suit brought there. An estimate of the inconveniences that would result to the corporation from a trial away from its "home" is relevant. To require a corporation to defend a suit away from home where its contact has been casual or isolated activities has been thought to lay too unreasonable a burden on it. However, even single or occasional acts may, because of their nature, quality, and circumstances, be deemed sufficient to render a corporation liable to suit. Hence, the criteria to determine whether jurisdiction is justified, is not simply mechanical or quantitative. Satisfaction of due process depends on the quality and nature of the activity in relation to the fair and orderly administration of the laws. In this case, International's (D) activities were neither irregular nor casual. Rather, they were systematic and continuous. The obligation sued upon here arose out of these activities. They were sufficient to establish adequate contacts or ties to make it reasonable to permit Washington to enforce the obligations International (D) incurred there. Affirmed.

DISSENT: (Black, J.) The U.S. Constitution leaves to each state the power to tax and to open the doors of its courts for its citizens to sue corporations who do business in the state. It is a judicial deprivation to condition the exercise of this power on this Court's notion of "fair play."

▶ ANALYSIS

Before this decision, three theories had evolved to provide for suits by and against foreign corporations. The first was the consent theory. It rested on the proposition that since a foreign corporation could not carry on its business within a state without the permission of that state, that state could require a corporation to appoint an agent to receive service of process within the state. However, it soon became established law that a foreign corporation could not be prevented by a state from carrying on interstate commerce within its borders. The presence doctrine required that the corporation was "doing business" and "present" in the state. The third theory used either the present or consent doctrine, and it was necessary to determine whether the corporation was doing business within the state either to decide whether its consent could properly be implied or to discover whether the corporation was present.

■■■■

Continued on next page.

Quicknotes

CONSENT JURISDICTION The forum having jurisdiction over a lawsuit as agreed upon by the parties prior to litigation.

DUE PROCESS CLAUSE Clauses, found in the Fifth and Fourteenth Amendments to the United States Constitution, providing that no person shall be deprived of "life, liberty, or property, without due process of law."

FAIR PLAY NOTION Equitable notion that persons must deal with each other fairly and justly.

IN PERSONAM JURISDICTION The jurisdiction of a court over a person as opposed to his interest in property.

INTERSTATE COMMERCE Commercial dealings between two parties located in different states or located in one state and accomplished through a point in another state or a foreign country; commercial dealings transacted between two states.

MINIMUM CONTACTS The minimum degree of contact necessary in order to sustain a cause of action within a particular forum, consistent with the requirements of due process.

STATUTE A law enacted pursuant to the legislature's power and consistent with specified procedure so that it regulates a particular activity.

■▬■

World-Wide Volkswagen Corp. v. Woodson

Automobile distributor (P) v. Court (D)

444 U.S. 286 (1980).

NATURE OF CASE: Petition for a writ prohibiting the exercise of in personam jurisdiction.

FACT SUMMARY: World-Wide Volkswagen Corp. (P) sought a writ of prohibition to keep district court Judge Woodson (D) from exercising in personam jurisdiction over it, alleging it did not have sufficient "contacts" with the forum state of Oklahoma to render it subject to such jurisdiction.

🏛 RULE OF LAW
A state court may exercise personal jurisdiction over a nonresident defendant only so long as there exists sufficient "minimum contacts" between him and the forum state such that maintenance of the suit does not offend "traditional notions of fair play and substantial justice."

FACTS: World-Wide Volkswagen Corp. (World-Wide) (P) was the regional distributor of Audi automobiles for the tristate area of New York, New Jersey, and Connecticut. It was the distributor of the particular Audi that the Robinsons purchased from a New York dealer and drove to Oklahoma, where three family members were severely burned when another car struck their Audi in the rear. The Robinsons brought a products liability action in an Oklahoma district court, suing the New York dealership and World-Wide (P) (a New York corporation). Claiming that no evidence showed it had any connection with Oklahoma whatsoever, World-Wide (P) sought a writ of prohibition to keep district court Judge Woodson (D) from exercising in personam jurisdiction. It argued that a lack of sufficient contacts with the forum state made assertion of such jurisdiction improper under the Due Process Clause. The Supreme Court of Oklahoma denied the writ, noting that World-Wide (P) could foresee that the automobiles it sold would be taken into other states, including Oklahoma. The U.S. Supreme Court granted certiorari.

ISSUE: Must a defendant have "minimum contacts" with the forum state before it can exercise in personam jurisdiction over him?

HOLDING AND DECISION: (White, J.) Yes. A state court may exercise personal jurisdiction over a nonresident defendant only so long as there exists sufficient "minimum contacts" between him and the forum state such that maintenance of the suit does not offend "traditional notions of fair play and substantial justice." Under the Due Process Clause, the exercise of in personam jurisdiction over a defendant is not constitutional unless he has sufficient "minimum contacts" with the forum state

so that maintenance of the suit does not offend "traditional notions of fair play and substantial justice." Here, World-Wide (P) had no "contacts, ties, or relations" with Oklahoma, so personal jurisdiction could not be exercised. As for the notion that it was foreseeable that cars sold in New York would wind up in Oklahoma, the foreseeability that is critical to due process analysis is not the mere likelihood that a product will find its way into the forum state. Rather, it is that the defendant's conduct and connection with the forum state are such that he should reasonably anticipate being hauled into court there. Such conduct and connection are simply missing in this case. Reversed.

DISSENT: (Brennan, J.) The automobile is designed specifically to facilitate travel from place to place, and the sale of one purposefully injects it into the stream of interstate commerce. Thus, this case is not unlike those where in personam jurisdiction is properly exercised over one who purposefully places his product into the stream of interstate commerce with the expectation it will be purchased by consumers in other states. Furthermore, a large part of the value of automobiles is the extensive, nationwide network of highways. State maintenance of such roads contributes to the value of World-Wide's (P) business. World-Wide (P) also participates in a network of related dealerships with nationwide service facilities. Having such facilities in Oklahoma also adds to the value of World-Wide's (P) business. Thus, it has the required minimum contacts with Oklahoma to render this exercise of personal jurisdiction constitutional.

DISSENT: (Marshall, J.) Reasonable minds may differ as to whether World-Wide (P) has sufficient minimum contacts with Oklahoma, but the majority reached its decision by taking an unnecessarily narrow view of World-Wide's (P) conduct, by focusing instead on the Robinsons' conduct. Thus, it determined that jurisdiction could not be asserted over World-Wide (P) because World-Wide (P) had no control over the Robinsons' unilateral decision to drive to Oklahoma. Jurisdiction is based on the deliberate and purposeful actions of World-Wide (P), and, here, World-Wide (P) chose to engage in the global business of marketing and servicing automobiles. The product it sells has value only in the fact that it is mobile. People buy cars in order to make short and long trips. Local dealers derive a substantial portion of their revenues from their service operations and thereby obtain a further economic benefit from the opportunity to

Continued on next page.

service cars that were sold in other states. Even though World-Wide (P) could not know in advance that this particular automobile would be driven to Oklahoma, it must have anticipated that a substantial portion of the cars it sold would travel out of New York. Knowing that some of its cars would be driven in all of the 50 states should alert a reasonable businessman to the likelihood that a defect in the product might manifest itself in another state, in the normal course of the operation of the car for its intended purpose. Foreseeability alone is not the only determinant of issues of jurisdiction. World-Wide (P) knowingly reached out of state and received economic advantage from the fact that its product can be moved out of state, and from the activities of dealers and distributors in other states. It intentionally became part of an interstate economic network. Thus, World-Wide (P) had reason to expect that it could be brought before an Oklahoma court. The majority correctly states that if the product is purchased in the forum state, the forum state may assert jurisdiction over everyone in the chain of distribution. But jurisdiction is not necessarily lacking if the product enters the state, not through the channels of distribution, but in the course of its intended use by the consumer.

DISSENT: (Blackmun, J.) It is the mobile nature of automobiles that ought to be the focus of this litigation. It is reasonable and constitutional to uphold Oklahoma jurisdiction.

▶ *ANALYSIS*

Over the years, modern transportation and communication have made foreign state suits much less of a burden to defendants. This resulted in a relaxing of the due process limits placed on state jurisdiction down to the "minimum contacts" concept. However, even if there were no inconvenience to the defendant, a state could not exercise personal jurisdiction over him if he had no "contacts, ties, or relations." This is true even if that state had a strong interest in applying its law to the controversy it was the most convenient location for litigation, etc. The reason is that the Due Process Clause serves two distinct functions: The first is as a guarantor against inconvenient litigation, but the second is as a guardian of interstate federalism. It is in this second capacity that the Due Process Clause would prevent assumption of jurisdiction in the aforementioned instance by recognizing the "territorial limitations on the power of the respective states."

■══■

Quicknotes

CERTIORARI A discretionary writ issued by a superior court to an inferior court in order to review the lower court's decisions; the Supreme Court's writ ordering such review.

DUE PROCESS CLAUSE Clauses, found in the Fifth and Fourteenth Amendments to the United States Constitution, providing that no person shall be deprived of "life, liberty, or property, without due process of law."

FAIR PLAY NOTION Equitable notion that persons must deal with each other fairly and justly.

FORUM STATE The state in which a court, or other location in which a legal remedy may be sought, is located.

IN PERSONAM JURISDICTION The jurisdiction of a court over a person as opposed to his interest in property.

INTERSTATE COMMERCE Commercial dealings between two parties located in different states or located in one state and accomplished through a point in another state or a foreign country; commercial dealings transacted between two states.

MINIMUM CONTACTS The minimum degree of contact necessary in order to sustain a cause of action within a particular forum, consistent with the requirements of due process.

WRIT OF PROHIBITION A writ issued by a superior court prohibiting a lower court from exceeding its jurisdiction or from usurping jurisdiction beyond that authorized by law.

■══■

Calder v. Jones

Magazine publisher (D) v. Libel complainant (P)

465 U.S. 783 (1984).

NATURE OF CASE: Appeal from reinstatement of complaint after it had been quashed for lack of personal jurisdiction.

FACT SUMMARY: Shirley Jones (P), a California resident, brought a libel suit against Calder (D) in a California court. Calder (D) was served with process by mail in Florida and moved to quash such service on jurisdictional grounds. The trial court granted the motion, and the state appellate court reversed.

🏛 RULE OF LAW
A state court may exercise jurisdiction over an out-of-state party whose intentional conduct is calculated to cause, and does cause, injury to the complainant in the forum state.

FACTS: Shirley Jones (P), who lived and worked in California, sued Calder (D) in California. Calder (D) was president and editor of a national magazine published in Florida (*The National Enquirer*). The magazine had a large circulation in California. Calder (D) was served with process by mail in Florida and caused a special appearance to be entered on his behalf, moving to quash such service on the grounds of lack of jurisdiction. The trial court granted the motion, and the state appellate court reversed, reinstating the complaint.

ISSUE: May a state court exercise jurisdiction over an out-of-state party whose intentional conduct in the second state is calculated to cause, and does cause, injury to the complainant in the forum state?

HOLDING AND DECISION: (Rehnquist, J.) Yes. A state court may exercise jurisdiction over an out-of-state party whose intentional conduct is calculated to cause, and does cause, injury to the complainant in the forum state. *The National Enquirer* is a Florida corporation with its principal place of business in Florida and publishes a national weekly newspaper with a circulation of over 5 million. 600,000 of those copies, almost twice the level of the next highest state, are sold in California. The Due Process Clause of the Fourteenth Amendment permits personal jurisdiction over a defendant in any state with which the defendant has "certain minimum contacts," such that the maintenance of the suit does not offend "traditional notions of fair play and substantial justice." Here, Jones (P), a resident of California, was the focus of the activities of Calder (D), the publisher, out of which the suit arose. Specifically, the allegedly libelous story concerned the California activities of a California resident and impugned the professionalism of an entertainer whose television career was centered in California. An individual injured in California need not go to Florida to seek redress from persons who, though remaining in Florida, knowingly cause the injury in California. Affirmed.

▶ ANALYSIS

In reaching its decision, the Court noted that here the defendant newspaper wrote and published an article that it knew would have a potentially devastating impact upon Jones (P) and that the newspaper (D) knew also that the brunt of the injury would be felt by Jones (P) in the state in which she lived and worked (California) and in which the newspaper (D) had its largest circulation.

■=■

Quicknotes

COMPLAINT The initial pleading commencing litigation that sets forth a claim for relief.

DUE PROCESS CLAUSE Clauses, found in the Fifth and Fourteenth Amendments to the United States Constitution, providing that no person shall be deprived of "life, liberty, or property, without due process of law."

FAIR PLAY NOTION Equitable notion that persons must deal with each other fairly and justly.

FORUM STATE The state in which a court, or other location in which a legal remedy may be sought, is located.

JURISDICTION The authority of a court to hear and declare judgment in respect to a particular matter.

LIBEL A false or malicious publication subjecting a person to scorn, hatred or ridicule, or injuring him or her in relation to his or her occupation or business.

MINIMUM CONTACTS The minimum degree of contact necessary in order to sustain a cause of action within a particular forum, consistent with the requirements of due process.

QUASH To vacate, annul, void.

■=■

Asahi Metal Industry Co., Ltd. v. Superior Court of California, Solano County

Tire valve manufacturer (P) v. Court (D)

480 U.S. 102 (1987).

NATURE OF CASE: Appeal from discharge of writ quashing service of summons.

FACT SUMMARY: Asahi Metal Industry Co., Ltd. (Ashai) (P) appealed from a decision of the California Supreme Court discharging a peremptory writ issued by the appeals court quashing service of summons in Cheng Shin's indemnity action, contending there did not exist minimum contacts between California and Asahi (P) sufficient to sustain jurisdiction.

🏛 RULE OF LAW
Minimum contacts sufficient to sustain jurisdiction are not satisfied simply by the placement of a product into the stream of commerce coupled with awareness that its product would reach the forum state.

FACTS: Asahi Metal Industry Co., Ltd. (Ashai) (P), a Japanese corporation, manufactured tire valve assemblies in Japan, selling some of them to Cheng Shin, a Taiwanese company, which incorporated them into the motorcycles it manufactured. Zurcher was seriously injured in a motorcycle accident, and a companion was killed. He sued Cheng Shin, alleging the motorcycle tire, manufactured by Cheng Shin, was defective. Cheng Shin sought indemnity from Asahi (P), and the main action settled. Asahi (P) moved to quash service of summons, contending that jurisdiction could not be maintained by California, the state in which Zurcher filed his action, consistent with the Due Process Clause of the Fourteenth Amendment. The evidence indicated that Asahi's (P) sales to Cheng Shin took place in Taiwan, and shipments went from Japan to Taiwan. Cheng Shin purchased valve assemblies from other manufacturers. Sales to Cheng Shin never amounted to more than 1.5 percent of Asahi's (P) income. Approximately 20 percent of Cheng Shin's sales in the United States are in California. In declaration, an attorney for Cheng Shin stated he made an informal examination of tires in a bike shop in Solano County, where Zurcher was injured, finding approximately 20 percent of the tires with Asahi's (P) trademark (25 percent of the tires manufactured by Cheng Shin). The Superior Court (D) denied the motion to quash, finding it reasonable that Asahi (P) defend its claim of defect in their product. The court of appeals issued a peremptory writ commanding the Superior Court (D) to quash service of summons. The state supreme court reversed and discharged the writ, finding that Asahi's (P) awareness that some of its product would reach California by placing it in the stream of commerce satisfied minimum contacts

sufficient to sustain jurisdiction. From this decision, Asahi (P) appealed.

ISSUE: Are minimum contacts sufficient to sustain jurisdiction satisfied by the placement of a product into the stream of commerce, coupled with the awareness that its product would reach the forum state?

HOLDING AND DECISION: (O'Connor, J.) No. Minimum contacts sufficient to sustain jurisdiction are not satisfied by the placement of a product in the stream of commerce, coupled with the awareness that its product would reach the forum state. To satisfy minimum contacts, there must be some act by which the defendant purposefully avails itself of the privilege of conducting activities within the forum state. Although the courts that have squarely addressed this issue have been divided, the better view is that the defendant must do more than place a product in the stream of commerce. The unilateral act of a consumer bringing the product to the forum state is not sufficient. Asahi (P) has not purposefully availed itself of the California market. It does not do business in the state, conduct activities, maintain offices or agents, or advertise. Nor did it have anything to do with Cheng Shin's distribution system, which brought the tire valve assembly to California. Assertion of jurisdiction based on these facts exceeds the limits of due process. [The Court went on to consider the burden of defense on Asahi (P) and the slight interests of the state and Zurcher, finding the assertion of jurisdiction unreasonable and unfair.] Reversed and remanded.

CONCURRENCE: (Brennan, J.) The state supreme court correctly concluded that the stream of commerce theory, without more, has satisfied minimum contacts in most courts that have addressed the issue, and it has been preserved in the decision of this Court.

CONCURRENCE: (Stevens, J.) The minimum contacts analysis is unnecessary; the Court has found by weighing the appropriate factors that jurisdiction under these facts is unreasonable and unfair.

▶ *ANALYSIS*

The Brennan concurrence is quite on point in criticizing the plurality for its characterization that this case involves the act of a consumer in bringing the product within the forum state. The argument presented in *World-Wide Volkswagen Corp. v. Woodson,* 444 U.S. 286 (1980), cited by the

Continued on next page.

plurality, seems more applicable to distributors and retailers, than to manufacturers of component parts.

■■■■

Quicknotes

DUE PROCESS CLAUSE Clauses, found in the Fifth and Fourteenth Amendments to the United States Constitution, providing that no person shall be deprived of "life, liberty, or property, without due process of law."

FORUM STATE The state in which a court, or other location in which a legal remedy may be sought, is located.

INDEMNITY The duty of a party to compensate another for damages sustained.

MINIMUM CONTACTS The minimum degree of contact necessary in order to sustain a cause of action within a particular forum, consistent with the requirements of due process.

PEREMPTORY WRIT Writ directing the sheriff to have the defendant appear before the court so long as the plaintiff has provided adequate security in order to prosecute the action.

QUASH To vacate, annul, void.

■■■■

J. McIntyre Machinery, Ltd. v. Nicastro

Product manufacturer (D) v. Injured worker (P)

131 S. Ct. 2780 (2011).

NATURE OF CASE: Appeal of judgment by state supreme court.

FACT SUMMARY: A person who was injured when he used a piece of heavy machinery sued the foreign manufacturer in New Jersey state court. The company disputed the state's jurisdiction.

🏛 RULE OF LAW
In products liability cases, the "stream-of-commerce" doctrine cannot displace the general rule that the exercise of judicial power is not lawful unless the defendant purposefully avails itself of the privilege of conducting activities within the forum state, thus invoking the benefits and protections of its laws.

FACTS: Robert Nicastro (P) injured his hand while using a metal-shearing machine that was manufactured by J. McIntyre Machinery, Ltd. (J. McIntyre) (D). The machine was manufactured in England, where J. McIntyre (D) is incorporated and operates, and the injury occurred in New Jersey. Nicastro (P) filed suit in New Jersey. The New Jersey Supreme Court found that it had jurisdiction over J. McIntyre (D) because J. McIntyre (D) machines were sold in the United States, the company attended annual conventions for the scrap recycling industry to advertise, and four machines were identified in New Jersey, and J. McIntyre (D) guided advertising and sales efforts for the U.S. distributor. J. McIntyre (D) appealed.

ISSUE: In products liability cases, can the "stream-of-commerce" doctrine displace the general rule that the exercise of judicial power is not lawful unless the defendant purposefully avails itself of the privilege of conducting activities within the forum state, thus invoking the benefits and protections of its laws?

HOLDING AND DECISION: (Kennedy, J.) No. In products liability cases, the "stream-of-commerce" doctrine cannot displace the general rule that the exercise of judicial power is not lawful unless the defendant purposefully avails itself of the privilege of conducting activities within the forum state, thus invoking the benefits and protections of its laws. The Supreme Court of New Jersey held that New Jersey's courts can exercise jurisdiction over a foreign manufacturer of a product as long as the manufacturer knows or reasonably should know that its products are distributed through a nationwide distribution system that might lead to those products being sold in any of the fifty states. That rule is from *Asahi Metal Industry Co. v. Superior Court of Cal, Solano County*, 480 U.S. 102 (1987). Based on that test, the court concluded that the British manufacturer of scrap metal machines was subject to New Jersey jurisdiction, even though the company had at no time advertised in, sent goods to, or in any way targeted the state. Those who live or operate primarily outside a state have a due process right not to be subjected to judgment in its courts, as a general rule. Where the individual or corporation explicitly consents to jurisdiction, is present in a state at the time a suit starts, is a citizen or has a domicile within the state, or is incorporated in the state, jurisdiction is proper, because all of those situations indicate an intent to submit to the laws of the state. The stream-of-commerce exception to the general rule refers to the movement of goods from manufacturers through distributors to consumers, and advocates of the exception argue that the placement of goods into the stream of commerce with the expectation that they will be purchased by consumers indicates purposeful availment. But the exception only holds where the activities manifest an intention to submit to the power of the sovereign. In this case, J. McIntyre (D) directed marketing and sales efforts at the United States, but not directly to New Jersey, and because of that, a federal court might have jurisdiction, but a New Jersey state court does not. It is J. McIntyre's (D) purposeful contacts with New Jersey, not with the United States, that are relevant. Because J. McIntyre has not engaged in conduct purposefully directed at New Jersey, New Jersey state courts did not have jurisdiction to hear the case. Reversed.

CONCURRENCE: (Breyer, J.) The judgment is correct, but it is determined by precedent. There is no reason to construct new general rules that limit jurisdiction, since on the basis of existing precedent, the case can be decided. No precedent finds that a single isolated sale, even if accompanied by the sales here, is sufficient. Nicastro (P) failed to meet his burden of showing that it was constitutionally proper to exercise jurisdiction over petitioner J. McIntyre (D).

DISSENT: (Ginsburg, J.) J. McIntyre (D) wanted to establish a market for its product in the United States and took steps to do so. Where in the United States buyers of the product live or operate is irrelevant to the manufacturer. The company simply wants to sell its product in the United States. Under *International Shoe*, 326 U.S. 310 (1945), personal jurisdiction is established.

▶ ANALYSIS

The absence of a majority opinion makes it difficult to identify a reliable rule: Three justices voted to reverse on

Continued on next page.

the basis of a new rule that limits jurisdiction more severely than precedent; three voted to reverse on the basis of precedent, with making a new rule; and three voted to affirm on the basis of precedent.

■═■

Quicknotes

FORUM STATE The state in which a court, or other location in which a legal remedy may be sought, is located.

JURISDICTION The authority of a court to hear and declare judgment in respect to a particular matter.

■═■

Burger King Corp. v. Rudzewicz

Franchisor (P) v. Defaulting franchisee (D)

471 U.S. 462 (1985).

NATURE OF CASE: Appeal from dismissal for lack of personal jurisdiction.

FACT SUMMARY: Rudzewicz (D), a Michigan resident, contended the Florida court lacked personal jurisdiction over him even though he had long conducted business in Florida and his franchise contract provided for adjudication of disputes in Florida.

🏛 RULE OF LAW
A party who establishes purposeful minimum contacts with a state is subject to that state's exercise of personal jurisdiction over him.

FACTS: Rudzewicz (D) entered into a franchise agreement with Burger King Corp. (P). Burger King (P) was a Florida corporation, and the contract held that it was to be governed by Florida law. All periodic payments for licensing and franchising were sent to Florida. Rudzewicz (D) defaulted on the obligations, and Burger King (P) brought a diversity suit against Rudzewicz (D), a Michigan resident. Rudzewicz (D) moved to dismiss on the basis that personal jurisdiction was lacking. The trial court denied the motion, and the court of appeals reversed. Burger King (P) appealed.

ISSUE: Is a party who establishes purposeful minimum contacts with a state subject to that state's exercise of personal jurisdiction over him?

HOLDING AND DECISION: (Brennan, J.) Yes. A party who establishes purposeful minimum contacts with a state is subject to personal jurisdiction in that state. In this case, the franchise contract allowed Rudzewicz (D) to enjoy the advantages of an association with a Florida corporation. This advantage was protected and governed by the laws of Florida. Therefore, Rudzewicz (D) had purposeful minimum contacts with Florida and personal jurisdiction existed. Reversed and remanded.

DISSENT: (Stevens, J.) It is a violation of fundamental fairness to force a franchisee to litigate a claim in a forum chosen unilaterally by the franchisor.

▶ ANALYSIS

The Court cites *McGee v. International Life Insurance Co.,* 355 U.S. 220 (1957), in support of its holding in this case. In *McGee,* personal jurisdiction was found based on the single transaction involved in the case. A single insurance policy was sufficient to find personal jurisdiction. The key was that the policy was the document being sued on.

■══■

Quicknotes

FRANCHISE An agreement whereby one party (the franchisor) grants another (the franchisee) the right to market its product or service.

MINIMUM CONTACTS The minimum degree of contact necessary in order to sustain a cause of action within a particular forum, consistent with the requirements of due process.

PERSONAL JURISDICTION The court's authority over a person or parties to a lawsuit.

■══■

ALS Scan, Inc. v. Digital Service Consultants, Inc.

Owner of copyright (P) v. Internet service provider (D)

293 F.3d 707 (4th Cir. 2002).

NATURE OF CASE: Interlocutory appeal from the dismissal of a complaint for lack of personal jurisdiction.

FACT SUMMARY: ALS Scan, Inc. (P) brought a copyright infringement claim against several defendants including Digital Service Consultants, Inc. (D), an Internet Service Provider (ISP). Digital Service Consultants, Inc. (D) filed a motion to dismiss the claim under Fed. R. Civ. P. 12(b)(2) and the district court granted the motion. ALS Scan (P) appealed.

RULE OF LAW

A state may not exercise personal jurisdiction over an out-of-state person whose only contact with the state is through Internet activity that is not directed at the state.

FACTS: ALS Scan, Inc. (P) is a Maryland corporation that creates and markets photographs for distribution over the Internet. ALS Scan (P) brought an action for copyright infringement against Digital Service Consultants, Inc. (Digital) (D) and Digital's customers, Robert Wilkins (D) and Alternative Products, Inc. (D) (collectively, Alternative Products (D)). All defendants are located in Georgia. The suit alleges that Alternative Products (D) gained revenue by publishing on its web site photographs owned by ALS Scan (P) without first securing permission from ALS Scan (P) to do so. The suit also alleges that Digital (D), as the Internet Service Provider (ISP) for Alternative Products (D), enabled Alternative Products (D) to publish the photographs on the Internet. Digital (D) did not itself publish the photographs, but only provided the other defendants with bandwidth to publish their own web site. Digital (D) filed a motion to dismiss on grounds that under Fed. R. Civ. P. 12(b)(2), the district court lacked personal jurisdiction over it. In support of the motion, Digital (D) claimed, among other things, that other than through the Internet, Digital (D) has no contacts with the State of Maryland. The district court granted Digital's (D) motion to dismiss for lack of personal jurisdiction. ALS Scan (P) then filed this interlocutory appeal from the court's ruling.

ISSUE: May a state exercise personal jurisdiction over an out-of-state person whose only contact with the state is through Internet activity that is not directed at the state?

HOLDING AND DECISION: (Niemeyer, J.) No. A state may not exercise personal jurisdiction over an out-of-state person whose only contact with the state is through Internet activity that is not directed at the state. Despite advances in technology, the state's judicial power over persons remains limited to persons within the state's boundaries and to those persons outside of the state who have minimum contacts with the state, such that the state's exercise of judicial power over the person would not offend traditional notions of fair play and substantial justice. A court may assume power over an out-of-state defendant either by a proper finding of specific jurisdiction based on conduct connected to the suit, or by a proper finding of general jurisdiction. ALS Scan (P) argues that Digital's (D) activity in enabling Alternative Products' (D) publication of the infringing photographs on the Internet, thereby causing ALS Scan (P) injury in Maryland, forms a proper basis for the district court's specific jurisdiction over Digital (D). The question then becomes whether a person electronically transmitting or enabling the transmission of information via the Internet to Maryland, causing injury there, subjects the person to the jurisdiction of a court in Maryland. The traditional standard for establishing specific jurisdiction must be adapted so that it makes sense in the Internet context. In *Zippo Manufacturing Co. v. Zippo Dot Com*, 952 F. Supp. 1119 (W.D. Pa. 1997), the court established the "sliding scale" test to evaluate the nature and quality of a defendant's Internet activity. That court stated: At one end of the spectrum are situations where a defendant clearly does business over the Internet. . . . At the opposite end are situations where a defendant has simply posted information on an Internet web site that is accessible to users in foreign jurisdictions. . . . The middle ground is occupied by interactive web sites where a user can exchange information with the host computer. In these cases, the exercise of jurisdiction is determined by examining the level of interactivity and commercial nature of the exchange of information that occurs on the web site. Thus, under *Zippo*, a state may, consistent with due process, exercise judicial power over a person outside of the state when that person (1) directs electronic activity into the state, (2) with the manifested intent of engaging in business or other interactions within the state, and (3) that activity creates, in a person within the state, a potential cause of action cognizable in the state's courts. Under this model, a person who simply places information on the Internet does not subject himself to jurisdiction in each state into which the electronic signal is transmitted and received. Specific jurisdiction in the Internet context may be based only on an out-of-state person's Internet activity directed at the state and causing injury that gives rise to a potential claim cognizable in the state. Digital (D) did not direct its electronic activity specifically at any target in Maryland.

Continued on next page.

It did not manifest intent to engage in a business or some other interaction in Maryland. None of its conduct in enabling a web site created a cause of action in Maryland. And while it is true that even in the absence of specific jurisdiction, general jurisdiction may exist when the defendant has sufficient contacts with the forum state, a state may not obtain general jurisdiction over out-of-state persons who regularly and systematically transmit electronic signals into the state via the Internet based solely on those transmissions. More would have to be demonstrated, but what and how much more will be decided at another time. Other than maintain its web site on the Internet, which did not carry the photographs at issue in this case, Digital (D) has engaged in no activity in Maryland. Its only contacts with the state occur when persons in Maryland access Digital's (D) web site. Such transmissions do not add up to the quality of contacts necessary for a state to have jurisdiction over the person for all purposes. Affirmed.

▶ *ANALYSIS*

Over the past several years, U.S. courts have wrestled with the issue of what types of online activities might subject a defendant to the jurisdiction of a distant state court. As recently as 1997, some federal district courts determined that simply maintaining a web site accessible within the forum state was sufficient to subject a defendant to the forum court's jurisdiction. See *Superguide Corp. v. Kegan,* 987 F. Supp. 481 (W.D.N.C. 1997); *Inset Sys. v. Instruction Set,* 937 F. Supp. 161 (D. Conn. 1996). With the introduction of new technology and new functionality, some U.S. courts, like the Pennsylvania court in *Zippo,* went so far as to craft specific and distinct analytical frameworks for evaluating whether personal jurisdiction could be obtained in Internet cases. *ALS Scan* is such a decision, and, as recently as January 2003, the U.S. Supreme Court chose not to hear, and thereby let stand, the *ALS Scan* decision.

■━■

Quicknotes

COPYRIGHT INFRINGEMENT A violation of one of the exclusive rights granted to an artist pursuant to Article I, section 8, clause 8 of the United States Constitution over the reproduction, display, performance, distribution, and adaptation of his work for a period prescribed by statute.

DUE PROCESS CLAUSE Clauses, found in the Fifth and Fourteenth Amendments to the United States Constitution, providing that no person shall be deprived of "life, liberty, or property, without due process of law."

FAIR PLAY NOTION Equitable notion that persons must deal with each other fairly and justly.

FORUM STATE The state in which a court, or other location in which a legal remedy may be sought, is located.

GENERAL JURISDICTION Refers to the authority of a court to hear and determine all cases of a particular type.

INTERLOCUTORY APPEAL The appeal of an issue that does not resolve the disposition of the case but is essential to a determination of the parties' legal rights.

MINIMUM CONTACTS The minimum degree of contact necessary in order to sustain a cause of action within a particular forum, consistent with the requirements of due process.

PERSONAL JURISDICTION The court's authority over a person or parties to a lawsuit.

■━■

Shaffer v. Heitner

Corporation (D) and corporate officers (D) v. Nonresident shareholder (P)

433 U.S. 186 (1977).

NATURE OF CASE: Appeal from a finding of state jurisdiction.

FACT SUMMARY: Heitner (P) brought a derivative suit against Greyhound (D) directors for antitrust losses it had sustained in Oregon. The suit was brought in Delaware, Greyhound's (D) state of incorporation.

🏛 RULE OF LAW
Jurisdiction cannot be founded on property within a state unless there are sufficient contacts within the meaning of the test developed in *International Shoe*.

FACTS: Heitner (P) owned one share of Greyhound (D) stock. Greyhound (D) had been subjected to a large antitrust judgment in Oregon. Heitner (P), a nonresident of Delaware, brought a derivative suit in Delaware, the state of Greyhound's (D) incorporation. Jurisdiction was based on sequestration of Greyhound (D) stock that was deemed to be located within the state of incorporation. The Delaware sequestration statute allowed property within the state to be seized ex parte to compel the owner to submit to the in personam jurisdiction of the court. None of the stock was actually in Delaware, but a freeze order was placed on the corporate books. Greyhound (D) made a special appearance to challenge the court's jurisdiction to hear the matter. Greyhound (D) argued that the sequestration statute was unconstitutional under the line of cases beginning with *Sniadach v. Family Finance Corp.*, 395 U.S. 337 (1969). Greyhound (D) also argued that there were insufficient contacts with Delaware to justify an exercise of jurisdiction. The Delaware courts found that the sequestration statute was valid since it was not a per se seizure of the property and was merely invoked to compel out-of-state residents to defend actions within the state. Little or no consideration was given to the "contact" argument based on a finding that the presence of the stock within the state conferred quasi-in-rem jurisdiction.

ISSUE: May a state assume jurisdiction over an issue merely because defendant's property happens to be within the state?

HOLDING AND DECISION: (Marshall, J.) No. Mere presence of property within a state is insufficient to confer jurisdiction on a court absent independent contacts within the meaning of *International Shoe*, 326 U.S. 310 (1945), which would make acceptance constitutional. We expressly disapprove that line of cases represented by *Harris v. Balk*, 198 U.S. 215 (1905), that permits jurisdiction merely because the property happens to be within the state. If sufficient contacts do not exist to assume jurisdiction absent the presence of property within the state, it cannot be invoked on the basis of property within the court's jurisdiction. We base this decision on the fundamental concepts of justice and fair play required under the Due Process and Equal Protection Clauses of the Fourteenth Amendment. Here, the stock is not the subject of the controversy. There is no claim to ownership of it or injury caused by it. The defendants do not reside in Delaware or have any contacts there. The injury occurred in Oregon. No activities complained of were done within the forum. Finally, Heitner (P) is not even a Delaware resident. Jurisdiction was improperly granted. Reversed.

CONCURRENCE: (Powell, J.) Property permanently within the state, e.g., real property, should confer jurisdiction.

CONCURRENCE: (Stevens, J.) Purchase of stock in the marketplace should not confer in rem jurisdiction in the state of incorporation.

CONCURRENCE AND DISSENT: (Brennan, J.) The Delaware sequestration statute's sole purpose is to force in personam jurisdiction through a quasi-in-rem seizure. The opinion is purely advisory in that if the Court finds the statute invalid, the rest of the opinion is not required. Delaware never argued that it was attempting to obtain in rem jurisdiction. Further, a derivative suit may be brought in the state of incorporation. Greyhound's (D) choice of incorporation in Delaware is a prima facie showing of submission to its jurisdiction.

▶ ANALYSIS

While the corporation could be sued in its state of incorporation under the dissents' theory, the suit is against the directors and neither the site of the wrong nor the residence of a defendant is in Delaware. The decision will only have a major impact in cases such as herein where the state really has no reason to want to adjudicate the issue. Of course, real property would still be treated as an exception.

■━■

Quicknotes

ANTITRUST Body of federal law prohibiting business conduct that constitutes a restraint on trade.

DERIVATIVE SUIT Action asserted by a shareholder in order to enforce a cause of action on behalf of the corporation.

does away with inrem/in personam.

Continued on next page.

DUE PROCESS CLAUSE Clauses, found in the Fifth and Fourteenth Amendments to the United States Constitution, providing that no person shall be deprived of "life, liberty, or property, without due process of law."

EX PARTE A proceeding commenced by one party.

FAIR PLAY NOTION Equitable notion that persons must deal with each other fairly and justly.

FORUM STATE The state in which a court, or other location in which a legal remedy may be sought, is located.

IN PERSONAM JURISDICTION The jurisdiction of a court over a person as opposed to his interest in property.

IN REM JURISDICTION A court's authority over an object so that its judgment is binding in respect to the rights and interests of all parties in that object.

MINIMUM CONTACTS The minimum degree of contact necessary in order to sustain a cause of action within a particular forum, consistent with the requirements of due process.

PRIMA FACIE An action in which the plaintiff introduces sufficient evidence to submit an issue to the judge or jury for determination.

QUASI-IN-REM PROCEEDING A proceeding in order to determine the interest of a specified person in particular property.

SEQUESTRATION ORDER A court order requiring the attachment of property or funds, pending a final disposition in the action.

■══■

Burnham v. Superior Court of California

Husband (P) v. Court (D)

495 U.S. 604 (1990).

NATURE OF CASE: Review of order denying motion to quash service of summons.

FACT SUMMARY: Burnham (P) was personally served with process while temporarily in California on business, while visiting his children.

🏛 RULE OF LAW
The Fourteenth Amendment does not deny a state jurisdiction over a person personally served with process while temporarily in a state, in a suit unrelated to his activities in the state.

FACTS: The Burnhams lived in New Jersey. After they separated, the wife moved to California. Mrs. Burnham filed a divorce action in California. At one point, Mr. Burnham (P) came to California on business. He had no other contacts with California. On this trip, he was served with the divorce action papers. He moved to quash, contending that his contacts with California were insufficient to confer jurisdiction. The trial court denied the motion, and the state court of appeal denied his petition for mandamus. The U.S. Supreme Court granted review.

ISSUE: Does the Fourteenth Amendment deny a state jurisdiction over a person personally served with process while temporarily in a state, in a suit unrelated to his activities in the state?

HOLDING AND DECISION: (Scalia, J.) No. The Fourteenth Amendment does not deny a state jurisdiction over a person personally served with process while temporarily in a state, in a suit unrelated to his activities in the state. It is a firmly established principle of personal jurisdiction that courts of a state have jurisdiction over persons physically present in a state. The cases decided by this Court that raise Fourteenth Amendment due process considerations are those where a state attempts to exercise jurisdiction over a nonresident who is not physically present. In a situation where the nonresident is served while physically present, no due process implication is made by service of process, no matter what the reason for his presence may be. Affirmed.

CONCURRENCE: (White, J.) The rule here is so well-established that no facial or as-applied challenge can be made.

CONCURRENCE: (Brennan, J.) The plurality incorrectly emphasizes the historical acceptance of the rule. This is an incorrect approach, as this Court may strike down a well-established rule it finds unconstitutional.

Rather, in any fairness analysis, it does not offend notions of fair play and justice to subject a physically present nonresident to jurisdiction.

CONCURRENCE: (Stevens, J.) The various opinions give excessive analysis to a very easy case whose result was self-evident.

▶ ANALYSIS

Supreme Court jurisprudence in this area goes back to 1877 with *Pennoyer v. Neff*, 95 U.S. 714. Since that case, the Court has fashioned a rule that out-of-state service may only be had on defendants having certain contacts with the state. The present case represents a total rejection of the notion of applying the same test to a physically-in-state defendant.

Quicknotes

DUE PROCESS CLAUSE Clauses, found in the Fifth and Fourteenth Amendments to the United States Constitution, providing that no person shall be deprived of "life, liberty, or property, without due process of law."

FAIR PLAY NOTION Equitable notion that persons must deal with each other fairly and justly.

FOURTEENTH AMENDMENT No person shall be deprived of life, liberty, or property, without the due process of law.

PERSONAL JURISDICTION The court's authority over a person or parties to a lawsuit.

QUASH To vacate, annul, void.

WRIT OF MANDAMUS A court order issued commanding a public or private entity, or an official thereof, to perform a duty required by law.

Goodyear Dunlop Tires Operations, S.A. et al. v. Brown et ux., Co-Administrators of the Estate of Brown, et al.

Foreign subsidiaries of U.S. corporation (D) v. Decedents' parents (P)

131 S. Ct. 2846 (2011).

NATURE OF CASE: Appeal of state court's assertion of jurisdiction.

FACTS SUMMARY: The parents of two American boys killed in a bus accident in France brought suit in North Carolina, where the boys lived, against the tire company.

🏛 RULE OF LAW
A state may not exercise general personal jurisdiction over a foreign subsidiary of a U.S. corporation where the subsidiary lacks continuous and systematic business contacts with the state.

FACTS: The parents (P) of two American boys who were killed in a bus accident in France brought suit in North Carolina state court against Goodyear Tire and Rubber Company (D) and three Goodyear subsidiaries (D) operating in Turkey, France, and Luxembourg. The parents (P) claimed that the accident resulted from a defective tire manufactured at the Turkish subsidiary's plant. Although Goodyear USA (D) operates in North Carolina, the three foreign subsidiaries (D) have no place of business, employees, or bank accounts in the state and neither solicit nor do business in the state. A small percentage of the subsidiaries' (D) tires were distributed in North Carolina by other Goodyear USA (D) affiliates, however. The subsidiaries (D) moved to dismiss the claims against them for lack of personal jurisdiction. The trial court denied the motion, and the North Carolina Court of Appeals affirmed, holding that the court had general jurisdiction over the subsidiaries (D) because their tires had reached the state through "the stream of commerce."

ISSUE: May a state exercise general personal jurisdiction over a foreign subsidiary of a U.S. corporation where the subsidiary lacks continuous and systematic business contacts with the state?

HOLDING AND DECISION: (Ginsburg, J.) No. A state may not exercise general personal jurisdiction over a foreign subsidiary of a U.S. corporation where the subsidiary lacks continuous and systematic business contacts with the state. As stated in *International Shoe Co. v. Washington*, 326 U. S. 310, 316 (1945), and its progeny, a distinction exists between general and specific personal jurisdiction. General personal jurisdiction arises from a defendant's "continuous and systematic" affiliation with a state and permits a state to exercise personal jurisdiction over the defendant for any claim, regardless of whether the claim itself has any connection to the defendant's activities in the state. Specific personal jurisdiction arises from a connection between the state and the underlying claim, and permits a state to exercise jurisdiction only with respect to that claim. In this case, the North Carolina courts conflated the two types of jurisdiction, improperly using the isolated presence of the subsidiaries' products in the state as a result of others' actions to justify jurisdiction over the subsidiaries for claims having nothing to do with those products. Reversed.

⬤ ANALYSIS

Key to this case is the distinction between two types of personal jurisdiction: general and specific. General jurisdiction is all-purpose, in the sense that it allows any claim to be brought against a defendant as long as the defendant has "systematic and continuous" contacts with that forum. Specific jurisdiction exists where there is a connection between a forum and a particular controversy, and it is limited to that controversy. In this case, only general jurisdiction was in issue: The site of the accident and the factory where the tires were made were both outside of North Carolina, so there was no connection between the state and the controversy, and specific jurisdiction was therefore not properly at issue. As to whether general jurisdiction existed, the Court focused on "stream-of-commerce," and reached the conclusion that jurisdiction did not exist.

■═■

Quicknotes

FORUM A court or other location in which a legal remedy may be sought.

GENERAL JURISDICTION Refers to the authority of a court to hear and determine all cases of a particular type.

IN PERSONAM JURISDICTION The power of a court over a person, as opposed to a court's power over a person's interest in property.

PERSONAL JURISDICTION The court's authority over a person or parties to a lawsuit.

■═■

Carnival Cruise Lines, Inc. v. Shute

Cruise line (D) v. Passenger (P)

499 U.S. 585 (1991).

NATURE OF CASE: Appeal from reversal of a grant of defendant's motion for summary judgment in an admiralty case.

FACT SUMMARY: After being injured while on a Carnival Cruise Lines (D) cruise, Shute (P) brought this action in the state of Washington, despite a forum-selection clause in the tickets providing for litigation only in Florida.

RULE OF LAW
A forum-selection clause in a form ticket contract will be reasonable and fair as long as it does not limit all liability of the carrier or avoid the right of any claimant to a trial by a court of competent jurisdiction.

FACTS: While on a Carnival Cruise Lines, Inc. (Carnival) (D) cruise off the western coast of Mexico, Shute (P) sustained an injury when she slipped on a deck mat. She filed suit in her home state of Washington, claiming that her injuries had been caused by the negligence of Carnival (D) and its employees. The passage contract tickets contained a forum-selection clause stipulating that any disputes would be litigated only in a court in the state of Florida, where Carnival's (D) principal place of business was located. The district court granted Carnival's (D) motion for summary judgment, holding its contacts with Washington constitutionally insufficient to support the exercise of personal jurisdiction. The court of appeals reversed, concluding that Carnival's (D) solicitation of business in Washington constituted sufficient contacts within the state. Carnival (D) appealed.

ISSUE: Will a forum-selection clause in a form ticket contract be reasonable and fair so long as it does not limit all liability of the carrier or avoid the right of any claimant to a trial by a court of competent jurisdiction?

HOLDING AND DECISION: (Blackmun, J.) Yes. A forum-selection clause in a form ticket contract will be reasonable and fair so long as it does not limit all liability of the carrier or avoid the right of any claimant to a trial by a court of competent jurisdiction. Without a reasonable forum clause, a cruise line could be subjected to litigation in several different fora. Additionally, such a clause dispels any confusion about where suits arising from the contract must be brought and defended. Passengers also benefit from reduced fares reflecting the savings that the cruise line enjoys by limiting the fora in which it may be sued. Finally, because the clause allows for judicial resolution of claims against Carnival (D) without limiting Carnival's (D)

liability for negligence, it does not violate 46 U.S.C. App. § 183c. Reversed.

DISSENT: (Stevens, J.) The fact that the cruise line (D) can reduce its litigation costs, and therefore its liability insurance premiums, by forcing this choice on its passengers does not suffice to render the provision reasonable. Long before the turn of the century, courts consistently held such clauses unenforceable under federal admiralty law.

► ANALYSIS

Both parties argued vigorously that the Court's opinion in *The Bremen v. Zapata Off-Shore Co.,* 407 U.S. 1 (1972), governed this case. However, the Court noted that in *The Bremen,* the Court addressed the enforceability of a forum-selection clause in a contract between two business corporations of different nations for the towing of an extremely costly piece of equipment. It was entirely reasonable to have expected the parties in that case to negotiate with care the selection of a forum for the resolution of disputes arising from their towing contract. In contrast, the passage contract at issue here was routine and nearly identical to every commercial passage contract issued by Carnival (D) and most other cruise lines.

Quicknotes

ADMIRALTY That area of law pertaining to navigable waters.

PERSONAL JURISDICTION The court's authority over a person or parties to a lawsuit.

SUMMARY JUDGMENT Judgment rendered by a court in response to a motion by one of the parties, claiming that the lack of a question of material fact in respect to an issue warrants disposition of the issue without consideration by the jury.

Mullane v. Central Hanover Bank & Trust Co.

Guardian of trust beneficiaries (P) v. Bank (D)

339 U.S. 306 (1950).

NATURE OF CASE: Challenge to state law.

FACT SUMMARY: Under a state statute, the rights of out-of-state residents who are beneficiaries of a common trust fund could be conclusively determined.

🏛 RULE OF LAW
A state may determine the rights of nonresident beneficiaries in the settlement of trust accounts if the notice provided is constitutionally adequate.

FACTS: New York allowed institutions to adopt common trust funds under which many small trusts could be combined for efficient administration. Notice of the new law to beneficiaries was by publication and by mail of the initial decision. Notice of the filing of accountings was by publication. Acceptance of the accounting by the court was a nonappealable final determination of rights. An administrator was appointed to represent the interests of all beneficiaries. Mullane (P) challenged the validity of the statute to bind out-of-state beneficiaries.

ISSUE: May a state determine the rights of nonresident beneficiaries in the settlement of trust accounts if the notice provided is constitutionally adequate?

HOLDING AND DECISION: (Jackson, J.) Yes. A state may determine the rights of nonresident beneficiaries in the settlement of trust accounts if the notice provided is constitutionally adequate. Trusts are created and administered pursuant to state law. Supervision by state courts is so rooted in customs to establish beyond doubt the right to determine the interests of all claimants, provided the procedure provides adequate due process procedures. It is immaterial whether the accounting procedure is deemed in rem, quasi in rem, etc. The paramount state interest in finally determining rights and interests in its trusts is sufficiently great as to overcome any due process challenges. The statute is valid as applied to nonresidents. However, publication alone is a reliable means of acquainting interested parties with the fact that their rights are before the courts only with respect to those beneficiaries whose interests or whereabouts could not with due diligence be ascertained. As to them, the statutory notice is sufficient. However great the odds that publication will never reach such unknown parties, it is not much more likely to fail than any of the other methods for providing notice open to legislators who try to prescribe the best notice practicable. The constitutional objections to published notice are overruled insofar as they are urged on behalf of any beneficiaries whose interests or addresses are unknown to the trustee. As to known present beneficiaries of known place of residence, however, notice by publication stands on a different footing. Even though there are exceptions, the rule is that within the limits of practicability, notice must be reasonably calculated to reach interested parties. Where the names and post office addresses of those affected by a proceeding are at hand, the reasons disappear for resorting to means less likely than the mails to apprise them of them. Reversed.

DISSENT: (Burton, J.) On the issue of whether the state provided adequate notice: The common trusts may be used only when the instrument creating the individual trusts permits it. There is no constitutional question here because whether notice is sufficient is within the state's discretion.

▶ ANALYSIS

It is typical that a state may decide in rem proceedings even though it may not have personal jurisdiction over some claimants or parties. The power inheres in the concept of state sovereignty. Without the ability to render such a final determination of rights in property in the state, the integrity of state court judgments would be threatened, and no judgments would be certain.

━━■

Quicknotes

COMMON TRUST FUND Trust fund managed by a financial institution as trustee wherein funds of many estates are commingled for purposes of efficient administration.

DUE PROCESS CLAUSE Clauses, found in the Fifth and Fourteenth Amendments to the United States Constitution, providing that no person shall be deprived of "life, liberty, or property, without due process of law."

IN REM An action against property.

PERSONAL JURISDICTION The court's authority over a person or parties to a lawsuit.

QUASI IN REM A court's authority over the defendant's property within a specified geographical area.

Piper Aircraft Co. v. Reyno

Aircraft company (D) v. Crash victims' representative (P)

454 U.S. 235 (1981).

NATURE OF CASE: Appeal of reversal of order of dismissal.

FACT SUMMARY: Reyno (P) sought to prevent transfer of this action from the district court in Pennsylvania to the courts of Scotland on the ground that the law of Scotland was less favorable to Reyno (P) than the law of Pennsylvania.

🏛 RULE OF LAW
Dismissal may not be barred solely because of the possibility of an unfavorable change in law.

FACTS: In July 1976, a small commercial aircraft, which had been manufactured by Piper Aircraft Co. (Piper) (D), crashed in the Scottish highlands, instantly killing the pilot and the plane's five passengers. The airplane's propellers had been manufactured in Ohio by Hartzell Propeller, Inc. (Hartzell) (D), and it was registered in Great Britain but operated by a Scottish air taxi service. In July 1977, a California probate court appointed Reyno (P) administratrix of the estates of the passengers, and she then commenced several wrongful death actions on behalf of the respective estates in the California Superior Court. Subsequently, Piper (D) successfully moved to have the case transferred to the United States District Court for the Middle District of Pennsylvania. In May 1978, both Hartzell (D) and Piper (D) moved to dismiss the action on the grounds of forum non conveniens. The district court granted these motions after applying a balancing test and determining that Scotland was the proper locus for the trial. The court of appeals reversed, after noting that the doctrine of strict liability was not applicable in the Scottish courts. The appellate panel held that dismissal is automatically barred where the law of the alternative forum is less favorable to a plaintiff than the law of the forum chosen by the plaintiff. Piper (D) and Hartzell (D) then brought this appeal.

ISSUE: May dismissal be barred solely because of the possibility of an unfavorable change in law?

HOLDING AND DECISION: (Marshall, J.) No. Dismissal may not be barred solely because of the possibility of an unfavorable change in law. Dismissal will ordinarily be appropriate where trial in the plaintiff's chosen forum imposes a heavy burden on the defendant or the court and where the plaintiff is unable to offer any specific reasons of convenience supporting his choice. The possibility of a change in substantive law should ordinarily not be given conclusive or even substantial weight in the forum non conveniens inquiry. A plaintiff's choice of forum is entitled to greater deference when the plaintiff has chosen a home forum. Because the central purpose of any forum non conveniens inquiry is to ensure that the trial is convenient, a foreign plaintiff's choice deserves less deference. Here, although the relatives of the decedents may not be able to rely on a strict liability theory, and although their potential damage award may be smaller, there is no danger that they will be deprived of any remedy or treated unfairly. Scotland has a very strong interest in litigation. The accident occurred in its airspace. All of the decedents were Scottish. Apart from Piper (D) and Hartzell (D), all potential plaintiffs and defendants are either Scottish or British. Reversed.

Scotland is proper

▶ ANALYSIS

As the Court noted in this case, at the outset of any forum non conveniens inquiry, the court must determine whether there exists an alternative forum. Ordinarily, this requirement will be satisfied if the defendant is amenable to process in the other jurisdiction. The court must then balance the competing factors, and if the balance of conveniences suggests that trial in the chosen forum would be unnecessarily burdensome for the defendant or the court, dismissal is proper.

■■■

Quicknotes

FORUM NON CONVENIENS An equitable doctrine permitting a court to refrain from hearing and determining a case when the matter may be more properly and fairly heard in another forum.

MOTION TO DISMISS Motion to terminate a trial based on the adequacy of the pleadings.

STRICT LIABILITY Liability for all injuries proximately caused by a party's conducting of certain inherently dangerous activities without regard to negligence or fault.

WRONGFUL DEATH An action brought by the beneficiaries of a deceased person, claiming that the deceased's death was the result of wrongful conduct by the defendant.

■■■

1404(a)

missing in law of Scotland

Reyno (CA) ⟶ Piper (PA), Hartzell (OH)

finding of fact not looked at in trial crt
• discretion is something to look at in appeal.
• hard to overturn trial crt in Venue discretion

The Choice of an Appropriate Court: Subject Matter Jurisdiction and Removal

Quick Reference Rules of Law

Louisville & Nashville Railroad Co. v. Mottley

Railroad (D) v. Injured passenger (P)

211 U.S. 149 (1908).

NATURE OF CASE: Appeal of a decision overruling a demurrer in an action for specific performance of a contract.

FACT SUMMARY: Mottley (P) was injured on a train owned by Louisville & Nashville Railroad Co. (D) and he was granted a lifetime free pass by the railroad, which he sought to enforce.

🏛 RULE OF LAW
Alleging an anticipated constitutional defense in the complaint does not give a federal court jurisdiction if there is no diversity of citizenship between the litigants.

FACTS: In 1871, Mottley (P) and his wife were injured while riding on the Louisville & Nashville Railroad. (D). The Mottleys (P) released their claims for damages against the Louisville & Nashville Railroad Co. (D) upon receiving a contract granting free transportation during the remainder of their lives. In 1907, the Louisville & Nashville Railroad (D) refused to renew the Mottleys' (P) passes, relying upon an act of Congress that forbade the giving of free passes or free transportation. The Mottleys (P) filed an action in a circuit court of the United States for the western district of Kentucky. The Mottleys (P) and the Louisville & Nashville Railroad (D) were both citizens of Kentucky. Therefore, the Mottleys (P) attempted to establish federal jurisdiction by claiming that the Louisville & Nashville Railroad (D) would raise a constitutional defense in their answer, thus raising a federal question. The Louisville & Nashville Railroad (D) filed a demurrer to the complaint for failing to state a cause of action. The demurrer was denied. On appeal, the U.S. Supreme Court did not look at the issue raised by the litigants but on their own motion raised the issue of whether the federal courts had jurisdiction to hear the case.

ISSUE: Does an allegation in the complaint that a constitutional defense will be raised in the answer, raise a federal question that would give a federal court jurisdiction if no diversity of citizenship is alleged?

HOLDING AND DECISION: (Moody, J.) No. Alleging an anticipated constitutional defense in the complaint does not give a federal court jurisdiction if there is no diversity of citizenship between the litigants. The Supreme Court reversed the lower court's ruling and remitted the case to that court with instructions to dismiss the suit for want of jurisdiction. Neither party to the litigation alleged that the federal court had jurisdiction in this case, and neither party challenged the jurisdiction of the federal court to hear the case. Because the jurisdiction of the circuit court is defined and limited by statute, the Supreme Court stated that it is their duty to see that such jurisdiction is not exceeded. Both parties to the litigation were citizens of Kentucky, and so there was no diversity of citizenship. The only way that the federal court could have jurisdiction in this case would be if there was a federal question involved. Mottley (P) did allege in his complaint that the Louisville & Nashville Railroad (D) based its refusal to renew the free pass on a federal statute. Mottley (P) then attempted to allege information that would defeat the defense of the Louisville & Nashville Railroad (D). This is not sufficient. The plaintiff's complaint must be based upon the federal laws of the Constitution to confer jurisdiction on the federal courts. Mottley's (P) cause of action was not based on any federal laws or constitutional privileges; it was based on a contract. Even though it is evident that a federal question will be brought up at the trial, plaintiff's cause of action must be based on a federal statute or the Constitution in order to have a federal question that would grant jurisdiction to the federal courts. Reversed and remanded.

▌ *ANALYSIS*

If Mottley (P) could have alleged that he was basing his action on a federal right, it would have been enough to have given the federal court jurisdiction. The federal court would have had to exercise jurisdiction at least long enough to determine whether there actually was such a right. If the federal court ultimately concludes that the claimed federal right does not exist, the complaint would be dismissed for failure to state a claim upon which relief can be granted rather than for lack of jurisdiction. The court has the power to determine the issue of subject matter jurisdiction on its own motion, as it did in this case. Subject matter jurisdiction can be challenged at any stage of the proceeding.

■━■

Quicknotes

DEMURRER The assertion that the opposing party's pleadings are insufficient and that the demurring party should not be made to answer.

DIVERSITY OF CITIZENSHIP Parties are citizens of different states, or one party is an alien; a factor, along with a statutorily set dollar value of the matter in controversy,

facts are true, but the P. shudn't win

Continued on next page.

that allows a federal district court to exercise its authority to hear a lawsuit based on diversity jurisdiction.

JURISDICTION The authority of a court to hear and declare judgment in respect to a particular matter.

SPECIFIC PERFORMANCE An equitable remedy whereby the court requires the parties to perform their obligations pursuant to a contract.

■━■

Ochoa v. PV Holding Corp.

Injured motorist (P) v. Out-of-state tortfeasor (D)

2007 WL 496612 (E.D. La. 2007).

NATURE OF CASE: Motion to remand the case to state court on grounds that federal court lacks jurisdiction.

FACT SUMMARY: A motorist, who caused an accident with another motorist in Louisiana thereby injuring her, removed the case to federal court, claiming that even though he had been a resident of Louisiana, he has, since Hurricane Katrina, lived in Texas and intended to stay there indefinitely. The injured motorist moved to remand to state court.

RULE OF LAW
Evidence of recent employment in a state, along with a subjective statement of intent to live in the state indefinitely, do not necessarily satisfy a party's burden of showing diverse citizenship in order to invoke a court's subject matter jurisdiction.

FACTS: Paul Gulley (D) had lived in Orleans Parish, Louisiana, but evacuated to Arlington, Texas, after Hurricane Katrina. While visiting family in Louisiana, Gulley (D) rear-ended the vehicle driven by Angela Ochoa (P), injuring her. Ochoa (P) is a resident of Louisiana. Gulley (D) was driving a rental car. Gulley (D) and the rental car company, PV Holding Corporation (D), removed the case to federal court, claiming that even though Gulley (D) had been a resident of Louisiana, he (D) has, since the hurricane, lived in Texas and intended to stay in Texas indefinitely. Gulley (D) lives and works in Texas, but he (D) has a Louisiana driver's license. He (D) has family in New Orleans, and he (D) had lived in New Orleans all his life, until being forced to leave.

ISSUE: Do evidence of recent employment in a state, along with a subjective statement of intent to live in the state indefinitely, necessarily satisfy a party's burden of showing diverse citizenship in order to invoke a court's subject matter jurisdiction?

HOLDING AND DECISION: (Feldman, J.) No. Evidence of recent employment in a state, along with a subjective statement of intent to live in the state indefinitely, do not necessarily satisfy a party's burden of showing diverse citizenship in order to invoke a court's subject matter jurisdiction. The lack of objective evidence to support Gulley's (D) statement of intent, his ties to New Orleans, and the fact that he was in New Orleans when the accident occurred undermine his claim that his domicile was Texas at the time the complaint was filed several months prior. Because he failed to carry his burden to show he was a citizen of Texas at the time the complaint

was filed, the court lacks removal jurisdiction based on diversity of citizenship and Ochoa's (P) motion to remand is granted.

ANALYSIS

Establishing a new domicile—and demonstrating intent to establish a new domicile—is not difficult under the law. Objective evidence to support a statement of intent to remain in a state might take form in a new driver's license, a new bank account, or a lease on a new apartment.

Quicknotes

DIVERSITY OF CITIZENSHIP Parties are citizens of different states, or one party is an alien; a factor, along with a statutorily set dollar value of the matter in controversy, that allows a federal district court to exercise its authority to hear a lawsuit based on diversity jurisdiction.

DOMICILE A person's permanent home or principal establishment to which he has an intention of returning when he is absent therefrom.

REMAND To send back for additional scrutiny or deliberation.

SUBJECT MATTER JURISDICTION The authority of the court to hear and decide actions involving a particular type of issue or subject.

United Mine Workers of America v. Gibbs

International union (D) v. Threatened superintendent (P)

383 U.S. 715 (1966).

NATURE OF CASE: Review of award of damages for violation of § 303 of the Labor Management Relations Act and for interference with a business interest.

FACT SUMMARY: Gibbs (P) lost his job as superintendent of a coal mining company because of alleged unlawful influence of United Mine Workers (D).

🏛 RULE OF LAW
Under pendent jurisdiction, federal courts may decide state issues that are closely related to the federal issues being litigated.

FACTS: There was a dispute between United Mine Workers (D) and the Southern Labor Union over who should represent the coal miners in that area. Tennessee Consolidated Coal Company closed down a mine where over 100 men belonging to United Mine Workers (D) were employed. Later, Grundy Company, a wholly owned subsidiary of Tennessee Consolidated Coal Company, hired Gibbs (P) to open a new mine using members of the Southern Labor Union. Gibbs (P) was also given a contract to haul the mine's coal to the nearest railroad loading point. Members of Local 5881 of the United Mine Workers (D) forcibly prevented the opening of the mine. Gibbs (P) lost his job and never entered into performance of his haulage contract. He soon began to lose other trucking contracts and mine leases he held in the area. Gibbs (P) claimed this was a result of a concerted union plan against him. He filed suit in the United States District Court for the Eastern District of Tennessee for violation of § 303 of the Labor Management Relations Act and a state law claim, based on the doctrine of pendent jurisdiction, that there was an unlawful conspiracy and boycott aimed at him to interfere with his contract of employment and with his contract of haulage. The jury's verdict was that the United Mine Workers (D) had violated both § 303 and the state law. On motion, the trial court set aside the award of damages for the haulage contracts and entered a verdict for United Mine Workers (D) on the issue of violation of § 303, which was the federal claim. The award as to the state claim was sustained. The court of appeals affirmed.

ISSUE: Can federal courts decide state issues that are closely related to the federal issues being litigated?

HOLDING AND DECISION: (Brennan, J.) Yes. When there are both state and federal claims involved in the same set of facts and the claims are such that the plaintiff would ordinarily be expected to try them all in one judicial proceeding, the federal court has the power to hear both the state and the federal claims. The federal claims must have substance sufficient to confer subject matter jurisdiction on the court. This is the doctrine of pendent jurisdiction. The court isn't required to exercise this power in every case. It has consistently been recognized that pendent jurisdiction is a doctrine of discretion, not of plaintiff's right. The court should look at judicial economy, convenience, and fairness to litigants in deciding whether to exercise jurisdiction over the state claims. If the factual relationship between the state and federal claims is so close that they ought to be litigated at the same trial, the court ought to grant pendent jurisdiction in order to save an extra trial. If the issues are so complicated that they are confusing to the jury, then the court probably should dismiss the state claims. The issue of whether pendent jurisdiction has been properly assumed is one that remains open throughout the litigation. If, before the trial, the federal claim is dismissed, then the state claim should also be dismissed. The court went on to hold that the plaintiff could not recover damages for conspiracy under the state claim. Reversed.

▶ ANALYSIS

This case helped clarify the law that had been established by the case of *Hurn v. Oursler*, 289 U.S. 238 (1933). That case set the rule for determining if a federal court could hear the state claim. If a case had two distinct grounds in support of a single cause of action, one of which presents a federal question, then the court could hear the state claim. But if a case had two separate and distinct causes of action and only one was a federal question, then the court could not hear the state claim. Now, the state and federal claims can state separate causes of action so long as they are factually closely related.

◼══◼

Quicknotes

BOYCOTT A concerted effort to refrain from doing business with a particular person or entity.

CONSPIRACY Concerted action by two or more persons to accomplish some unlawful purpose.

LABOR MANAGEMENT RELATIONS ACT Federal law prohibiting secondary boycotts.

PENDENT JURISDICTION A doctrine granting authority to a federal court to hear a claim that does not invoke diversity jurisdiction if it arises from the same transaction or occurrence as the primary action.

◼══◼

Owen Equipment and Erection Company v. Kroger

Crane company (D) v. Wife of electrocuted decedent (P)

437 U.S. 365 (1978).

NATURE OF CASE: Appeal from an action for damages for wrongful death.

FACT SUMMARY: Kroger (P), the widow of decedent, filed a wrongful death action against Omaha Public Power District after her husband was electrocuted when a steel crane hit a power line.

🏛 RULE OF LAW
In an action in which federal jurisdiction is based on diversity, a plaintiff may not assert a claim against a third-party defendant when there is no independent basis for federal jurisdiction over that claim.

FACTS: James Kroger was electrocuted when the boom of a steel crane next to which he was walking came too close to a high-tension electric power line. Kroger (P), the decedent's widow, filed a wrongful death action in the U.S. District Court for Nebraska against Omaha Public Power District (Omaha). Kroger's (P) complaint alleged that Omaha's negligence had caused her husband's death. Federal jurisdiction was based on diversity, since Kroger (P) was a citizen of Iowa and Omaha was a Nebraska corporation. Omaha then filed a third-party complaint pursuant to Rule 14 against Owen Equipment and Erection Company (Owen) (D), alleging that the crane was owned and operated by Owen (D) and that Owen's (D) negligence had been the proximate cause of Kroger's (P) death. While a motion for summary judgment on the part of Omaha was pending, Kroger (P) was granted leave to file an amended complaint naming Owen (D) as an additional defendant. Omaha's motion was granted, and the case went to trial between Kroger (P) and Owen (D). At trial, it was disclosed that Owen (D) was an Iowa corporation and not a Nebraska corporation as was alleged and that Kroger (P) and Owen (D) were, thus, both citizens of Iowa. Owen (D) moved to dismiss the complaint for lack of jurisdiction. The court reserved decision on the motion, and the jury returned a verdict in favor of Kroger (P). Then the court denied the motion to dismiss. The judgment was affirmed on appeal. The court of appeals held that the district court had power to adjudicate the claim because it arose from the core of operative facts giving rise to both Kroger's (P) claim against Omaha and Omaha's claim against Owen (D). Owen (D) appealed.

ISSUE: In an action in which federal jurisdiction is based on diversity, may the plaintiff assert a claim against a third-party defendant when there is no independent basis for federal jurisdiction over that claim?

HOLDING AND DECISION: (Stewart, J.) No. In an action in which federal jurisdiction is based on diversity, the plaintiff may not assert a claim against a third-party defendant when there is no independent basis for federal jurisdiction over that claim. Section 1332 confers upon federal courts jurisdiction over civil actions where the matter in controversy exceeds the sum of $10,000 and is between citizens of different states. Thus, it is clear that Kroger (P) could not originally have brought suit in federal court naming Owen (D) and Omaha as codefendants, since citizens of Iowa would have been on both sides of the litigation. Yet, the identical lawsuit resulted when Kroger (P) amended her complaint. Complete diversity was destroyed just as surely as if Kroger (P) had sued Owen (D) initially. If, as the court of appeals thought, a common nucleus of operative fact were the only requirement for ancillary jurisdiction in a diversity case, there would be no principled reason why Kroger (P) could not have joined her cause of action against Owen (D) in her original complaint as ancillary to her cause against Omaha. Congress's requirement of complete diversity would thus have been evaded completely. Reversed.

▶ ANALYSIS

The court of appeals relied upon the doctrine of ancillary jurisdiction as enunciated in *Mine Workers v. Gibbs,* 383 U.S. 715 (1966). However, the *Gibbs* case differed from this one in that it involved pendent jurisdiction, which concerns the resolution of a plaintiff's federal and state law claims against a single defendant in one action. In this claim, there was no claim based on substantive federal law.

■━■

Quicknotes

28 U.S.C. § 1332 Provides for original jurisdiction in federal district court all civil actions between citizens of different states.

ANCILLARY JURISDICTION Authority of a federal court to hear and determine issues related to a case over which it has jurisdiction, but over which it would not have jurisdiction if such claims were brought independently.

DIVERSITY OF CITIZENSHIP Parties are citizens of different states, or one party is an alien; a factor, along with a statutorily set dollar value of the matter in controversy, that allows a federal district court to exercise its authority to hear a lawsuit based on diversity jurisdiction.

Continued on next page.

PENDENT JURISDICTION   A doctrine granting authority to a federal court to hear a claim that does not invoke diversity jurisdiction if it arises from the same transaction or occurrence as the primary action.

SUMMARY JUDGMENT   Judgment rendered by a court in response to a motion by one of the parties, claiming that the lack of a question of material fact in respect to an issue warrants disposition of the issue without consideration by the jury.

WRONGFUL DEATH   An action brought by the beneficiaries of a deceased person, claiming that the deceased's death was the result of wrongful conduct by the defendant.

■■■■

- SBJ is never waived, you can raise it whenever.

- Scalia says must have SBJ, Common nucleus thing doesn't work for supp. juris.

P (IA) ——— v. ——> OPP D (NE)

kroger

no diversity

moved for summary judg

PVS (NE)
Owner (NE) (third party plaintiff)
filed motion for SJ.

Finley v. United States

Federal Tort Claims Act claimant (P) v. Federal government (D)

490 U.S. 545 (1989).

NATURE OF CASE: Appeal from denial of pendent-party jurisdiction.

FACT SUMMARY: Finley's (P) husband and children were killed in a plane crash. In her federal suit under the Federal Tort Claims Act against the Federal Aviation Administration, she sought to include claims against certain state defendants on the basis of pendent-party jurisdiction.

🏛 RULE OF LAW
The Federal Tort Claims Act does not permit the assertion of pendent-party jurisdiction over additional parties.

FACTS: Finley's (P) husband and children were killed in a plane crash that Finley (P) believed resulted from the negligence of a power company against which she brought suit in state court, alleging the negligent illumination of runway lights and negligent positioning of electric transmission lines of the power company. Subsequently, Finley (P) learned that the party responsible for maintaining runway lights was the Federal Aviation Administration, and she filed a Federal Tort Claims Act suit against the United States (D) in federal district court. A year later, Finley (P) moved to amend the federal complaint to include claims against the original state-court defendants, as to which no independent basis for federal jurisdiction existed. The district court granted the motion. The court of appeals reversed, and the U.S. Supreme Court affirmed the reversal.

ISSUE: Does the Federal Tort Claims Act permit the assertion of pendent-party jurisdiction over additional parties?

HOLDING AND DECISION: (Scalia, J.) No. The added claims in this case involve added parties over whom no independent basis of jurisdiction exists. The relationship between the added claims and the original complaint is one of mere "factual similarity," which is of no consequence, as neither the convenience of the litigants nor considerations of judicial economy can suffice to justify extension of the doctrine of ancillary jurisdiction. The Federal Tort Claims Act confers jurisdiction over "civil actions on claims against the United States," but the Act does *not* say "civil actions on claims that include requested relief against the United States" or "civil actions in which there is a claim against the United States." The latter would be formulations one might expect if the presence of a claim against the United States constituted merely a minimum jurisdictional

requirement, rather than a definition of the permissible scope of Federal Tort Claims Act actions. Affirmed.

DISSENT: (Blackmun, J.) Because congressional preference here made the federal forum the only possible one in which to hear the constitutional case as a whole, pendent-party jurisdiction should be permitted.

DISSENT: (Stevens, J.) The congressional grant of jurisdiction to hear "civil actions on claims against the United States" authorizes the federal courts to hear state-law claims against a pendent party. Forcing a federal plaintiff to litigate a case in both federal and state courts impairs the ability of the federal court to grant full relief and imparts a fundamental bias against utilization of the federal forum owing to the deterrent effect imposed by the needless requirement of duplicate litigation if the federal forum is chosen.

▶ ANALYSIS

The Court majority made clear that due regard for the rightful independence of state governments requires that federal courts scrupulously confine their own jurisdiction to the precise limits that a federal statute (in this case the Federal Tort Claims Act) has defined. Subsequent to *Finley,* Congress enacted a new supplemental jurisdiction statute that allows for pendent-party jurisdiction unless a federal statute specifically precludes it.

■==■

Quicknotes

ANCILLARY JURISDICTION Authority of a federal court to hear and determine issues related to a case over which it has jurisdiction, but over which it would not have jurisdiction if such claims were brought independently.

FEDERAL TORT CLAIMS ACT (FTCA) Legislation that provides a limited waiver of the federal government's sovereign immunity when its employees are negligent within the scope of their employment. The government is liable if a law enforcement officer commits assault, battery, false imprisonment, false arrest, abuse of process, or malicious prosecution. The government is not liable if the claim against law enforcement officers is for libel, slander, misrepresentation, deceit, or interference with contract. Congress has not waived the government's sovereign immunity against all law enforcement acts or omissions.

Continued on next page.

JURISDICTION The authority of a court to hear and declare judgment in respect to a particular matter.

PENDENT JURISDICTION A doctrine granting authority to a federal court to hear a claim that does not invoke diversity jurisdiction if it arises from the same transaction or occurrence as the primary action.

■━■

this is now allowed as long as there is "same case or controversy".

Finley ——1331——> FAA
    no SJJ, no divest ——> SDGE (CA)

Arising under 1331

- Common nucleus analysis doesn't work like scalia decided.
- this closes the state juris & fed juris
   └> that's why 1367(b) was made by congress.

° 1367 - overruls Finley & codifies Gibbs & kroger
      └> it reinstates "the same case or controversy".

CHAPTER 9

Choice of Federal or State Law—The *Erie* Doctrine

Quick Reference Rules of Law

Erie Railroad Co. v. Tompkins

Railroad (D) v. Injured (P)

304 U.S. 64 (1938).

(handwritten margin note, left side, rotated): 1) they should apply unwritten law of the statood declared by the highest court

NATURE OF CASE: Action to recover damages for personal injury allegedly caused by negligent conduct.

FACT SUMMARY: In a personal injury suit, federal district court trial judge refused to apply applicable state law because such law was "general" (judge-made) and not embodied in any statute.

🏛 RULE OF LAW
Although the 1789 Rules of Decision Act left federal courts unfettered to apply their own rules of procedure in common law actions brought in federal court, state law governs substantive issues. State law includes not only statutory law but case law as well.

FACTS: Tompkins (P) was walking in a right-of-way parallel to some railroad tracks when an Erie Railroad Co. (Erie) (D) train came by. Tompkins (P) was struck and injured by what he would, at trial, claim to be an open door extending from one of the railcars. Under Pennsylvania case law (the applicable law since the accident occurred there), state courts would have treated Tompkins (P) as a trespasser in denying him recovery for other than wanton or willful misconduct on Erie's (D) part. Under "general" law, recognized in federal courts, Tompkins (P) would have been regarded as a licensee and would only have been obligated to show ordinary negligence. Because Erie (D) was a New York corporation, Tompkins (P) brought suit in a federal district court in New York, where he won a judgment for $30,000. Upon appeal to a federal circuit court, the decision was affirmed.

ISSUE: Was the trial court in error in refusing to recognize state case law as the proper rule of decision in deciding the substantive issue of liability?

HOLDING AND DECISION: (Brandeis, J.) Yes. The Court's opinion is in four parts. (1) *Swift v. Tyson*, 41 U.S. (16 Pet.) 1 (1842), which held that federal courts exercising jurisdiction on the ground of diversity of citizenship need not, in matters of general jurisprudence, apply the unwritten law of the state as declared by its highest court, is overruled. Section 34 of the Federal Judiciary Act of 1789, c. 20, 28 U.S.C. § 725, requires that federal courts, in all matters except those where some federal law is controlling, apply as their rules of decision the law of the state, unwritten as well as written. Up to this time, federal courts had assumed the power to make "general law" decisions even though Congress was powerless to enact "general law" statutes. (2) *Swift* had numerous political and social defects. The hoped-for uniformity among state courts had not occurred; there was no satisfactory way

to distinguish between local and general law. On the other hand, *Swift* introduced grave discrimination by noncitizens against citizens. The privilege of selecting the court for resolving disputes rested with the noncitizen who could pick the more favorable forum. The resulting far-reaching discrimination was due to the broad province accorded "general law" in which many matters of seemingly local concern were included. Furthermore, local citizens could move out of the state and bring suit in a federal court if they were disposed to do so; corporations, similarly, could simply reincorporate in another state. More than statutory relief is involved here; the unconstitutionality of *Swift* is clear. (3) Except in matters governed by the federal Constitution or by acts of Congress, the law to be applied in any case is the law of the state. There is no federal common law. The federal courts have no power derived from the Constitution or by Congress to declare substantive rules of common law applicable in a state whether they are "local" or "general" in nature. (4) The federal district court was bound to follow the Pennsylvania case law, which would have denied recovery to Tompkins (P). Reversed.

CONCURRENCE: (Reed, J.) It is unnecessary to go beyond interpreting the meaning of "laws" in the Rules of Decision Act. Article III, and the Necessary and Proper Clause of Article I of the Constitution, might provide Congress with the power to declare rules of substantive law for federal courts to follow.

▌ *ANALYSIS*

Erie can fairly be characterized as the most significant and sweeping decision on civil procedure ever handed down by the U.S. Supreme Court. As interpreted in subsequent decisions, *Erie* held that while federal courts may apply their own rules of procedure, issues of substantive law must be decided in accord with the applicable state law—usually the state in which the federal court sits. Note, however, how later Supreme Court decisions have made inroads into the broad doctrine enunciated here.

■=■

Quicknotes

DIVERSITY OF CITIZENSHIP Parties are citizens of different states, or one party is an alien; a factor, along with a statutorily set dollar value of the matter in controversy, that allows a federal district court to exercise its authority to hear a lawsuit based on diversity jurisdiction.

Continued on next page.

FEDERAL JUDICIARY ACT § 34   The laws of the states shall be regarded as rules of decisions in trials at common law in the federal courts.

JURISDICTION   The authority of a court to hear and declare judgment in respect to a particular matter.

NECESSARY AND PROPER CLAUSE, ACT I, § 8 OF THE CONSTITUTION   Enables Congress to make all laws that may be "necessary and proper" to execute its other, enumerated powers.

NEGLIGENCE   Conduct falling below the standard of care that a reasonable person would demonstrate under similar conditions.

PERSONAL INJURY   Harm to an individual's person or body.

RULES OF DECISION ACT   Provides that the laws of the several states shall be regarded as rules of decisions in civil action, except where the Constitution, treaties, or acts of Congress otherwise provide.

■═■

Guaranty Trust Co. v. York

Trust company (D) v. Injured class members (P)

326 U.S. 99 (1945).

NATURE OF CASE: Class action suit for breach of trust.

FACT SUMMARY: York (P) brought a class action suit against Guaranty Trust Co. (D) in federal court on diversity jurisdiction. The action was barred in the state courts by the statute of limitations, and summary judgment was granted to Guaranty Trust (D) on that basis.

> 🏛 **RULE OF LAW**
> In all cases where a federal court is exercising diversity jurisdiction, the outcome of the case should be substantially the same, so far as legal rules determine outcome, as it would be if tried in state court.

FACTS: York (P) brought suit in federal district court in New York on behalf of a class of persons allegedly damaged by Guaranty Trust Co.'s (D) breach of trust. The suit was brought in 1942 but complained of transactions occurring in 1931. Guaranty Trust (D) was granted a summary judgment on the grounds that the action was barred by the New York statute of limitations and that this suit being heard on diversity jurisdiction was governed by the statute. The court of appeals reversed, stating that suits in equity were not controlled by the state statute of limitations.

ISSUE: Where a suit brought in federal court on diversity jurisdiction would be barred by statute if brought in the state court, may the federal court nonetheless hear the case on its merits?

HOLDING AND DECISION: (Frankfurter, J.) No. In all cases where a federal court is exercising diversity jurisdiction, the outcome of the case should be substantially the same, so far as legal rules determine outcome, as it would be if tried in state court. Since this Court's decision in *Erie Railroad Co. v. Tompkins*, 304 U.S. 64 (1938), a considerable amount of divergence has developed over what matters are procedural and what are substantive. Since these two concepts are fluid and situation-controlled in most instances, the debate misses the underlying rationale of *Erie*. When sitting in diversity jurisdiction, a federal court is but another state court. The controlling factor is whether, by reason of application of differing federal rules, an outcome substantially different would result than if the case were brought in state court. The rules of law applied to the case cannot allow or bar recovery in the federal court where an opposite result would occur in the state court. For that reason, the summary judgment granted by the trial court is sustained. Reversed and remanded.

▶ **ANALYSIS**

Guaranty Trust, which clarified *Erie,* may itself be in the process of being slowly eroded by modern courts. *Hanna v. Plumer,* 380 U.S. 460 (1965), held that where state law conflicts with the Federal Rules of Civil Procedure, the latter prevails regardless of the effect on outcome of the litigation. And in *Byrd v. Blue Ridge Rural Electric Cooperative, Inc.,* 356 U.S. 525 (1958), the Court suggested that some constitutional doctrines (there, the right to a jury trial in federal court) are so important as to be controlling over state law—once again, the outcome notwithstanding.

■━■

Quicknotes

CLASS ACTION SUIT A suit commenced by a representative on behalf of an ascertainable group that is too large to appear in court, who shares a commonality of interests and who will benefit from a successful result.

DIVERSITY JURISDICTION The authority of a federal court to hear and determine cases involving parties who are of different states and an amount in controversy greater than a statutorily set amount.

STATUTE OF LIMITATIONS A law prescribing the period in which a legal action may be commenced.

SUMMARY JUDGMENT Judgment rendered by a court in response to a motion by one of the parties, claiming that the lack of a question of material fact in respect to an issue warrants disposition of the issue without consideration by the jury.

■━■

Byrd v. Blue Ridge Rural Electric Cooperative, Inc.

Employee of subcontractor (P) v. General contractor (D)

356 U.S. 525 (1958).

NATURE OF CASE: Negligence action for damages.

FACT SUMMARY: Byrd (P) was injured while connecting power lines for a subcontractor of Blue Ridge Rural Electric Cooperative, Inc. (D).

🏛 RULE OF LAW
The *Erie* doctrine requires that federal courts in diversity cases must respect the definitions of rights and obligations created by state courts, but state laws cannot alter the essential characteristics and functions of the federal courts, and the jury function is such an essential function (provided for in the Seventh Amendment).

FACTS: Byrd (P) was injured while connecting power lines as an employee of a subcontractor of Blue Ridge Rural Electric Cooperative, Inc. (Blue Ridge) (D). He sued Blue Ridge (D) in federal court on a negligence theory. Because he was a citizen of North Carolina and Blue Ridge (D) was a South Carolina corporation, jurisdiction was grounded in diversity of citizenship. At trial, Blue Ridge (D) offered an affirmative defense based on a South Carolina law that would limit Byrd (P) to workmen's compensation benefits by defining him as a statutory employee of Blue Ridge (D) as well as the subcontractor (thereby precluding any collateral negligence action). The trial court refused to allow the defense to be offered, but the U.S. Supreme Court reversed and remanded the case to the trial court for a new trial allowing the defense. Under South Carolina law, however, the issue of immunity from negligence was to be tried by a judge. Blue Ridge (D) claimed that despite the *Erie* doctrine, South Carolina law cannot be allowed to preclude his right to a jury.

ISSUE: Do *Erie* doctrine considerations require that all state determinations of rights be upheld regardless of their intrusions into federal determinations?

HOLDING AND DECISION: (Brennan, J.) No. The *Erie* doctrine requires that federal courts in diversity cases must respect the definitions of rights and obligations created by state courts, but state laws cannot alter the essential characteristics and functions of the federal courts, and the jury function is such an essential function (provided for in the Seventh Amendment). The South Carolina determination here that immunity is a question of law to be tried by a judge is merely a determination of the form and mode of enforcing immunity. It does not involve any essential relationship or determination of right created by the state. Of course, the *Erie* doctrine will reach even such form and mode determinations where no affirmative

countervailing considerations can be found. Here, however, the Seventh Amendment makes the jury function an essential factor in the federal process protected by the Constitution. Reversed and remanded. On remand, the court must permit a jury trial.

▶ ANALYSIS

This case points up a major retreat by the Court in its interpretation of the *Erie* doctrine. The *Guaranty Trust* case, 326 U.S. 99 (1945), had stated that the *Erie* doctrine required that federal courts not tamper with state remedies for violations of state-created rights. In *Byrd,* the Court retreats, stating that questions of mere "form and mode" of remedy (i.e., trial by jury or judge) are not necessarily the province of the states where essential federal rights (i.e., Seventh Amendment) are involved. Note that the Court does not abandon the *Guaranty Trust* rationale, however (that the outcome of a case should not be affected by the choice of court in which it is filed). The Court expresses doubt that the permitting of trial by jury here will make any difference in the final argument here, since the Court first states that trial by jury is an essential right, and then states that it is really insignificant after all.

■═■

Quicknotes

DIVERSITY OF CITIZENSHIP Parties are citizens of different states, or one party is an alien; a factor, along with a statutorily set dollar value of the matter in controversy, that allows a federal district court to exercise its authority to hear a lawsuit based on diversity jurisdiction.

IMMUNITY Exemption from a legal obligation.

NEGLIGENCE Conduct falling below the standard of care that a reasonable person would demonstrate under similar conditions.

SEVENTH AMENDMENT Provides that no fact tried by a jury shall be otherwise re-examined in any court of the United States, other than according to the rules of the common law.

■═■

Hanna v. Plumer

Injured (P) v. Estate executor (D)

380 U.S. 460 (1965).

NATURE OF CASE: Appeal of summary judgment in federal diversity tort action.

FACT SUMMARY: Hanna (P) filed tort action in federal court in Massachusetts, where Plumer (D) resided, for an auto accident that occurred in South Carolina.

🏛 RULE OF LAW

The *Erie* doctrine mandates that federal courts are to apply state substantive law and federal procedural law, but, where matters fall roughly between the two and are rationally capable of classification as either, the Constitution grants the federal court system the power to regulate their practice and pleading (procedure).

FACTS: Hanna (P), a citizen of Ohio, filed a tort action in federal court in Massachusetts against Plumer (D), the executor of the estate of Louise Plumer Osgood, a Massachusetts citizen. It was alleged that Mrs. Osgood caused injuries to Hanna (P) in an auto accident in South Carolina. Service on Plumer (D) was accomplished pursuant to Fed. R. Civ. P. 4(d)(1) by leaving copies of the summons with Plumer's (D) wife. At trial, motion for summary judgment should have been accomplished pursuant to Massachusetts law (by the *Erie* doctrine), which requires service by hand to the party personally. On appeal, Hanna (P) contended Rules of Civil Procedure apply to this case. Plumer (D), however, contended that: (1) a substantive law question under *Erie* is any question in which permitting application of federal law would alter the outcome of the case (the so-called "outcome determination" test); (2) the application of federal law here i.e., 4[d][1] will necessarily affect the outcome of the case (from a necessary dismissal to litigation); and, so, therefore (3) *Erie* requires that the state substantive law requirement of service by hand be upheld along with the trial court's summary judgment.

ISSUE: Does the *Erie* doctrine classification of "substantive law questions" extend to embrace questions involving both substantive and procedural considerations merely because such a question might have an effect on the determination of the substantive outcome of the case?

HOLDING AND DECISION: (Warren, C.J.) No. The *Erie* doctrine mandates that federal courts are to apply state substantive law and federal procedural law, but, where matters fall roughly between the two and are rationally capable of classification as either, the Constitution grants the federal court system the power to regulate their practice and pleading (procedure). It is well settled that the

Enabling Act for the Federal Rules of Civil Procedure requires that a procedural effect of any rule on the outcome of a case be shown to actually "abridge, enlarge or modify" the substantive law in a case for the *Erie* doctrine to come into play. Where, as here, the question only goes to procedural requirements (e.g., service of summons; a dismissal for improper service here would not alter the substantive right of Hanna (P) to serve Plumer (D) personally and refile or effect the substantive law of negligence in the case), Article III and the Necessary and Proper Clause provide that the Congress has a right to provide rules for the federal court system such as Fed. R. Civ. P. 4(d)(1). "Outcome determination analysis was never intended to serve as a talisman" for the *Erie* doctrine. Reversed.

CONCURRENCE: (Harlan, J.) Justice Harlan agrees with the result of the Court and its rejection of the outcome determination lest. He argues, however, that the Court was wrong in stating that anything arguably procedural is constitutionally placed within the province of the federal government to regulate.

▶ *ANALYSIS*

This case points a return to the basic rationales of *Erie R. Co. v. Tompkins*, 304 U.S. 64 (1938). First, the Court asserts that one important consideration in determining how a particular question should be classified (substantive or procedural) is the avoidance of "forum shopping" (the practice of choosing one forum, such as federal, in which to file in order to gain the advantages of that forum), which permits jurisdictions to infringe on the substantive law defining powers of each other. Second, the Court seeks to avoid inequitable administration of the laws that would result from allowing jurisdictional considerations to determine substantive rights. Justice Warren, here, in rejecting the "outcome determination" test asserts that any rule must be measured ultimately against the Federal Rules Enabling Act and the Constitution.

■=■

Quicknotes

ARTICLE III, U.S. CONSTITUTION Limits federal judicial power to cases and controversies.

DIVERSITY ACTION An action commenced by a citizen of one state against a citizen of another state or against an alien, involving an amount in controversy set by statute, over which the federal court has jurisdiction.

Continued on next page.

ENABLING ACT A statute that confers new powers upon a person or entity.

FED. R. CIV. P. 4(d)(1) Governs service of process.

JURISDICTION The authority of a court to hear and declare judgment in respect to a particular matter.

NECESSARY AND PROPER CLAUSE, ACT I, § 8 OF THE CONSTITUTION Enables Congress to make all laws that may be "necessary and proper" to execute its other, enumerated powers.

SUMMARY JUDGMENT Judgment rendered by a court in response to a motion by one of the parties, claiming that the lack of a question of material fact in respect to an issue warrants disposition of the issue without consideration by the jury.

TORT A legal wrong resulting in a breach of duty, which is intentionally or purposefully committed by the wrongdoer.

Walker v. Armco Steel Corp.

Injured carpenter (P) v. Nail manufacturer (D)

446 U.S. 740 (1980).

NATURE OF CASE: Appeal from dismissal of complaint for personal injuries.

FACT SUMMARY: Walker (P) contended that Fed. R. of Civ. P. 3 governed the manner in which an action is commenced in federal court for all purposes, including the tolling of the state statute of limitations.

🏛 RULE OF LAW
In diversity actions, Fed. R. Civ. P. 3 governs the date from which timing requirements of the federal rules begin to run but does not affect state statutes of limitations.

FACTS: Walker (P), a carpenter, was injured on August 22, 1975, while pounding a Sheffield nail manufactured by Armco Steel Corp. (Armco) (D) into a cement wall. Since there was diversity of citizenship, suit was brought in the U.S. District Court for the Western District of Oklahoma. The complaint was filed on August 19, 1977, but service of process was not made until December 1, 1977. On January 5, 1978, Armco (D) filed a motion to dismiss the complaint on the ground that the action was barred by the Oklahoma statute of limitations, which stated that an action is not commenced for purposes of the statute of limitations until service of the summons on the defendant. In his reply brief, Walker (P) admitted that his case would be foreclosed in state court but argued that Fed. R. Civ. P. 3 governs the manner in which an action is commenced in federal court for all purposes, including the tolling of the state statute of limitations. Fed. R. Civ. P. 3 states that an action is commenced by filing a complaint with the court. After the court of appeals affirmed the district court's dismissal of the action as barred by the Oklahoma two-year statute of limitations, Walker (P) appealed.

ISSUE: In diversity actions, does Fed. R. Civ. P. 3 affect state statutes of limitations?

HOLDING AND DECISION: (Marshall, J.) No. In diversity actions, Fed. R. Civ. P. 3 governs the date from which various timing requirements of the federal rules begin to run but does not affect state statutes of limitations. Rule 3 simply states that a civil action is commenced by filing a complaint with the court. There is no indication that the rule was intended to toll a state statute of limitations, much less that it purported to displace state tolling rules for purposes of state statutes of limitations. In contrast to Rule 3, the Oklahoma statute is a statement of a substantive decision by that state that actual service on and actual notice on the defendant are integral parts of the several policies served by the statute of limitations. Affirmed.

▶ ANALYSIS

The Court in this case applied the rules enunciated in *Erie Railroad Co. v. Tompkins,* 304 U.S. 64 (1938), regarding the application of state law in federal diversity actions. In the *Erie* case, the Court held that "except in matters governed by the Federal Constitution or by Acts of Congress, the law to be applied in any (diversity) case is the law of the State." Id. at 78.

Quicknotes

COMPLAINT The initial pleading commencing litigation that sets forth a claim for relief.

DIVERSITY OF CITIZENSHIP Parties are citizens of different states, or one party is an alien; a factor, along with a statutorily set dollar value of the matter in controversy, that allows a federal district court to exercise its authority to hear a lawsuit based on diversity jurisdiction.

STATUTE OF LIMITATIONS A law prescribing the period in which a legal action may be commenced.

Gasperini v. Center for Humanities, Inc.

Journalist (P) v. Educational publisher (D)

518 U.S. 415 (1996).

NATURE OF CASE: Review of appeal overturning a jury verdict as excessive in action for breach of contract, conversion, and negligence.

FACT SUMMARY: A federal circuit court, hearing a case on diversity jurisdiction, let stand a jury verdict of $450,000 for Gasperini's (P) lost photographic slides; the court of appeals, applying New York law governing excessive damage awards, set aside the verdict.

🏛 RULE OF LAW
A federal trial court can apply state law governing the excessiveness or inadequacy of compensation awards without running afoul of the Seventh Amendment's prohibition against re-examination of a fact tried by jury so long as the state standard is applied by the federal trial court judge, and appellate control of the trial court ruling is limited to review for "abuse of discretion."

FACTS: Gasperini (P), a journalist, agreed to supply his original color transparencies to the Center for Humanities, Inc. (Center) (D) for use in an educational videotape. He selected 300 slides; the Center (D) agreed to return the slides, but it could not find them at the end of the project. Gasperini (P) filed suit in the U.S. District Court for the Southern District of New York, invoking the court's diversity jurisdiction. He alleged several state law claims. The Center (D) conceded liability, and the issue of damages was tried before a jury. The jury awarded Gasperini (P) $450,000 in compensatory damages. The Center (D) attacked the verdict on excessiveness grounds. The district court denied the motion. On appeal, the court of appeals vacated the jury verdict. Applying New York's CPLR § 5501(c), which permits the ordering of a new trial where an award deviates materially from what is reasonable compensation, the court concluded that evidence at trial was insufficient to determine such a damage award. The appellate court ordered a new trial unless Gasperini (P) accepted an award of $100,000. Gasperini (P) appealed to the U.S. Supreme Court.

ISSUE: Can a federal trial court apply state law governing the excessiveness or inadequacy of compensation awards without running afoul of the Seventh Amendment's prohibition against re-examining a fact tried by jury?

HOLDING AND DECISION: (Ginsburg, J.) Yes. A federal trial court can apply state law governing the excessiveness or inadequacy of compensation awards without running afoul of the Seventh Amendment's prohibition against re-examination of a fact tried by jury so long as the state standard is applied by the federal trial court judge, and appellate control of the trial court ruling is limited to review for "abuse of discretion." The Seventh Amendment, which governs proceedings in federal court but not in state court, provides that "no fact tried by a jury, shall be otherwise re-examined in any Court of the United States. . . ." When a federal court hears a case under diversity jurisdiction, the court applies state substantive law and federal procedural law. However, classification of a law as substantive or procedural is often difficult. The various circuits have at times set aside awards using "abuse of discretion" as their standard. In such cases, the appellate courts have held that the damages award is no longer a question of fact, but a question of law. However, the federal system and the constraints of the Seventh Amendment must be harmonized with the application of state law. Thus, the district court has the responsibility to apply state laws governing excessive damages awards, and the appellate court must review for abuse of discretion. In this case, the district court should have applied § 5501(c) to determine whether the award deviated materially from reasonableness. The appellate court was constrained to review for abuse of discretion. The judgment of the appellate court is vacated, and that court is instructed to remand so that the trial judge may test the jury's verdict against CPLR § 5501(c)'s "deviates materially" standard.

▶ ANALYSIS

The seminal case, *Erie Railroad Co. v. Tompkins,* 304 U.S. 64 (1938), first specified the "substantive" versus "procedural" distinction mentioned in this case. The goal of *Erie* was to prevent forum shopping between state and federal courts. However, Justice Scalia argued that by adopting different standards for appellate review between the state and federal courts, the incentive to forum shop was enhanced. This raises the question, though, as to just how influential a deviation in appellate review standards will be when parties are selecting the lower court forum in which to litigate their claims.

■➡■

Quicknotes

BREACH OF CONTRACT Unlawful failure by a party to perform its obligations pursuant to contract.

CONVERSION The act of depriving an owner of his property without permission or justification.

Continued on next page.

DIVERSITY JURISDICTION The authority of a federal court to hear and determine cases involving $10,000 or more and in which the parties are citizens of different states, or in which one party is an alien.

NEGLIGENCE Conduct falling below the standard of care that a reasonable person would demonstrate under similar conditions.

SEVENTH AMENDMENT Provides that no fact tried by a jury shall be otherwise re-examined in any court of the United States, other than according to the rules of the common law.

■══■

Shady Grove Orthopedic Associates v. Allstate Insurance Company

Medical association (P) v. Insurance company (D)

130 S. Ct. 1431 (2010).

NATURE OF CASE:
Grant of a writ of certiorari.

FACT SUMMARY:
Shady Grove Orthopedics Associates (P) sued Allstate Insurance Company (Allstate) (D) for the insurance company's (D) alleged failure to pay interest on overdue insurance payments, on behalf of itself and a class of plaintiffs. The district court dismissed the case on the grounds that New York law prevented a class action lawsuit to recover "penalties," and the Second Circuit affirmed.

RULE OF LAW
Federal Rule of Civil Procedure 23 preempts state law as to when a class action lawsuit may be filed in federal court.

FACTS:
Shady Grove Orthopedic Associates (Shady Grove) (P) provided medical care to Sonia Galvez for her injuries resulting from a car accident. Galvez had an automobile insurance policy from Allstate Insurance Company (Allstate) (D). Shady Grove (P) submitted a claim to Allstate (D) for Galvez's treatment. Allstate's (D) payment to Shady Grove (P) was late, and Allstate (D) refused to pay interest, a charge for which is allowable under New York law. Shady Grove (P) then filed a class action lawsuit in federal court, arguing that Allstate (D) violated New York law by failing to pay interest to policyholders. Allstate (D) moved to dismiss, arguing that under Section 901(b) of the New York Civil Practice Law and Rules, Shady Grove (P) and Galvez could not use a class action lawsuit to collect a statutory penalty unless specifically authorized under the statute, and that such a lawsuit was not specifically authorized by statute. Shady Grove (P) and Galvez argued that § 901(b) did not apply in federal courts because it was a procedural rule and it conflicted with Federal Rule of Civil Procedure 23, which governs class action lawsuits in federal court. The U.S. District Court for the Eastern District of New York held that Shady Grove's (P) class action claim was not authorized and thus dismissed its claim. The court found that New York insurance laws did not specifically authorize a class action for the recovery of interest, and, therefore, § 901(b) prevented the filing of the class action. On appeal, Shady Grove (P) argued that the New York law conflicts with Rule 23 and thus was not applicable. The U.S. Court of Appeals for the Second Circuit disagreed with Shady Grove (P) and affirmed the district court, reasoning that the New York rules of civil procedure did not conflict with Rule 23, and Rule 23 therefore did not control.

ISSUE:
Does Federal Rule of Civil Procedure 23 preempt state law as to when a class action lawsuit may be filed in federal court?

HOLDING AND DECISION:
(Scalia, J.) Yes. Federal Rule of Civil Procedure 23 preempts state law as to when a class action lawsuit may be filed in federal court. Section 901(b) of the New York rules of civil procedure does not preclude a federal court sitting in diversity from hearing a class action under Rule 23 of the federal rules of civil procedure. If Rule 23 answers the question in dispute, it governs, unless it exceeds its statutory authorization or Congress's rulemaking power. Here, Rule 23 answers the question in dispute—the question being whether Shady Grove's (P) suit may proceed as a class action—and is therefore controlling. The Rules Enabling Act, not *Erie*, controls the validity of a federal rule of civil procedure, even if that results in opening the federal courts to class actions that cannot proceed in state court. The concurrence's analysis conflicts with the Court's precedent in *Sibbach v. Wilson & Co.*, 312 U.S. 1 (1941)—that the federal rules "really regulate procedure." Reversed and remanded.

CONCURRENCE:
(Stevens, J.) Rule 23 applies in this case, but it also must be recognized that in some cases federal courts should apply state procedural rules in diversity cases, because they function as part of the state's definition of substantive rights and remedies.

DISSENT:
(Ginsburg, J.) The majority opinion used Rule 23 to override New York's statutory restriction on the availability of damages and consequently turned a $500 case into a $5,000,000 one. It is important to interpret the federal rules with sensitivity to state regulatory policies.

ANALYSIS

Forum shopping is a likely and important consequence of *Shady Grove*. If the federal rules preempt state statutes limiting class actions, as in this case, litigants will likely try to file in federal court. *Shady Grove* may therefore increase the number of class actions brought in federal court, and also might raise strategic considerations about removal for defendants sued in state courts. The plurality recognized this risk, acknowledging "the reality that keeping the federal-court door open to class actions that cannot proceed in state court will produce forum shopping."

Continued on next page.

Quicknotes

CLASS ACTION A suit commenced by a representative on behalf of an ascertainable group that is too large to appear in court, who shares a commonality of interests and who will benefit from a successful result.

FORUM SHOPPING Refers to a situation in which one party to an action seeks to have the matter heard and determined by a court or in a jurisdiction that will provide it with the most favorable result.

Finality and Preclusion

Quick Reference Rules of Law

Car Carriers, Inc. v. Ford Motor Company

Transport company (P) v. Major customer (D)

789 F.2d 589 (7th Cir. 1989).

NATURE OF CASE: Appeal from dismissal of suit on grounds of *res judicata*.

FACT SUMMARY: In 1982, Car Carriers, Inc. (P), an automobile transporter, sued Ford Motor Company (Ford) (D), its major customer, under the Sherman Antitrust Act. The district court dismissed the complaint with prejudice. In 1983, Car Carriers (P) brought a new complaint against Ford (D), utilizing the same basic fact situation, this time for alleged violations of the Racketeer Influenced and Corrupt Organizations Act (RICO) and the Interstate Commerce Act. The district court dismissed this suit based on *res judicata*.

> ### 🏛 RULE OF LAW
> *Res judicata* bars a second lawsuit arising from the same operative set of facts even when an analysis of the rights, duties, and injuries involved in the second lawsuit reveals that they are materially different from those at issue in the first.

FACTS: Car Carriers, Inc. (P), a company that hauled automobiles, alleged that Ford Motor Company (Ford) (D), its major customer, had for many years been entering into conspiracy against trade agreements. In 1982, Car Carriers (P) sued Ford (D) and others under the Sherman Antitrust Act. The district court dismissed the complaint on the grounds that the plaintiff did not suffer the type of harm that antitrust laws were designed to recompense. The court further found that because this defect was noncurable, the claims were dismissed with prejudice. In 1983 Car Carriers (P) brought a new complaint against Ford (D), utilizing the same basic fact situation, this time based on alleged violations of RICO and Interstate Commerce Act legislation. The district court dismissed this suit based on res judicata.

ISSUE: Does res judicata bar a second lawsuit arising from the same set of operative facts even when an analysis of the rights, duties, and injuries involved in the second lawsuit reveals that they are materially different from those in issue in the first?

HOLDING AND DECISION: (Ripple, J.) Yes. Under res judicata, a final judgment on the merits bars further claims by parties or their privies based on the same cause of action. A "cause of action" consists of a single core of operative facts that give rise to a remedy, a test that is decidedly fact oriented. Thus, a mere change in legal theory, as here, does *not* create a new cause of action. Therefore, the prior litigation as to these plaintiffs acts as a bar not only to those issues that were raised and decided in their earlier litigation but also to those issues that could have been raised in that litigation. In this case, plaintiff's Sherman Act, RICO, and Interstate Commerce claims essentially all arose from the same set of operative facts. Affirmed.

▶ ANALYSIS

The approach of this court is consistent with the general litigation scheme established by the Federal Rules of Civil Procedure in which litigants have great latitude in joining claims and amending pleadings. Thus, to further the purpose of the Federal Rules, courts have appropriately defined res judicata with sufficient breadth to encourage parties to present all their related claims at one time.

■━■

Quicknotes

COMPLAINT The initial pleading commencing litigation that sets forth a claim for relief.

CONSPIRACY Concerted action by two or more persons to accomplish some unlawful purpose.

INTERSTATE COMMERCE Commercial dealings between two parties located in different states or located in one state and accomplished through a point in another state or a foreign country; commercial dealings transacted between two states.

RACKETEER INFLUENCED AND CORRUPT ORGANIZATIONS ACT (RICO) Federal and state statutes enacted for the purpose of prosecuting organized crime.

RES JUDICATA The rule of law a final judgment by a court precludes subsequent litigation between the parties regarding the same cause of action.

■━■

Brent Taylor v. Robert A. Sturgell et al.

Private citizen (P) v. Government (D)

553 U.S. 880 (2008).

NATURE OF CASE: Grant of certiorari.

FACT SUMMARY: After a federal appeals court determined that Brent Taylor (P) could not pursue a suit in federal court because he had been "virtually represented" by an associate in a previous suit, Robert Taylor (Acting Administrator of the Federal Aviation Administration) (P) sought relief in the U.S. Supreme Court.

🏛 RULE OF LAW
The dismissal of a claim does not preclude a second individual, based on the concept of "virtual representation," from bringing a similar claim when both claims involve the same project and the parties to each suit are represented by the same attorney.

FACTS: Greg Herrick filed a Freedom of Information Act (FOIA) request seeking the plans and specifications for a rare aircraft from the Federal Aviation Administration (FAA) (D). The FAA (D) refused to turn over the plans as "protected trade secrets," and Herrick filed suit against the FAA (D) to recover the plans. The district court found for the FAA (D), and the U.S. Court of Appeals for the Tenth Circuit affirmed. A month later, Brent Taylor (P), represented by Herrick's attorney, filed another FOIA request seeking the plans. When the request was again denied, Taylor (P) filed suit in federal court in the District of Columbia. The district court determined that Robert A. Taylor (P) had been "virtually represented" by Herrick in the first suit and therefore could not pursue the second suit in federal court. The U.S. Court of Appeals for the D.C. Circuit affirmed. Taylor (P) sought relief in the U.S. Supreme Court, arguing that the D.C. Circuit's finding that Taylor (P) and Herrick enjoyed a close enough relationship for virtual representation to apply conflicted with tests employed by several other circuits.

ISSUE: Does the dismissal of a claim preclude a second individual, based on the concept of "virtual representation," from bringing a similar claim when both claims involve the same project and the parties to each suit are represented by the same attorney?

HOLDING AND DECISION: (Ginsburg, J.) No. The dismissal of a claim does not preclude a second individual, based on the concept of "virtual representation," from bringing a similar claim when both claims involve the same project and the parties to each suit are represented by the same attorney. "Nonparty preclusion" must be balanced against the historic tradition that everyone should have her own day in court. The general rule is against nonparty preclusion, but the general rule has some exceptions

that fall into six categories. First, a person who agrees to be bound by a judgment will be bound according to the terms of the agreement. Second, pre-existing substantive legal relationships between a non-party and party can bind a non-party to a judgment. Third, a non-party may be precluded from bringing his own claim, if he was adequately represented by someone with the same interests, and who was a party to a previous suit. Fourth, a non-party who assumes control over a case may be bound by the judgment in that case. Fifth, a party may not re-litigate an issue by using a proxy, such as an undisclosed agent. Sixth, special statutory schemes may prohibit repetitive litigation by non-parties if the scheme is consistent with due process. In this case, only the fifth category could apply. Thus, the case has to be remanded to determine whether Taylor (P) was Herrick's "undisclosed agent." If the courts below find that Taylor (P) is Herrick's agent, then nonparty claim preclusion will apply. Virtual representation should be applied rarely and under delineated exceptions to the general rule. The D.C. Circuit's decision is vacated and the case sent back to the district court for a new trial.

▶ ANALYSIS

By definition, the doctrine of virtual representation deprives litigants of their right to a day in court by binding them to judgments in cases in which they were not parties and in which they did not have the opportunity to defend their own interests. This decision sets forth the unanimous disapproval by the Supreme Court of the doctrine of virtual representation, and more clearly defines its previous decisions on non-party claim preclusion. As the Court indicated, virtual representation is in direct conflict with the "day-in-court" ideal, and because of this tension, virtual representation has always been the subject of controversy in lower courts.

■=■

Gonzalez v. Banco Central Corp.

Land purchasers (P) v. Real estate developer (D)

27 F.3d 751 (1st Cir. 1994).

NATURE OF CASE: Appeal from dismissal of complaint on grounds of *res judicata*.

FACT SUMMARY: Gonzalez (P) constituted a group of real estate purchasers who brought suit against Banco Central Corp. (Banco) (D), the seller, for fraud. The Gonzalez group (P) had attempted unsuccessfully to join with a prior group of real estate purchasers who had earlier sued Banco (D) and against whom a directed verdict had been rendered.

> 🏛 **RULE OF LAW**
> Nonparties may be barred from bringing suit by *res judicata* in a prior suit based on the same facts if, and only if, there is identicality between them and the parties in the earlier case.

FACTS: Real estate purchasers (P) brought a fraud suit against Banco Central Corp. (Banco) (D), which was the selling developers of worthless swampland in Florida. The court rendered a directed verdict against the purchasers, known as the "Rodriguez" plaintiffs. Subsequently, another group of allegedly defrauded real estate purchasers, the Gonzalez group (P), brought its own suit against Banco (D). The Gonzalez group (P) had tried in vain to join the Rodriguez group in the original suit. The district court dismissed the complaint of the Gonzalez group (P) on the grounds of res judicata, holding that the Gonzalez group (P) was in privity with the Rodriguez plaintiffs in the earlier suit and, hence, that there was identicality of parties in the two cases.

ISSUE: Does identicality of parties bar plaintiffs on res judicata grounds from bringing an action arising from the same facts previously litigated by another group of plaintiffs against the same defendants?

HOLDING AND DECISION: (Selya, J.) No. Identicality of parties exists only if the Gonzalez (P) plaintiffs were in privity with the Rodriguez plaintiffs in the earlier case. Privity, in turn, depends on whether the present Gonzalez (P) plaintiffs had substantial control over the earlier Rodriguez plaintiffs or were "virtually represented" by them. Although there are no bright-line tests of either factor, it is clear that the Gonzalez (P) plaintiffs in the instant case were not in privity with the earlier Rodriguez plaintiffs. Tellingly, the fact that the Gonzalez (P) plaintiffs were initially rebuffed in attempting to join the Rodriguez plaintiffs, but five years later were asked by those same plaintiffs to join the ongoing litigation strongly indicates that the Gonzalez (P) group had no involvement—let alone control—in that first litigation. Second, a balancing of the equities results in finding that the Gonzalez (P) plaintiffs were not "virtually represented" by the earlier plaintiffs. There was no evidence that the Gonzalez (P) plaintiffs had timely notice of the earlier suit or that the earlier Rodriguez plaintiffs were in any way responsible for or accountable to the Gonzalez (P) plaintiffs. There was no "special type of close relationship" between the two groups, and no evidence existed that the Gonzalez (P) group ever consented—explicitly or implicitly—to be bound by the verdict in the earlier Rodriquez case. The latter is particularly evident by the fact that the Gonzalez (P) group initiated their action while the earlier case was still pending. Reversed and remanded.

▶ **ANALYSIS**

There is no bright-line test for gauging substantial control. The inquiry must be case specific, and fact patterns are almost endlessly variable. Hence, the court must consider the totality of the circumstances to determine whether they justify a reasonable inference of a nonparty's potential of actual involvement as a decision maker in the earlier litigation.

■■■

Quicknotes

COMPLAINT The initial pleading commencing litigation that sets forth a claim for relief.

DIRECTED VERDICT A verdict ordered by the court in a jury trial.

RES JUDICATA The rule of law a final judgment by a court precludes subsequent litigation between the parties regarding the same cause of action.

■■■

David P. Hoult v. Jennifer Hoult

Father (P) v. Daughter (D)

157 F.3d 29 (1st Cir. 1998).

NATURE OF CASE: Plaintiff's appeal from dismissal of suit on grounds that he was estopped from relitigating issue resolved in earlier lawsuit.

FACT SUMMARY: A father brought defamation suit against his daughter that daughter claimed should be dismissed on grounds of collateral estoppel.

🏛 RULE OF LAW
Doctrine of collateral estoppel precludes relitigation of the central issue in a prior suit.

FACTS: Jennifer Hoult (D) sued David Hoult (her father) (P) for assault, battery, and intentional infliction of emotional distress, presenting evidence that he (P) had sexually abused and raped her (D) over a period of many years. The jury found in her (D) favor and awarded damages. Subsequently, the daughter (D) wrote to several professional associations in which she (D) repeated the charge that her father (P) had raped her. The father (P) then brought the present defamation action against the daughter (D). The daughter (D) moved to dismiss the father's (P) complaint on the grounds the jury verdict in her earlier assault action had determined that the father (P) had raped her, thus he (P) should be barred by collateral estoppel from relitigating this finding.

ISSUE: Does the doctrine of collateral estoppel preclude relitigation of the central issue in a prior suit?

HOLDING AND DECISION: (Boudin, J.) Yes. Even though the jury in the prior suit did not make an explicit finding that David Hoult (P) had raped Jennifer Hoult (D), such finding was a "necessary component of the decision reached" by the prior jury, which had held that Jennifer's father had in many ways sexually abused her. In the daughter's prior suit, the rape charges were pivotal and constituted the "centerpiece" of her case, and both her counsel as well as defense counsel in the prior suit referred to rape. The father's (P) present lawsuit against his daughter (D) simply seeks, in the guise of a defamation action, to retry the central issue in the prior assault case between the same litigants. Affirmed.

▶ ANALYSIS

The court stressed that here the key issue of rape, ultimately a credibility contest between the two opposing parties, was resolved by the jury at the first trial, whose decision about what happened was therefore not open to relitigation.

━■━

Quicknotes

ASSAULT AND BATTERY Any unlawful touching of another person without justification or excuse.

COLLATERAL ESTOPPEL A doctrine whereby issues litigated and determined in a prior proceeding are binding upon all subsequent litigation between the parties regarding that issue.

COMPLAINT The initial pleading commencing litigation that sets forth a claim for relief.

DEFAMATION An intentional false publication, communicated publicly in either oral or written form, subjecting a person to scorn, hatred or ridicule, or injuring him or her in relation to his or her occupation or business.

ESTOPPEL An equitable doctrine precluding a party from asserting a right to the detriment of another whom justifiably relied on the conduct.

RAPE Unlawful sexual intercourse with a woman by a man by means of fear or force and without her consent.

━■━

Jarosz v. Palmer

Individual (P) v. Attorney (D)

Mass. Sup. Jud. Ct., 436 Mass. 526 (2002).

NATURE OF CASE: Appeal from the dismissal of a claim on the basis of issue preclusion.

FACT SUMMARY: Jarosz (P) hired Palmer (D), to assist Jarosz (P) and his three partners in the acquisition of a company. Two lawsuits were then filed. The first lawsuit was filed by Jarosz (P) against his partners and the corporation after the partners terminated him as an employee and officer of the company. The company and partners retained Palmer (D) as their attorney. Jarosz (P) moved to disqualify Palmer (D) on the basis of his previous relationship with Palmer (D) in the corporate acquisition. His motion was denied, and the trial judge ruled that Jarosz (P) failed to prove that Palmer (D) had previously represented him individually. Jarosz (P) filed a second lawsuit, this one against Palmer (D) for alleged malpractice. The trial judge ruled that because of the decision denying the motion to disqualify in the first case, issue preclusion prevented Jarosz from asserting that Palmer (D) represented him individually in the business transaction. The trial judge dismissed Jarosz's (P) claim. Jarosz (P) appealed.

🏛 RULE OF LAW

The requirement of the doctrine of issue preclusion that the issue decided be "essential to the judgment" requires that the issue be essential to the merits of the underlying case.

FACTS: Jarosz (P) and his three partners acquired a company known as Union Products. Jarosz (P) had engaged Palmer (D), an attorney, to assist in the acquisition and financing of the business. When the relationship between Jarosz (P) and his partners soured, Jarosz (P) was terminated as an employee and officer of the company. Jarosz (P) filed suit against his former partners and the company for wrongful termination and breach of fiduciary duty. In that case, Palmer (D) represented the partners and the company. Jarosz (P) moved to disqualify Palmer (D) from representing the partners and the company, on the basis that Palmer (D) had previously represented him individually. The motion was denied on grounds that Jarosz (P) did not establish that an attorney-client relationship existed between himself and Palmer (D) during the acquisition dealings. Thereafter, Jarosz (P) filed this complaint against Palmer (D), alleging breach of contract, breach of fiduciary duty, legal malpractice, and violations of M.G.L. c. 93A. Palmer (D) defended these claims on the grounds that he never represented Jarosz (P) individually. Palmer (D) moved for judgment on the pleadings, arguing that the denial of Jarosz's (P) motion to disqualify in the first lawsuit

in another court precluded Jarosz (P) from relitigating the issue in the second. The court granted Palmer's (D) motion, finding that the three requirements for issue preclusion had been met: the issue had been actually litigated, it was the subject of a valid and final judgment, and it was essential to the judge's decision. The court dismissed Jarosz's (P) complaint against Palmer (D). Jarosz (P) appealed the dismissal of his suit against Palmer (D).

ISSUE: Does the requirement of doctrine of issue preclusion that the issue decided be "essential to the judgment" require that the issue be essential to the merits of the underlying case?

HOLDING AND DECISION: (Cowin, J.) Yes. The requirement of doctrine of issue preclusion that the issue decided be "essential to the judgment" requires that the issue be essential to the merits of the underlying case. Under the doctrine of issue preclusion, when an issue has been "actually litigated and determined by a valid and final judgment, and the determination is essential to the judgment, the determination is conclusive in a subsequent action between the parties whether on the same or different claim." Jarosz (P) claims that the issue was not actually litigated and that it was not essential to the decision. However, the issue of Jarosz's (P) alleged attorney-client relationship with Palmer (D) was actually litigated. The requirement for actual litigation of an issue does not require that a court hold an evidentiary hearing or trial before issue preclusion can apply. The appropriate question is whether there has been an "adversary presentation" and a "consequent judgment" that was not the result of the parties' consent. In the present matter, the issue of Jarosz's (P) attorney-client relationship had been briefed, and there had been a hearing, and the judge made a determination. As a result, the issue had been actually litigated. The denial of the motion to disqualify was not essential to the judgment in the underlying case, however. The requirement that the issue be essential to the judgment necessitates that the issue be essential to the underlying case. The nature of Jarosz's (P) attorney-client relationship with Palmer (D) was clearly not essential to a determination on the merits of his claim against his partner and the company, and the issue was therefore not essential to the judgment. Issue preclusion cannot apply. Reversed.

▶ ANALYSIS

An interesting question is whether issue preclusion will be available when the prior case was terminated by a

Continued on next page.

stipulation of dismissal. A key requirement for application of the doctrine of issue preclusion is that the issue "actually be litigated" and is "essential" to the underlying judgment. When parties stipulate to dismiss a case, nothing has been litigated, and because any claim has more than one element, it will be the rare case that a party can show that an "issue" was essential to that dismissal.

■━■

Quicknotes

BREACH OF CONTRACT Unlawful failure by a party to perform its obligations pursuant to contract.

BREACH OF FIDUCIARY DUTY The failure of a fiduciary to observe the standard of care exercised by professionals of similar education and experience.

EVIDENTIARY HEARING Hearing pertaining to the evidence of the case.

ISSUE PRECLUSION When a particular issue has already been litigated, further litigation of the same issue is barred.

LEGAL MALPRACTICE Conduct on the part of an attorney falling below that demonstrated by other attorneys of ordinary skill and competency under the circumstances, resulting in damages.

■━■

Parklane Hosiery Co., Inc. v. Shore

Corporation (D) v. Stockholders (P)

439 U.S. 322 (1979).

NATURE OF CASE: Appeal from stockholders' class action.

FACT SUMMARY: Shore (P) and other stockholders brought this action, alleging that Parklane Hosiery Co., Inc. (D) had issued a materially false and misleading proxy statement.

🏛 RULE OF LAW
A litigant who was not a party to a prior judgment may use that judgment "offensively" to prevent a defendant from relitigating issues resolved in the earlier proceeding.

FACTS: Shore (P) and other stockholders brought this class action against Parklane Hosiery Co., Inc. (Parklane) (D), alleging that the company had issued a materially false and misleading proxy statement that violated various federal securities laws. Before this action came to trial, the Securities and Exchange Commission (SEC) filed suit against Parklane (D), making the same allegations as Shore. Injunctive relief was requested. The court found that the proxy was false and misleading and entered a declaratory judgment to that effect. The court of appeals affirmed. Shore (P), in the present case, then moved for partial summary judgment against Parklane (D), asserting that it was collaterally estopped from relitigating the issues that had been resolved against it in the action brought by the SEC. The district court denied the motion on the ground that such an application of collateral estoppel would deny Parklane (D) its Seventh Amendment right to jury trial. The court of appeals reversed, holding that a party who has had issues of fact determined against him after a full and fair opportunity to litigate in a nonjury trial is collaterally estopped from obtaining a subsequent jury trial of these same issues of fact. Parklane (D) appealed.

ISSUE: May a litigant who was not a party to a prior judgment use that judgment "offensively" to prevent a defendant from relitigating issues resolved in the earlier proceeding?

HOLDING AND DECISION: (Stewart, J.) Yes. A litigant who was not a party to a prior judgment may use that judgment "offensively" to prevent a defendant from relitigating issues resolved in the earlier proceeding. Unless the application of offensive estoppel would be unfair to the defendant, a trial court has broad discretion to determine when it should be applied. In this case, none of the considerations that would justify a refusal to allow the use of estoppel is present. Since Parklane (D) received a full and fair opportunity to litigate its claims in the SEC action, the

contemporary law of collateral estoppel leads inescapably to the conclusion that Parklane (D) is collaterally estopped from relitigating the question of whether the proxy statements were materially false and misleading. Affirmed.

DISSENT: (Rehnquist, J.) At common law as it existed in 1791, petitioners would have been entitled to have a jury determine the facts in the private action. In 1791, collateral estoppel was permitted only where the parties in the first action were identical to, or in privity with, the parties to the subsequent action. The judge-made doctrine of collateral estoppel cannot contract the right to a jury trial that the defendant would have enjoyed in 1791. Here, the use of collateral estoppel eliminates the right to trial by jury and, therefore, contravenes the Seventh Amendment. And even if there were no violation of the Seventh Amendment, the use of collateral estoppel here is unfair, since the party who is sought to be estopped has not had an opportunity to have the facts of his case determined by a jury. The petitioners were not entitled to a jury trial in the SEC lawsuit.

▶ ANALYSIS

In both the defensive and offensive use of collateral estoppel, the party against whom estoppel is asserted has litigated and lost in an earlier action. Nevertheless, several reasons have been advanced why the two situations should be treated differently. First, offensive use of collateral estoppel does not promote judicial economy in the same manner as defensive use does. Defensive estoppel precludes a plaintiff from relitigating identical issues by merely switching adversaries. Secondly, offensive estoppel may be unfair to a defendant.

■▬■

Quicknotes

CLASS ACTION SUIT A suit commenced by a representative on behalf of an ascertainable group that is too large to appear in court, who shares a commonality of interests and who will benefit from a successful result.

DECLARATORY JUDGMENT An adjudication by the courts which grants not relief but is binding over the legal status of the parties involved in the dispute.

DEFENSIVE COLLATERAL ESTOPPEL A doctrine that may be invoked by a defendant against a plaintiff, whereby the plaintiff is prohibited from relitigating issues litigated and determined in a prior proceeding against another defendant.

Continued on next page.

INJUNCTIVE RELIEF A court order issued as a remedy, requiring a person to do, or prohibiting that person from doing, a specific act.

OFFENSIVE COLLATERAL ESTOPPEL A doctrine that may be invoked by a plaintiff whereby a defendant is prohibited from relitigating issues litigated and determined in a prior proceeding against another plaintiff.

PROXY STATEMENT A statement, containing specified information by the Securities and Exchange Commission, in order to provide shareholders with adequate information upon which to make an informed decision regarding the solicitation of their proxies.

SEVENTH AMENDMENT Provides that no fact tried by a jury shall be otherwise re-examined in any court of the United States, other than according to the rules of the common law.

SUMMARY JUDGMENT Judgment rendered by a court in response to a motion by one of the parties, claiming that the lack of a question of material fact in respect to an issue warrants disposition of the issue without consideration by the jury.

■■■

Hardy v. Johns-Manville Sales Corporation

Exposed workers (P) v. Asbestos manufacturer (D)

681 F.2d 334 (5th Cir. 1982).

NATURE OF CASE: Appeal of collateral estoppel order in action for damages for personal injury.

FACT SUMMARY: A trial court entered a collateral estoppel order regarding a failure-to-warn basis for products liability, although the jury in the prior action could have based its finding on one of several theories.

🏛 RULE OF LAW
Collateral estoppel may be applied only where there is an identity of issues.

FACTS: A class of plaintiffs sued various defendants' products for personal injury related to asbestos exposure. One theory of recovery was products liability based on a failure to warn. The plaintiffs moved for a collateral estoppel order based on a jury finding in a prior case that the same defendants had failed to warn of the danger of asbestos. However, it was unclear from the record of the prior case as to when the jury believed the duty to warn came into being. In the present action, warnings were placed by Johns-Manville Sales Corporation (Johns-Manville) (D) at various times from 1964 through 1969. The district court entered summary adjudication as to the failure-to-warn theory, and Johns-Manville (D) appealed.

ISSUE: May collateral estoppel be applied only where there is an identity of issues?

HOLDING AND DECISION: (Gee, J.) Yes. Collateral estoppel may be applied only where there is an identity of issues. When the prior judgment is ambivalent, the doctrine is not to be utilized. Here, the jury in the prior action could have found that the duty to warn arose any time between 1963 and 1969, when it held the duty to have arisen is unclear from the record. Here, some defendants began issuing warnings as early as 1964. Therefore, it is possible that they fulfilled any duty to warn they may have had. This being so, collateral estoppel was incorrectly applied. Reversed.

▶ ANALYSIS

Most actions involve general verdicts without specific findings by juries. It is difficult to find an identity of issues in such situations. Collateral estoppel is usually more readily available when the prior case contained special interrogatories.

■■■

Quicknotes

COLLATERAL ESTOPPEL A doctrine whereby issues litigated and determined in a prior proceeding are binding upon all subsequent litigation between the parties regarding that issue.

DUTY-TO-WARN An obligation owed by an owner or occupier of land to persons who come onto the premises, to inform them of defects or active operations which may cause injury.

INTERROGATORY A method of pretrial discovery in which written questions are provided by one party to another who must respond in writing under oath.

PRODUCT LIABILITY The legal liability of manufacturers and sellers for damages and injuries suffered by buyers, users, and even bystanders, because of defects in goods purchased.

■■■

Federated Department Stores, Inc. v. Moitie

Department store (D) v. Government (P)

452 U.S. 394 (1981).

NATURE OF CASE: Appeal from reversal of dismissal of antitrust action.

FACT SUMMARY: Federated Department Stores, Inc. (D) contended that the doctrine of *res judicata* barred relitigation of an unappealed adverse judgment where other plaintiffs in similar actions had successfully appealed judgments against them.

RULE OF LAW

Res judicata bars relitigation of an unappealed adverse judgment where other plaintiffs in similar actions against common defendants successfully appealed the judgments against them.

FACTS: In 1976, the Government (P) brought an antitrust action against Federated Department Stores, Inc. (Federated) (D), alleging that it had violated § 1 of the Sherman Act by agreeing to fix the retail price of women's clothing sold in Northern California. Seven parallel civil actions were subsequently filed by private plaintiffs seeking treble damages on behalf of proposed classes of retail purchasers, including that of Moitie (P) *(Moitie I)* in state court and Brown (P) *(Brown I)* in federal district court. Each of these complaints tracked almost verbatim the allegations of the Government's (P) complaint, although the *Moitie I* complaint referred solely to state law. All of the actions, including *Moitie I*, were assigned to a single federal judge, who dismissed all of the actions because of pleading defects. The plaintiffs in five of the suits appealed that judgment to the federal court of appeals, while the single counsel representing Moitie (P) and Brown (P) chose not to appeal and instead refiled the two actions in state court, *(Moitie II* and *Brown II),* respectively. Federated (D) removed the new actions to federal district court, where they were dismissed on the grounds of *res judicata.* However, the court of appeals reversed, such as was obtained by the other five plaintiffs, when their position is closely interwoven with that of the appealing parties. Federated (D) appealed.

ISSUE: Does *res judicata* bar relitigation of an unappealed adverse judgment where other plaintiffs in similar actions against common defendants successfully appealed the judgments against them?

HOLDING AND DECISION: (Rehnquist, J.) Yes. Res judicata bars relitigation of an unappealed adverse judgment where other plaintiffs in similar actions against common defendants successfully appealed the judgments against them. A final judgment on the merits of an action precludes the parties or their privies from relitigating issues that were, or could have been, raised in that action. A judgment, merely voidable because it is based upon an erroneous view of the law, is not open to collateral attack but can be corrected only by a direct review and not by bringing another action upon the same cause of action. Here, both *Brown I* and *Moitie I* were final judgments on the merits and involved the same claims and the same parties as *Brown II* and *Moitie II.* Both those parties seek to be the windfall beneficiaries on an appellate reversal procured by other independent parties, and it is further apparent that Brown (P) and Moitie (P) made a calculated choice to forgo their appeals. Reversed and remanded.

CONCURRENCE: (Blackmun, J.) *Brown I* is *res judicata* on Brown's (P) state law claims. Even if the state and federal claims are distinct, Brown's (P) failure to allege the state claims in *Brown I* manifestly bars their allegation in *Brown II.*

DISSENT: (Brennan, J.) The Court today disregards statutory restrictions on federal court jurisdiction and, in the process, confuses rather than clarifies long-established principles of *res judicata.*

▶ ANALYSIS

The Court, in a footnote, agreed with the court of appeals that at least some of the claims had a sufficient federal character, such as would support removal to the federal court. Both the district court and the court of appeals had found that Brown (P) and Moitie (P) had attempted to avoid removal jurisdiction by artfully casting their essentially federal law claims as state-law claims.

◼━◼

Quicknotes

ANTITRUST Body of federal law prohibiting business conduct that constitutes a restraint on trade.

FINAL JUDGMENT A decision by the court settling a dispute between the parties on its merits and which is appealable to a higher court.

JUDGMENT ON THE MERITS A determination of the rights of the parties to litigation based on the presentation evidence, barring the party from initiating the same suit again.

JURISDICTION The authority of a court to hear and declare judgment in respect to a particular matter.

Continued on next page.

PLEADING   A statement setting forth the plaintiff's cause of action or the defendant's defenses to the plaintiff's claims.

REMOVAL   Petition by a defendant to move the case to another court.

RES JUDICATA   The rule of law a final judgment by a court precludes subsequent litigation between the parties regarding the same cause of action.

TREBLE DAMAGES   An award of damages triple of the amount awarded by the jury and provided for by statute for violation of certain offenses.

Allen v. McCurry

Policemen (D) v. Criminal defendant (P)

449 U.S. 90 (1980).

NATURE OF CASE: Action for damages for violation of constitutional rights.

FACT SUMMARY: McCurry (P) sought damages from Allen (D) and other policemen for allegedly violating his constitutional rights in seizing the evidence that was introduced at his criminal trial and which resulted in conviction; Allen (D) raised a collateral estoppel defense.

🏛 RULE OF LAW
Collateral estoppel can be raised as a defense to a § 1983 suit brought by one convicted of a crime who is precluded from pursuing federal habeas corpus relief.

FACTS: McCurry (P) was convicted in state court after his motion to suppress certain evidence on grounds of unconstitutional search and seizure was denied in part. His conviction was upheld on appeal, and he was unable to pursue federal habeas corpus relief because he did not assert that the state courts had denied him a "full and fair" opportunity" to litigate his search and seizure claim. So, he brought a suit in federal court under § 1983, seeking damages from Allen (D) and other policemen, who had been responsible for seizing the evidence, for an alleged violation of his constitutional rights. Allen (D) raised the state court's partial rejection of McCurry's (P) constitutional claim as a collateral estoppel defense to the § 1983 suit. The district court granted summary judgment for Allen (D), holding that collateral estoppel prevented McCurry (P) from relitigating the search and seizure question already decided against him in the state courts. The court of appeals reversed and remanded, concluding that since federal habeas corpus relief was precluded, the § 1983 suit was McCurry's (P) only route to a federal forum for his constitutional claim.

ISSUE: Can collateral estoppel be raised as a defense to a § 1983 suit brought by one convicted of a crime who is precluded from pursuing federal habeas corpus relief?

HOLDING AND DECISION: (Stewart, J.) Yes. The rules of *res judicata* and collateral estoppel generally apply and can be raised as a defense to a § 1983 suit for damages for violations of constitutional rights, and this remains the case even when the party bringing suit cannot pursue federal habeas corpus relief because he does not allege that he lacked a "full and fair" opportunity to litigate his constitutional claim in the state court criminal proceedings against him. Since § 1983 was designed to allow federal relief when state courts were unable or unwilling to protect federal rights, it might well support an exception

to *res judicata* and collateral estoppel where there was not a full and fair opportunity to litigate the constitutional claim or issue in the state court proceeding, but that is the precise general limit on rules of preclusion which already exists. The actual basis of the court of appeals' holding appears to be a generally framed principle that every person asserting a federal right is entitled to one unencumbered opportunity to litigate that right in a federal district court, regardless of the legal posture in which the federal claim arises. However, there is no authority for such a position either in the Constitution or in the language or legislative history of § 1983. The court of appeals erred in holding that McCurry's (P) inability to obtain federal habeas corpus relief upon his Fourth Amendment claim renders the doctrine of collateral estoppel inapplicable to his § 1983 suit. Reversed and remanded.

DISSENT: (Blackmun, J.) Whether or not the doctrine of preclusion is applicable in a § 1983 case should not be determined by simply inquiring whether there was a "full and fair opportunity" to litigate the constitutional claim during the state proceedings. All relevant factors should be considered in each case before concluding that preclusion is warranted.

▶ ANALYSIS

Even before this case was decided, it had been the virtually unanimous view of the court of appeals that § 1983 presented no categorical bar to the application of *res judicata* and collateral estoppel concepts. However, a few of the courts did suggest that the normal rules of claims preclusion should not apply in one particular instance: Where § 1983 plaintiff seeks to litigate in federal court a federal issue which he could have raised but did not raise in an earlier state court suit against the same adverse party. The Supreme Court has yet to decide that issue.

■—■

Quicknotes

42 U.S.C. § 1983 Provides that every person, who under color of state law subjects or causes to be subjected any citizen of the United States or person within its jurisdiction to be deprived of rights, privileges and immunities guaranteed by the federal Constitution and laws, is liable to the injured party at law or in equity.

COLLATERAL ESTOPPEL A doctrine whereby issues litigated and determined in a prior proceeding are binding

Continued on next page.

upon all subsequent litigation between the parties regarding that issue.

HABEAS CORPUS A proceeding in which a defendant brings a writ to compel a judicial determination of whether he is lawfully being held in custody.

■══■

CHAPTER 1

Class Actions: It All Comes Together

Quick Reference Rules of Law

Hansberry v. Lee

Purchaser of real property (D) v. Landowner (P)

311 U.S. 32 (1940).

NATURE OF CASE: A class action to enforce a racially restrictive covenant.

FACT SUMMARY: Lee (P) sought to enjoin a sale of land to Hansberry (D) on the grounds that the sale violates a racially restrictive covenant.

🏛 RULE OF LAW
There must be adequate representation of the members of a class action or the judgment is not binding on the parties not adequately represented.

FACTS: Hansberry (D), a Black, purchased land from a party who had signed a restrictive covenant forbidding the sale of the land to Blacks. Lee (P), one of the parties who signed the covenant, sought to have the sale enjoined because it breached the covenant. Lee (P) contended that the validity of the covenant was established in a prior case in which one of the parties was a class of landowners involved with the covenant. To be valid, 95 percent of the landowners had to sign the covenant, and the trial court in the prior case held that 95 percent of the landowners had signed the covenant. That case was appealed, and the Illinois Supreme Court upheld the decision, even though they found that 95 percent of the landowners had not signed the covenant, but the court held that since it was a class action, all members of the class would be bound by the decision of the court. Hansberry (D) claimed that he and the party selling the house to him were not bound by the *res judicata* effect of the prior decision, as they were not parties to the litigation. The lower court held that the decision of the Illinois Supreme Court would have to be challenged directly in order that it be set aside or reversed. Otherwise, their decision was still binding. The case was appealed to the U.S. Supreme Court.

ISSUE: For a judgment in a class action to be binding, must all of the members of the class be adequately represented by parties with similar interests?

HOLDING AND DECISION: (Stone, J.) Yes. It is not necessary that all members of a class be present as parties to the litigation in order to be bound by the judgment, if they are adequately represented by parties who are present. In regular cases, to be bound by the judgment, the party must receive notice and an opportunity to be heard. If due process isn't afforded the individual, then the judgment is not binding. The class action is an exception to the general rule. Because of the numbers involved in class actions, it is enough if the party is adequately represented by a member of the class with a similar interest. Hansberry (D) wasn't adequately represented by the class

of landowners. Their interests were not similar enough to even be considered members of the same class. Lee (P) and the landowners were trying to restrict Blacks from buying any of the land, and Hansberry (D) was a Black attempting to purchase land. When there is such a conflicting interest between members of a class, there is most likely not adequate representation of one of the members of the class. There must be a similarity of interest before there can even be a class. Since there was no similarity of interests between Lee (P) and Hansberry (D), Hansberry (D) could not be considered a member of the class: and so the prior judgment was not binding on Hansberry (D). Hansberry (D) was not afforded due process because of the lack of adequate representation. Reversed.

▶ *ANALYSIS*

Rule 23(c)(3) requires that the court describe those whom the court finds to be members of the class. The court is to note those to whom notice was provided and also those who had not requested exclusion. These members are considered members of the class and are bound by the decision of the court whether it is in their favor or not. The federal rules allow a member of the class to request exclusion from the class, and that party will not be bound by the decision of the court. Since a party must receive notice of the class action before he can request exclusion from the class, the court must determine if a party received sufficient notice of the action or if sufficient effort was made to notify him of the action. The rules state if the court finds that the party did have sufficient notice and was considered a member of the class, he is bound by the decision.

■■■■

Quicknotes

CLASS ACTION SUIT A suit commenced by a representative on behalf of an ascertainable group that is too large to appear in court, who shares a commonality of interests and who will benefit from a successful result.

COVENANT A written promise to do, or to refrain from doing, a particular activity.

DUE PROCESS CLAUSE Clauses, found in the Fifth and Fourteenth Amendments to the United States Constitution, providing that no person shall be deprived of "life, liberty, or property, without due process of law."

Continued on next page.

ENJOIN The ordering of a party to cease the conduct of a specific activity.

RES JUDICATA The rule of law that a final judgment by a court precludes subsequent litigation between the parties regarding the same cause of action.

■═■

Phillips Petroleum Co. v. Shutts

Oil land lessee (D) v. Royalty owners (P)

472 U.S. 797 (1985).

NATURE OF CASE: Appeal of award of damages in class action breach of contract lawsuit.

FACT SUMMARY: A state class action lawsuit involved a plaintiff class of which 97 percent had no contacts with the forum state.

🏛 RULE OF LAW
A state may exercise jurisdiction over a class action plaintiff even if the plaintiff's contacts with the state would not confer jurisdiction over a defendant.

FACTS: A class action lawsuit was filed in a Kansas court against Phillips Petroleum Co. (Phillips) (D) on behalf of around 33,000 royalty owners (P). The class was certified. Notice of the lawsuit was sent by first-class mail to each plaintiff, with an explanation that each plaintiff would be bound unless he or she "opted out" of the suit. At the end of the trial, damages were awarded against Phillips (D), and Phillips (D) sought certiorari to the Supreme Court, arguing that the Due Process Clause prevented the Kansas courts from exercising jurisdiction over the plaintiffs having no contacts with Kansas, these being 97 percent of the plaintiffs.

ISSUE: May a state exercise jurisdiction over a class action plaintiff even if the plaintiff's contacts with the state would not confer jurisdiction over a defendant?

HOLDING AND DECISION: (Rehnquist, J.) Yes. A state may exercise jurisdiction over a class action plaintiff even if the plaintiff's contacts with the state would not confer jurisdiction over a defendant. The "minimum contacts" test of *International Shoe Co. v. Washington*, 326 U.S. 310 (1945), is a recognition that due process demands that a defendant should not be subjected to the expense and uncertainty of defending in an alien forum unless he has sufficient contact with the forum that would make it reasonable that he be expected to so defend. A class action plaintiff is in nowhere nearly as perilous a position as a civil defendant. The class action plaintiff need not travel, need not retain counsel, and, in fact, can sit back and do nothing. The court must certify the class, so the danger of improper inclusion in a class is minimal. Since the class action plaintiff is in nowhere near the danger of a civil defendant, he requires less protection under the Due Process Clause. Here, each plaintiff was notified and given the opportunity to "opt out" of the suit. This was all due

process required. Affirmed in part, reversed in part, and remanded.

▶ ANALYSIS

The Court had to dispose of a threshold issue. It was contended that Phillips (D) did not have standing to raise the due process claims of the plaintiffs. The Court got past this argument by noting that the inclusion of the plaintiff class presented dangers to Phillips (D) independent of the rights of the plaintiffs, and, therefore, Phillips (D) had standing to complain of the plaintiff class.

◼═◼

Quicknotes

CLASS ACTION A suit commenced by a representative on behalf of an ascertainable group that is too large to appear in court, who share a commonality of interests and who will benefit from a successful result.

DUE PROCESS CLAUSE Clauses, found in the Fifth and Fourteenth Amendments to the United States Constitution, providing that no person shall be deprived of "life, liberty, or property, without due process of law."

◼═◼

Wal-Mart Stores, Inc. v. Dukes

Retail giant (D) v. Female employees (P)

131 S. Ct. 2541 (2011).

NATURE OF CASE: Class action based on gender discrimination.

FACT SUMMARY: A small group of women filed a gender discrimination claim against Wal-Mart Stores, Inc. (D). A class was certified, and the original small group of women who filed the claims wanted to represent the class. The class was the largest in history.

🏛 RULE OF LAW

(1) A class consisting of more than one million women employed by a single employer nationwide cannot be certified as a class if they do not meet the "commonality" threshold for class certification under Fed. R. Civ. P. 23(a)(2) because they cannot demonstrate all class members were subject to the same discriminatory employment policy.

(2) Claims for monetary relief may not be certified under Fed. R. Civ. P. 23(b)(2) where the monetary relief is not incidental to the injunctive or declaratory relief.

FACTS: Betty Dukes (P), a Wal-Mart "greeter" at a Pittsburg, California, store, and five other women filed a class-action lawsuit in which they alleged that the company's nationwide policies resulted in lower pay for women than men in comparable positions and longer wait for management promotions than men. The U.S. District Court for the Northern District of California certified the class, finding Plaintiffs satisfied the requirements of Fed. R. Civ. P. 23(a)(2) and 23(b)(2). The certified class was estimated to include more than 1.5 million women including all women employed by Wal-Mart nationwide at any time after December 26, 1998, making this the largest class action lawsuit in U.S. history. Wal-Mart (D) argued that the court should require employees to file on an individual basis, contending that class actions of this size—formed under Fed. R. Civ. P. 23(b) of the federal rules of civil procedure—are inherently unmanageable and unduly costly. The U.S. Court of Appeals for the Ninth Circuit upheld the class certification three times.

ISSUE:

(1) Can a class consisting of more than one million women employed by a single employer nationwide be certified as a class if they do not meet the "commonality" threshold for class certification under Fed. R. Civ. P. 23(a)(2) because they cannot demonstrate all class members were subject to the same discriminatory employment policy?

(2) May claims for monetary relief be certified under Fed. R. Civ. P. 23(b)(2) where the monetary relief is not incidental to the injunctive or declaratory relief?

HOLDING AND DECISION: (Scalia, J.)

(1) No. A class consisting of more than one million women employed by a single employer nationwide cannot be certified as a class if they do not meet the "commonality" threshold for class certification under Fed. R. Civ. P. 23(a)(2) because they cannot demonstrate all class members were subject to the same discriminatory employment policy. The class action is "an exception to the usual rule that litigation is conducted by and on behalf of the individual named parties only." In order to justify a departure from that rule, "a class representative must be part of the class and 'possess the same interest and suffer the same injury' as the class members." Rule 23(a) ensures that the named plaintiffs are appropriate representatives of the class whose claims they wish to litigate. The Rule's four requirements? numerosity, commonality, typicality, and adequate representation—effectively "limit the class claims to those fairly encompassed by the named plaintiff's claims." The second of the Rule's four requirements, "proof of commonality," necessarily overlaps with the group's argument that Wal-Mart (D) engages in a pattern or practice of discrimination. Under Title VII, the central inquiry involves the reason for a particular employment decision, and the plaintiffs wish to sue for millions of employment decisions at once. Without something holding together the alleged reasons for those employment decisions, it would be impossible to say that examination of all the class members' claims will produce a common answer to the crucial discrimination question. The testimony of the plaintiffs' social science expert who claimed that Wal-Mart's (D) culture was susceptible to gender bias is unpersuasive. The testimony is useless to the question of whether the plaintiffs could prove a general policy of discrimination. Also rejected, is the use of aggregate statistical analyses and the mere existence of gender disparities in pay, promotion, or representation to meet the commonality burden. Instead, to show commonality, a plaintiff would at least need to demonstrate store-by-store disparities. Third, affidavits from 120 individuals, or one out of every 12,500 class members, did not constitute "significant proof" that Wal-Mart (D) operates under a general policy of discrimination. The members of the plaintiffs' group held many different jobs, at different levels of

Continued on next page.

Wal-Mart's (D) hierarchy, for variable lengths of time, in 3,400 stores, across 50 states, with many different supervisors (male and female), subject to a variety of regional policies that all differed. Some thrived while others did not. They have little in common but their sex and this lawsuit.

(2) No. Claims for monetary relief may not be certified under Fed. R. Civ. P. 23(b)(2) where the monetary relief is not incidental to the injunctive or declaratory relief. After satisfying the elements of Rule 23(a), the proposed class must satisfy at least one of the three requirements listed in Rule 23(b). The plaintiffs sought certification under Rule 23(b)(2), which applies when "the party opposing the class has acted or refused to act on grounds that apply generally to the class, so that final injunctive relief or corresponding declaratory relief is appropriate respecting the class as a whole." But Rule 23(b)(2) applies only when a single injunction or declaratory judgment would provide relief to each member of the class. It does not authorize class certification when each individual class member would be entitled to a *different* injunction or declaratory judgment against the defendant. Similarly, it does not authorize class certification when each class member would be entitled to an individualized award of monetary damages. The "predominance test" established by the Ninth Circuit, which permitted the certification of claims for monetary damages as long as claims for injunctive relief "predominated" over the claims for monetary damages, is rejected. Rather, the "incidental damages" test, which permits certification of claims for monetary relief as long as that relief "flow[s] directly from liability to the class as a whole," which "should not require additional hearings," is more appropriate. The adoption of a bright-line rule prohibiting all money damages from ever being certified under Rule 23(b)(2) is not considered here.

Reversed.

CONCURRENCE AND DISSENT: (Ginsburg, J.) The class should not have been certified under Fed. R. Civ. P. 23(b)(2), because the plaintiffs, alleging discrimination in violation of Title VII, seek monetary relief that is not merely incidental to any injunctive or declaratory relief that might be available. But a class of this type may be certifiable under Rule 23(b)(3), if the plaintiffs show that common class questions "predominate" over issues affecting individuals, such as qualification for, and the amount of, back pay or compensatory damages, and that a class action is "superior" to other modes of adjudication. Whether the class the plaintiffs describe meets the specific requirements of Rule 23(b)(3) is not before the Court, and that matter should be reserved for consideration and decision on remand. But the majority disqualifies the class under 23(a)(2), holding that the plaintiffs cannot cross the "commonality" line, and by doing so imports into the Rule 23(a) determination concerns properly addressed in a Rule 23(b)(3) assessment. The majority errs in importing a "dissimilarities" notion suited to Rule 23(b)(3) into the Rule 23(a) commonality inquiry.

▶ *ANALYSIS*

This is a landmark case that was thoroughly analyzed in the media when it was released. Many criticized the decision as inappropriately and unfairly raising the bar for certification to the detriment of those with valid Title VII claims. District courts will now be required to scrutinize closely all alleged common questions of law and fact to determine if the proposed common questions generate common answers that are apt to drive resolution in each case. It will not be sufficient for plaintiffs to allege a "general policy" without proving the existence of the policy and its impact on each class member.

━■■■

Quicknotes

CLASS ACTION A suit commenced by a representative on behalf of an ascertainable group that is too large to appear in court, who shares a commonality of interests and who will benefit from a successful result.

CLASS CERTIFICATION Certification by a court's granting of a motion to allow individual litigants to join as one plaintiff in a class action against the defendant.

━■■■

Martin v. Wilks

Municipality (D) v. White firefighters (P)

490 U.S. 755 (1989).

NATURE OF CASE: Review of order reinstating reverse discrimination action.

FACT SUMMARY: In a reverse discrimination action, it was contended that an earlier consent decree mandating certain affirmative action procedures barred a subsequent reverse discrimination action by parties not involved in the prior action.

RULE OF LAW

A consent decree mandating affirmative action does not have preclusive effect upon a subsequent challenge to those programs brought by persons not parties to the prior action.

FACTS: Several black firefighters brought a discrimination action against the City of Birmingham, Alabama (D). The suit was settled by way of a consent decree wherein certain affirmative action programs were mandated. Subsequently, several white firefighters (P) brought suit, contending that the affirmative action programs constituted reverse discrimination in violation of federal civil rights laws. The district court dismissed, holding that the prior judgment had preclusive effect as to the validity of the programs. The court of appeals reversed. The U.S. Supreme Court granted review.

ISSUE: Does a consent decree mandating affirmative action have preclusive effect upon a subsequent challenge to those programs brought by persons not parties to the prior action?

HOLDING AND DECISION: (Rehnquist, C.J.) No. A consent decree mandating affirmative action does not have preclusive effect upon a subsequent challenge to those programs brought by persons not parties to the prior action. It is a principle of general application in Anglo-American jurisprudence that one is not bound by a judgment in personam in which he was not a party. This rule is part of our deep-seated tradition that everyone should have his own day in court. However, the argument is made here that because the plaintiffs in this action had notice of the prior action and could have intervened, they cannot now complain of the prior judgment. This is incorrect. Fed. R. Civ. P. 24, which deals with intervention, is cast in permissive, not compulsory, terms. Rule 19, dealing with joinder, can be compulsory. Where Rule 19 is not invoked

to join a nonconsenting party, as was not done here, a judgment cannot bind the nonparty. Affirmed.

DISSENT: (Stevens, J.) The Court has crafted a rule which, in essence, allows nonparties to appeal a final judgment an indeterminate time after it is entered.

► ANALYSIS

This decision, and several others handed down the same year, provoked a reaction in the civil rights community. Congress eventually passed the Civil Rights Restoration Act, which was vetoed in 1990 but signed in 1991. The rule of this case was legislatively overruled.

■■■

Quicknotes

AFFIRMATIVE ACTION A form of benign discrimination designed to remedy existing discrimination by favoring one group over another.

COLLATERAL ATTACK A proceeding initiated in order to challenge the integrity of a previous judgment.

CONSENT DECREE A decree issued by a court of equity ratifying an agreement between the parties to a lawsuit; an agreement by a defendant to cease illegal activity.

FED. R. CIV. P. 19 Governs compulsory party joinder.

FED. R. CIV. P. 24 Establishes intervention requirements.

JOINDER The joining of claims or parties in one lawsuit.

■■■

Glossary

Common Latin Words and Phrases Encountered in the Law

A FORTIORI: Because one fact exists or has been proven, therefore a second fact that is related to the first fact must also exist.

A PRIORI: From the cause to the effect. A term of logic used to denote that when one generally accepted truth is shown to be a cause, another particular effect must necessarily follow.

AB INITIO: From the beginning; a condition which has existed throughout, as in a marriage which was void ab initio.

ACTUS REUS: The wrongful act; in criminal law, such action sufficient to trigger criminal liability.

AD VALOREM: According to value; an ad valorem tax is imposed upon an item located within the taxing jurisdiction calculated by the value of such item.

AMICUS CURIAE: Friend of the court. Its most common usage takes the form of an amicus curiae brief, filed by a person who is not a party to an action but is nonetheless allowed to offer an argument supporting his legal interests.

ARGUENDO: In arguing. A statement, possibly hypothetical, made for the purpose of argument, is one made arguendo.

BILL QUIA TIMET: A bill to quiet title (establish ownership) to real property.

BONA FIDE: True, honest, or genuine. May refer to a person's legal position based on good faith or lacking notice of fraud (such as a bona fide purchaser for value) or to the authenticity of a particular document (such as a bona fide last will and testament).

CAUSA MORTIS: With approaching death in mind. A gift causa mortis is a gift given by a party who feels certain that death is imminent.

CAVEAT EMPTOR: Let the buyer beware. This maxim is reflected in the rule of law that a buyer purchases at his own risk because it is his responsibility to examine, judge, test, and otherwise inspect what he is buying.

CERTIORARI: A writ of review. Petitions for review of a case by the United States Supreme Court are most often done by means of a writ of certiorari.

CONTRA: On the other hand. Opposite. Contrary to.

CORAM NOBIS: Before us; writs of error directed to the court that originally rendered the judgment.

CORAM VOBIS: Before you; writs of error directed by an appellate court to a lower court to correct a factual error.

CORPUS DELICTI: The body of the crime; the requisite elements of a crime amounting to objective proof that a crime has been committed.

CUM TESTAMENTO ANNEXO, ADMINISTRATOR (ADMINISTRATOR C.T.A.): With will annexed; an administrator c.t.a. settles an estate pursuant to a will in which he is not appointed.

DE BONIS NON, ADMINISTRATOR (ADMINISTRATOR D.B.N.): Of goods not administered; an administrator d.b.n. settles a partially settled estate.

DE FACTO: In fact; in reality; actually. Existing in fact but not officially approved or engendered.

DE JURE: By right; lawful. Describes a condition that is legitimate "as a matter of law," in contrast to the term "de facto," which connotes something existing in fact but not legally sanctioned or authorized. For example, de facto segregation refers to segregation brought about by housing patterns, etc., whereas de jure segregation refers to segregation created by law.

DE MINIMIS: Of minimal importance; insignificant; a trifle; not worth bothering about.

DE NOVO: Anew; a second time; afresh. A trial de novo is a new trial held at the appellate level as if the case originated there and the trial at a lower level had not taken place.

DICTA: Generally used as an abbreviated form of obiter dicta, a term describing those portions of a judicial opinion incidental or not necessary to resolution of the specific question before the court. Such nonessential statements and remarks are not considered to be binding precedent.

DUCES TECUM: Refers to a particular type of writ or subpoena requesting a party or organization to produce certain documents in their possession.

EN BANC: Full bench. Where a court sits with all justices present rather than the usual quorum.

EX PARTE: For one side or one party only. An ex parte proceeding is one undertaken for the benefit of only one party, without notice to, or an appearance by, an adverse party.

EX POST FACTO: After the fact. An ex post facto law is a law that retroactively changes the consequences of a prior act.

EX REL.: Abbreviated form of the term "ex relatione," meaning upon relation or information. When the state brings an action in which it has no interest against an individual at the instigation of one who has a private interest in the matter.

FORUM NON CONVENIENS: Inconvenient forum. Although a court may have jurisdiction over the case, the action should be tried in a more conveniently located court, one to which parties and witnesses may more easily travel, for example.

GUARDIAN AD LITEM: A guardian of an infant as to litigation, appointed to represent the infant and pursue his/her rights.

HABEAS CORPUS: You have the body. The modern writ of habeas corpus is a writ directing that a person (body) being detained (such as a prisoner) be brought before the court so that the legality of his detention can be judicially ascertained.

IN CAMERA: In private, in chambers. When a hearing is held before a judge in his chambers or when all spectators are excluded from the courtroom.

IN FORMA PAUPERIS: In the manner of a pauper. A party who proceeds in forma pauperis because of his poverty is one who is allowed to bring suit without liability for costs.

INFRA: Below, under. A word referring the reader to a later part of a book. (The opposite of supra.)

IN LOCO PARENTIS: In the place of a parent.

IN PARI DELICTO: Equally wrong; a court of equity will not grant requested relief to an applicant who is in pari delicto, or as much at fault in the transactions giving rise to the controversy as is the opponent of the applicant.

IN PARI MATERIA: On like subject matter or upon the same matter. Statutes relating to the same person or things are said to be in pari materia. It is a general rule of statutory construction that such statutes should be construed together, i.e., looked at as if they together constituted one law.

IN PERSONAM: Against the person. Jurisdiction over the person of an individual.

IN RE: In the matter of. Used to designate a proceeding involving an estate or other property.

IN REM: A term that signifies an action against the res, or thing. An action in rem is basically one that is taken directly against property, as distinguished from an action in personam, i.e., against the person.

INTER ALIA: Among other things. Used to show that the whole of a statement, pleading, list, statute, etc., has not been set forth in its entirety.

INTER PARTES: Between the parties. May refer to contracts, conveyances or other transactions having legal significance.

INTER VIVOS: Between the living. An inter vivos gift is a gift made by a living grantor, as distinguished from bequests contained in a will, which pass upon the death of the testator.

IPSO FACTO: By the mere fact itself.

JUS: Law or the entire body of law.

LEX LOCI: The law of the place; the notion that the rights of parties to a legal proceeding are governed by the law of the place where those rights arose.

MALUM IN SE: Evil or wrong in and of itself; inherently wrong. This term describes an act that is wrong by its very nature, as opposed to one which would not be wrong but for the fact that there is a specific legal prohibition against it (malum prohibitum).

MALUM PROHIBITUM: Wrong because prohibited, but not inherently evil. Used to describe something that is wrong because it is expressly forbidden by law but that is not in and of itself evil, e.g., speeding.

MANDAMUS: We command. A writ directing an official to take a certain action.

MENS REA: A guilty mind; a criminal intent. A term used to signify the mental state that accompanies a crime or other prohibited act. Some crimes require only a general mens rea (general intent to do the prohibited act), but others, like assault with intent to murder, require the existence of a specific mens rea.

MODUS OPERANDI: Method of operating; generally refers to the manner or style of a criminal in committing crimes, admissible in appropriate cases as evidence of the identity of a defendant.

NEXUS: A connection to.

NISI PRIUS: A court of first impression. A nisi prius court is one where issues of fact are tried before a judge or jury.

N.O.V. (NON OBSTANTE VEREDICTO): Notwithstanding the verdict. A judgment n.o.v. is a judgment given in favor of one party despite the fact that a verdict was returned in favor of the other party, the justification being that the verdict either had no reasonable support in fact or was contrary to law.

NUNC PRO TUNC: Now for then. This phrase refers to actions that may be taken and will then have full retroactive effect.

PENDENTE LITE: Pending the suit; pending litigation under way.

PER CAPITA: By head; beneficiaries of an estate, if they take in equal shares, take per capita.

PER CURIAM: By the court; signifies an opinion ostensibly written "by the whole court" and with no identified author.

PER SE: By itself, in itself; inherently.

PER STIRPES: By representation. Used primarily in the law of wills to describe the method of distribution where a person, generally because of death, is unable to take that which is left to him by the will of another, and therefore his heirs divide such property between them rather than take under the will individually.

PRIMA FACIE: On its face, at first sight. A prima facie case is one that is sufficient on its face, meaning that the evidence supporting it is adequate to establish the case until contradicted or overcome by other evidence.

PRO TANTO: For so much; as far as it goes. Often used in eminent domain cases when a property owner receives partial payment for his land without prejudice to his right to bring suit for the full amount he claims his land to be worth.

QUANTUM MERUIT: As much as he deserves. Refers to recovery based on the doctrine of unjust enrichment in those cases in which a party has rendered valuable services or furnished materials that were accepted and enjoyed by another under circumstances that would reasonably notify the recipient that the rendering party expected to be paid. In essence, the law implies a contract to pay the reasonable value of the services or materials furnished.

QUASI: Almost like; as if; nearly. This term is essentially used to signify that one subject or thing is almost analogous to another but that material differences between them do exist. For example, a quasi-criminal proceeding is one that is not strictly criminal but shares enough of the same characteristics to require some of the same safeguards (e.g., procedural due process must be followed in a parole hearing).

QUID PRO QUO: Something for something. In contract law, the consideration, something of value, passed between the parties to render the contract binding.

RES GESTAE: Things done; in evidence law, this principle justifies the admission of a statement that would otherwise be hearsay when it is made so closely to the event in question as to be said to be a part of it, or with such spontaneity as not to have the possibility of falsehood.

RES IPSA LOQUITUR: The thing speaks for itself. This doctrine gives rise to a rebuttable presumption of negligence when the instrumentality causing the injury was within the exclusive control of the defendant, and the injury was one that does not normally occur unless a person has been negligent.

RES JUDICATA: A matter adjudged. Doctrine which provides that once a court of competent jurisdiction has rendered a final judgment or decree on the merits, that judgment or decree is conclusive upon the parties to the case and prevents them from engaging in any other litigation on the points and issues determined therein.

RESPONDEAT SUPERIOR: Let the master reply. This doctrine holds the master liable for the wrongful acts of his servant (or the principal for his agent) in those cases in which the servant (or agent) was acting within the scope of his authority at the time of the injury.

STARE DECISIS: To stand by or adhere to that which has been decided. The common law doctrine of stare decisis attempts to give security and certainty to the law by following the policy that once a principle of law as applicable to a certain set of facts has been set forth in a decision, it forms a precedent which will subsequently be followed, even though a different decision might be made were it the first time the question had arisen. Of course, stare decisis is not an inviolable principle and is departed from in instances where there is good cause (e.g., considerations of public policy led the Supreme Court to disregard prior decisions sanctioning segregation).

SUPRA: Above. A word referring a reader to an earlier part of a book.

ULTRA VIRES: Beyond the power. This phrase is most commonly used to refer to actions taken by a corporation that are beyond the power or legal authority of the corporation.

Addendum of French Derivatives

IN PAIS: Not pursuant to legal proceedings.

CHATTEL: Tangible personal property.

CY PRES: Doctrine permitting courts to apply trust funds to purposes not expressed in the trust but necessary to carry out the settlor's intent.

PER AUTRE VIE: For another's life; during another's life. In property law, an estate may be granted that will terminate upon the death of someone other than the grantee.

PROFIT A PRENDRE: A license to remove minerals or other produce from land.

VOIR DIRE: Process of questioning jurors as to their predispositions about the case or parties to a proceeding in order to identify those jurors displaying bias or prejudice.

Casenote® Legal Briefs